HITCHHIKING TO SERENDIP

IN WHICH A BRITISH SERVICEMAN IGNORES ALL
ADVICE AND HITCHHIKES ACROSS 1950s
PRE-REVOLUTIONARY AFRICA

by

JOHN J. FULFORD

Hitchhiking to Serendip by John J. Fulford

Copyright © 2013 by John J. Fulford

Published by Astoria Press, Long Beach, CA

Author services provided by Pedernales Publishing, LLC
www.pedernalespublishing.com

Cover by Christine Di Natale
www.dinataledesign.com

Interior maps by Sherry Wachter and Robert Cisneros

Editing services by Barbara Ardinger
www.barbaraardinger.com

Library of Congress Control Number: 2014931012

ISBN Number: 978-0-9831872-5-7 Paperback Edition
                      978-0-9831872-6-4 Digital Edition

Serendipity...you will understand it better by the derivation than by the definition. I once read a silly fairy tale, called *the three Princes of Serendip*: as their Highnesses travelled, they were always making discoveries, by accidents and sagacity, of things which they were not in quest of....

— *Letter from Horace Walpole to Sir Horace Mann, January 28, 1754*

CONTENTS

HITCHHIKING TO SERENDIP

INTRODUCTION

I was not supposed to go to Africa. It just happened, and that needs a little explanation. During my national service in the RAF, I was posted to a base in the south of England, where I was supposed to be trained as an armourer-bombs. I arrived at a dreary little camp in a deep forest where great stacks of bombs of every size stood rusting in the gloom. The food was uneatable, the barracks were uninsulated tin huts heated only by small wood-burning stoves, and there was no running hot water. It was a bad winter. When it wasn't raining, it was snowing. Most of my time was filled by just trying to keep warm and dry.

On one particularly miserable day, I marched into the HQ building and demanded to be posted overseas. "Where to?" asked the orderly, who was an old veteran that didn't think highly of conscripts. "To the hottest, driest place where the RAF has a base," I almost shouted. The orderly gave a sly smile, and a few weeks later I received note that I was going to be posted to Aden, which is on the southern tip of the Arabian peninsula. I knew enough geography to know that Aden was very hot. And it was dry, very dry indeed.

At the dispersal base in the north of England, where I spent a few days getting a score of inoculations, I ran across a man who had just returned from Aden. He told me that Aden was considered the worst place anybody could be posted. "Alcatraz or Devil's Island would be holiday camps in comparison," he cheerfully advised me.

The longer I listened to him, the more I wondered whether or not I had made a smart decision.

Suddenly, a short, overweight sergeant marched into the bunkhouse where we were sitting. He pointed to the nearest man, who happened to be me, and said, "Have you had all your shots?" I admitted that I had indeed been poked with every size needle. "Get your stuff and line up with the bunch outside. One of them has just gone down sick, so you replace him."

The sergeant had been ordered to put 36 live bodies on the plane, and he was going to do precisely that. Where I was supposed to go was of no interest to him. When I discovered that the group that I had joined was headed for Southern Rhodesia, I kept my mouth shut and my fingers crossed until I was safely seated on the plane.

We stopped in Malta and Libya, then went on to Khartoum and Entebbe in Uganda, but we were confined to the airports at those stops and only had tempting glimpses of those fascinating places. Eventually the plane circled over Bulawayo, Rhodesia, and I sat with my nose pressed to the little window. Below me, the grass was yellow, and under the few shade trees were little groups of round huts with thatched roofs. A tiny car raised a plume of dust from a dirt road. The sky was completely cloudless and pale blue with heat. I had arrived in Africa.

At the base a few miles out of town, the sergeant was not happy to see me. All the others from the plane had already been sent off to their various barracks and duties, but I remained standing to attention next to my duffle bag.

"An armourer!" the sergeant roared. "Bombs! We don't have

no bloody bombs here. This is a flight training base. We don't even have any bloody fireworks for Guy Fawkes Night." He sighed a great sigh and looked as if he was about to cry. "I asked for a coppersmith! A bloody coppersmith, and they sent you." He glared at me. "I hope you can read and write, because you're now my duty clerk." He pointed to his office and stalked off, leaving me staring at the ground trying to find my shadow. It had disappeared or, more accurately, I was standing on it. I suddenly felt ridiculously happy that I had scientific proof that I was really in tropical Africa.

Because most of Rhodesia is about three or four thousand feet above sea level, the climate is almost perfect. The nights are cool and the days are warm and dry, except during the short rainy season when the life-giving water arrives in astonishing quantities. The humidity is quite low, and although we were issued mosquito nets, we only used them during the rains.

There was almost no red tape or military bureaucracy, and as long as we kept the planes flying, everything was very relaxed. The local beer was good, cigarettes were cheap, and there was an excellent swimming pool for the men.

My new job was to make out all the duty rosters and issue leave passes. As I was the man who decided who was on guard duty and who was exempt, I became exceedingly popular. The best part was being able to make out leave passes. Every document was supposed to be checked and signed by the sergeant, but he signed everything I gave him without bothering to read it. It didn't take me long to recognize my good luck.

My family was scattered all over the world, and when I wrote and told my mother where I was, she replied immediately with the name of a second cousin who lived in Bulawayo. They were a charming family and extremely proud of Rhodesia. Every now and then, they invited me down for a weekend, and we took drives to somewhere scenic or historic. They had a long list of places that I just had to visit while I was in Africa, but my problem was that I did not have a car, or even a motorbike. When I suggested hitchhiking, they were horrified. "You can do that type of thing in Europe," they said, "but in Africa, a white man does not hitchhike!"

I didn't see why not. Many of the airmen hitched a lift into town with no problem, and there was that thick pad of leave passes on my desk, just asking to be used. Furthermore, I reasoned, since the government had already paid for my trip to Africa, it would be foolish of me, even ungrateful, not to take advantage of the opportunity.

So I bought a road map of Central Africa and slipped a very generous leave pass into the stack for the sergeant to sign. When the rains were well and truly over, I walked out of the gates in khaki shorts and shirt and carrying a small pack. I was off to see Africa.

I was only 20 years old in 1952. As a school-boy, I had read about Dr. David Livingstone and the Boer War. I had read Kipling's Just-So Stories and all about the Zulu Wars, too. But I had not paid much attention to politics, so I was quite unaware that I had arrived in Africa at a crucial turning point in the history of the continent. I was there during what we might call the calm before the storm. Just over the horizon and approaching swiftly was a storm that would, in a few short years, completely change the face of Africa.

In western Africa, Ghana had been independent for five years. Now other colonies were demanding independence. In Kenya, the Mau Mau Revolt had already started, and in South Africa the Afrikaner National Party was gaining strength and imposing strict apartheid laws. The Pax Britannica of the past thirty years was fast breaking down.

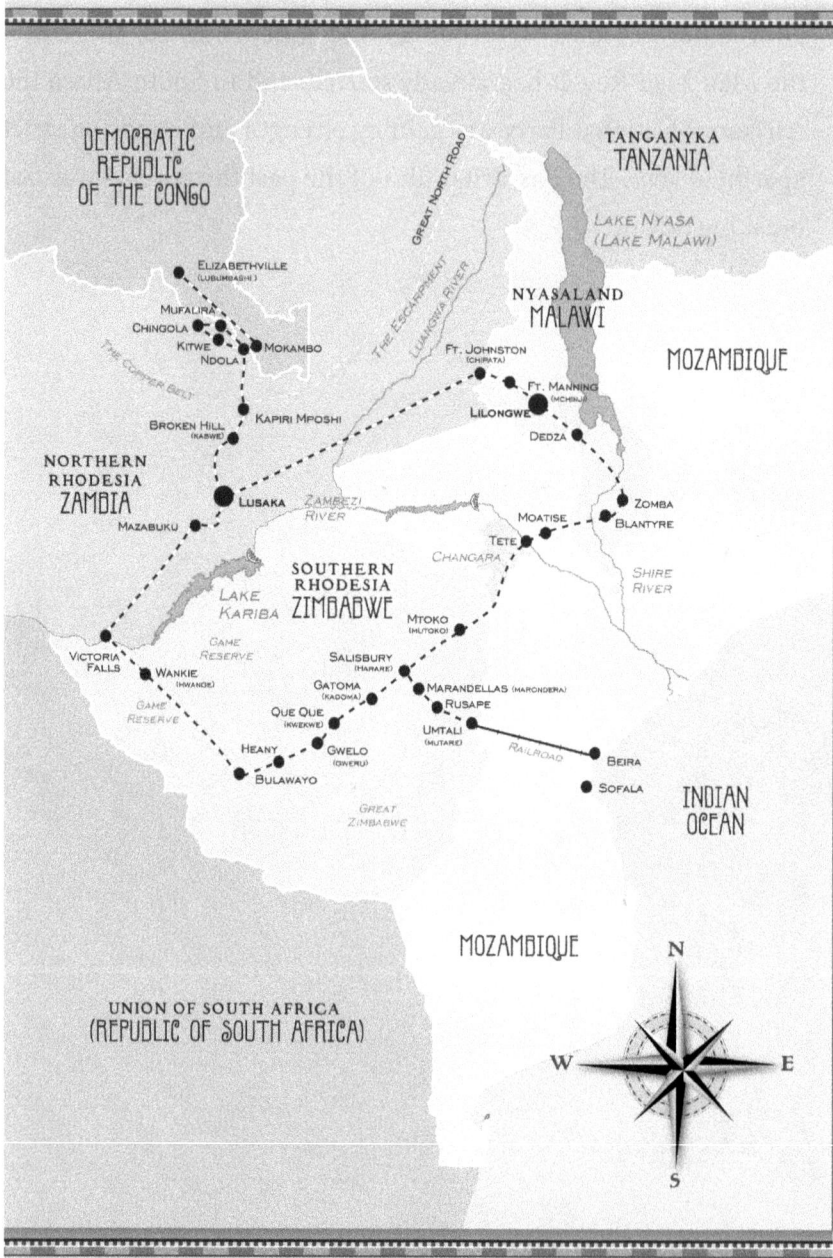

Map One. My First Trip. North into Mozambique, Nyasaland,
Northern Rhodesia, and the Belgian Congo

THE FIRST TRIP

Chapter One: Buluwayo to Umtali

Day 1

I had been walking for less than five minutes when a car stopped. The driver thought I was hitching into Bulawayo (now the second largest city in Zimbabwe, which was still Rhodesia when I was there in 1952) and had stopped to tell me that I was on the wrong side of the road. He was pleasantly surprised when I told him that I was off to see Rhodesia.

"Not enough of you boys get out and look around," he said. "Chance of a lifetime, and most of them spend it sitting in camp drinking beer and wishing they were in England." He laughed, "Silly buggers don't know what they're missing."

I told him of a man in my bunkhouse who was from Birmingham and had been in Rhodesia two years. A few weeks before he was due to go home he took a trip to Victoria Falls, where he bought some ivory trinkets. Then he tried to get a tan, but ended up with such a bad sunburn that he was charged with self-inflicted injuries and did guard duties for a week. On top of that, the ivory turned out to be plastic and was probably made in Birmingham.

We drove through fairly level farmland with huge fields of maize and small herds of healthy looking cattle. There were not many buildings and only a few trees in the pastures, and a few miles beyond the camp, the paved road became strips of paved road.

In a very big land with a very small taxpaying population, building roads was a problem. Outside the major towns, most roads were just gravel with two concrete strips down the middle. The narrow concrete strips were tricky to drive on, and they took a lot of punishment. In some places, they were worn away completely and for long stretches they were cracked and potholed. Sometimes the potholes were incredibly large with wickedly jagged edges. In theory, approaching cars had to give up one strip to oncoming cars, but in practice most drivers played a game of "chicken" and waited until the last few seconds before bouncing to one side. Swearing at the strips was part of the driving experience, and almost everybody preferred the gravel roads with their clouds of dust and flying rocks.

While we were changing the inevitable flat tire, I noticed that every car that passed slowed down and somebody offered help. Traffic was thin and the distances were long with little if any emergency road service, so neighborliness was automatic. When we stopped at a small hotel to wash down the dust, the bar was officially closed. But the proprietor gave a shout from his chair on the veranda, and ice-cold bottles immediately appeared. When I asked how a land that grew no hops and very little barley could make so much good beer, the two men winked at each other and one said, "Marvelous what science can do with good water."

My ride ended at Gwelo (now *Gweru),* a small town with a freshly painted look about it. The streets had curbs and street lights and there were plenty of well-tended flower beds. Since it was late afternoon, I checked into the hotel. I was satisfied with my progress for the first day, and after sunset. I set off to explore the town. It was a pretty little place, but I had seen it all in ten minutes so I stopped at a hot dog stand to have supper. The owner was a small cheerful man with a very broad cockney accent. He and his stand could have been on any corner in the East End of London instead of under a giant African moon.

"Been here five years now," he told me. "You won't catch me going back."

There were a few other people out strolling in the cool of the evening and as he served his delicious hot dogs and fat meat pies, he told me that Gwelo was actually a very old town that sprang up when gold was discovered by the original pioneers. Cecil Rhodes thought that it was an extension of the fabulously rich Rand, five hundred miles to the south, and hundreds of claims were staked. There was gold there, but unfortunately it was in hard quartz. Although mining continued, Gwelo was never a rival to Johannesburg.

"The real gold around here is growing in the fields." the vendor said. "Tobacco and maize."

In the hotel, I found notes offering and requesting rides posted in the hotel. In a land where distances are great and the roads are lonely, most travelers are glad of the company, especially if the other party will share the driving and help change a tire.

Day 2

I was awakened at sunrise by an African servant and a nice cup of tea. The hotel desk was still closed, but one of the staff made up my bill, took my money, and gave me change. I didn't think to get a receipt and when I returned to the military camp weeks later, I found the bill from the hotel waiting for me. It took some complicated correspondence to explain what had really happened.

Gwelo was very quiet early in the morning. I walked to the out-skirts and waited in the cool morning brightness. A mounted po-liceman gave me a curious glance as he ambled by, but he didn't say anything. A girl in a milk truck gave me a short ride, and then about 9 o'clock a large American car stopped and the driver offered me a lift to Que Que (now Kwekwe), about forty miles north. The driver was from Manchester, and we began talking about cars and roads. This subject proved to be the best ice-breaker with most drivers. All I had to say was, "How does this model stand up to the roads?" and conversation was good for the next two hours. The Rhodesians drove English or American cars, with no loyalty to any particular make. The rugged conditions brought out the weak points in every car, people switched or traded cars constantly, and everybody knew what car they would never drive again. I learned a great deal about cars. The manufacturers could have learned a lot, too.

Que Que, which claimed to have the largest gold mine in Rho-desia, turned out to be a very ugly industrial town filled with houses and factories that did not interest me. I picked my way across the railway tracks and walked out into the countryside, where I was soon picked up by a young man with a soft Devon accent who was driving an extremely battered car. He told me that he was a tele-phone line man and often went deep into the bush with a truckload of laborers. Almost always, they got stuck in dust or mud, depend-ing on the season.

"Only a month ago we got caught in the rains," he said. "Had to sit there for over a week while the river went down." He jerked his thumb towards the back of the car and laughed. "I don't go any-where now without shovels and grub."

As we were talking, we both noticed a burning smell. While I checked the tires, he opened the hood. The radiator cap shot up in a cloud of steam. Fortunately, he had a funnel and a can of water on the back seat, so we topped up the radiator and set off again, but not for long. We soon used up his water supply, and for the next 120 miles we stopped at every creek, mud hole, and irrigation ditch we came across. We got it down to a fine art, with me fetching the water and him under the hood, and we didn't lose much time. I was amazed at just how much water was still available in what appeared to be a rather dry landscape.

At Gatooma (now *Kadoma*), he pointed to some factory build-ings and said, "Chrome mine. Maybe the chrome on this car came from there. There's a gold mine over there, too." When I asked what was growing in the fields, he said, "Cotton. They grow an awful lot of cotton here." I had never seen cotton fields before and was surprised at how low the bushes were. Here and there, I saw black laborers working in the fields, but there was no sign of any white overseer.

The Southern Rhodesian countryside was still very open, but had become hillier, and soon we reached a paved road and the sub-urbs of Salisbury, the capital city that was renamed Harare in 1982. The houses spread out into the distance and were clearly going to spread even further, and my friend guessed that within five years the size of the city would double. "I don't know whether I like it or hate it," he said. "On one hand, it's astonishing just how much has been done. New towns and factories everywhere and business just booming along. We're building a great country out of nothing. But then again," he paused, "it's not the Africa that I came out to. I like the bush."

He dropped me off at a bus stop in an expensive-looking residential area with large houses and immaculate gardens. An almost new car pulled up, and a huge mustache with a cheerful red face behind it promptly offered me a lift. The owner of the gorgeous mustache was an RAF pilot who had trained in Rhodesia, probably at the same camp where I was stationed. Like so many that I was to meet, he had decided that life in post-war England, with its grey skies, grey buildings and overcrowded cities, was no pleasure, and he had immediately moved back to Rhodesia, where he had started a little business, married a local girl, and was "doing quite nicely, thank you." He dropped me off at a hotel where I looked over the notes. As nobody seemed to be going in my direction, I decided to press on.

Salisbury was a big, bustling, modern city, quite different from sleepy Bulawayo. The streets were filled with well-dressed people, the buildings were taller, the roads narrower and the shops full of everything that money could buy. But a large city was not what I had come to see, so I strolled east until I found myself at what looked like a major crossroads and waited under a shady tree.

The next car to stop was driven by a middle-aged lady who asked me where I was going. When I said Umtali (which became *Mutare in 1982),* she squealed with delight and pointed to the car in front of her. "He's got Umtali license plates. I bet he's going home."

Completely ignoring the traffic, she sped up and pulled alongside the other car and called out to the driver. Looking very startled, he slowed down, which gave her the opportunity to pull up in front of him with a wonderful squeal of brakes. She was really enjoying herself. I, on the other hand, was acutely embarrassed. Even so, he allowed me into his car. She gave a long blast on the horn and sped off.

Up to that point, everybody I had met was a recent immigrant to Rhodesia, but this man proved to be a third-generation Rhodesian. He was a farmer, and his farm was in the hills near Umtali. His family had been with the original settlers who had trekked their clumsy ox-wagons into the wilds of Mashonaland from Kimberley, the world-famous diamond district over a thousand miles away. They had survived the native uprisings, the droughts, the isolation, and the insects, and had put down deep roots. He was a quiet man, proud of what he and his ancestors had accomplished. As we drove along, he pointed out things that he thought I would be interested in.

We drove through rolling countryside that seemed to be very fertile, heavily populated, and with a wide variety of crops. Soon we began to pass huge fields of tobacco, and there were more trees including small forests of eucalyptus with their smooth white trunks and grey leaves. "Tree plantations," the driver said. "You have to have patience to grow trees. Just sitting and staring at them for seven years and worrying all the time about fires." He laughed. "I'll stick to fruit and veggies." In this part of Africa, he explained, the native trees are not suitable for telephone poles, railway ties, or building. "We have to import nearly all our lumber. But eucalyptus seems to stand up to termites." He laughed again. "In Rhodesia, what the bank doesn't own, the termites eat."

At Marandellas (now Marondera), we stopped to wash down the dust. It wasn't a large town, but it was clearly an important supply center for a huge farming region. There were warehouses and farm machine dealerships along the main street, and the hotel was large and prosperous. While we ate, I studied the other customers. The salesmen and businessmen mostly sat at the tables, while the farmers invariably perched on the bar stools. There was no standard dress. Khaki predominated, but it was mixed with loud checks. I also observed shorts and slacks, bush jackets and colorful blazers, sandals and cowboy boots, and a wonderful collection of headgear, including wide-brimmed bush hats with real leopard skin bands, ancient felt hats, Scots berets, and service berets from the red of the parachute regiment to air force blue. I even saw a deer stalker, a few tweedy caps, a scattering of American Stetsons and Australian hats with one side turned up. No two hats were quite alike, and I felt quite naked with nothing on my head. From the conversation I overheard, I gathered that most of the people were recent immigrants. I also got the impression of intelligent toughness and hard-working independence coupled with a rough, sunburned humor. These people could have emigrated to Australia, Canada, or even Brazil, but they had chosen Africa, in the 1950s, the last frontier.

We had about a hundred miles to go when we left Marandellas, and I estimated we should arrive in Umtali by sunset. There were long detours around road construction, plus ruts, potholes, exposed rocks, and tangled roots to slow us down, as well as an occasional stop at a service station to top up the radiator. As the road began to climb and the countryside grew hillier, with long ranges of rocky outcrop and domed hills covered with thorn trees, we began to see clusters of small hills that the farmer called *kopjes*, with weirdly balancing rocks on their peaks. There were fewer towns, and we crossed a number of swiftly flowing rivers where my host pointed, with evident amusement, at places where cars had been swept away during the rains.

We crossed on what were politely called "low level bridges." African rivers tend to be wide and seasonal, and in the early days, there was only a ford. In time, a rough road surface was laid on the river bed, which was dry for much of the year and this, of course, washed away quite regularly. The solution was a simple concrete causeway just a few feet above the river bed. These low level bridges are fine for most of the year, but they are quickly submerged during flash floods and are quite impassable for days on end during the rainy season. Now and then an impatient driver will try his luck, and, as my companion said as we splashed our way slowly over one, "Sometimes they do, but sometimes they end up swimming." He looked at me and laughed, "Don't worry. There are no crocs around here."

It was growing dark, and I was growing anxious about hotels. My anxiety vanished as I witnessed the majesty of the sunset. There was a sudden short blaze of orange in the west, then the sky turned scarlet while the yellow hills turned blue, then deep purple. For a few minutes there was color all around, then the darkening sky drew silver mists out of the valleys and hollows and we were wrapped in the cool of night.

We stopped at a lonely garage at the foot of the mountain to fill the radiator for the long slow climb over Christmas Pass. Neither the farmer nor the garage owner knew how the pass got its name, but driving it was no holiday. It seemed to go straight up at a very steep grade, and at times we were down to barely 20 miles per hour with the temperature gauge on red, and yet we actually passed another car. On the eastern side of the pass, the road twisted its way down and I caught brief glimpses of our destination, which looked like a cluster of glow worms nestled in the velvet darkness. After one final hairpin bend we were on a brightly lighted main street and I jumped out at the hotel.

Umtali (now Mutari) is a holiday resort as well as a frontier railway town, and as it was Easter week the hotel was crowded. The manager found me a room on my solemn promise that I would vacate it as soon as possible in the morning. After removing a few layers of red dust from my clothes and my body, I went down to dinner. It was a first-class hotel, and I was a little apprehensive about my casual traveling clothes, so I slipped behind a potted palm only to find that although the women were all dressed up, most of the men were wearing shorts and open necked shirts. It was part of the pleasant informality of the country where the dress codes and taboos of England were quietly ignored and a man could be comfortable yet still be a gentleman. After an excellent meal, I took a stroll along the tree lined streets which smelled cool and damply fresh after the dusty journey.

Chapter Two: Umtali to Beira and Back

Day 3

At the crack of dawn, I breakfasted and paid my bill, then sat in a little park opposite the post office. It was cool and quiet, and I had time to think where next to go. I had originally intended to go down to Beira, on the coast, then head north through Mozambique, but some people I had talked to in the hotel insisted that the road north barely existed and even the main road from Umtali down to Beira was flooded or washed out in places. Hitchhiking in Mozambique thus was definitely out. What I could do, I decided, was take the train down to Beira for a quick dip in the Indian Ocean.

At the railway station I learned that the train did not leave until 8:30 in the evening, so I bought a ticket, checked in my bag, and took a stroll around the town. It was Sunday and very quiet except for a few church goers. In less than an hour I had seen the whole town. Since it was still early morning, I bought some snacks at a stall and set off for a day in the hills.

Rhodesia (now Zimbabwe) has no coasts and no really large lakes. Umtali, nestled in the cool hills, is a popular vacation spot, and those who can afford it, own or rent villas in the surrounding hills. I walked along avenues of attractive houses surrounded by trees and neatly clipped hedges. In 1952, there was something very English about the beautiful gardens with their roses and neatly trimmed lawns. It could have been a small town in Sussex, were it not for the hibiscus and frangipani and the great yellow African sun overhead. I spent a delightful day wandering through woods and meadows, cooling my feet in little streams and picnicking in wonderful solitude on a hillside with the town spread out below, its roofs gleaming red and white among the brilliant green.

I was awakened from my nap by a cold wind and saw that huge grey clouds were boiling down from the peaks and rapidly filling the valley. Most of the mountains had vanished. I needed no other warning. With a great deal of haste and no dignity, I plunged down the slope in the general direction of the town and was safely under the veranda of a store when the heavens opened up. It was still early afternoon, so I spent the rest of the day staring moodily at the sheets of water pouring off the roof and swilling in a great flood down the street. My only companion was a bedraggled dog that was not inclined to be friendly.

By seven in the evening, the rain had still not stopped, so I dashed from cover to cover to the railway station, where a square meal in the restaurant soon improved my spirits. At 8:30, I stood waiting for the train on a suspiciously deserted platform. About 9:30, other passengers began to arrive. Obviously, the locals were familiar with the Mozambique railways and had given themselves plenty of time for a leisurely drink or two. As this was my first trip on a train in Africa, I was quite excited. The passenger berths were listed on a board, and when the train finally arrived, I learned that my companions were two English civil servants going home after their tour of duty and three Rhodesians going on a fishing holiday.

In Europe in 1952, crossing a border was an uncomplicated business, requiring only a passport. Most people did not need a visa.

As I set off in my odyssey through southern Africa, I neglected to check the regulations, taking it for granted that my English passport was also sufficient there. Now, when my companions learned that I had no visa, the Rhodesians immediately started talking about Portuguese prisons and chain gangs. They had had a few beers and put plenty of imagination and humor into their tales, but gradually the Englishmen became quite worried. "Tell you what," one of them said at last. "Just say that you're in transit to Blantyre in Nyasaland. That should work." Since I had a faint hope that I might be able to get as far as Nyasaland on my little trip, I could tell a lie with a perfectly straight face.

After a long wait, the train moved a few miles toward the border, where it stopped again, and for another hour we stood in the corridor watching a variety of officials bustling about, including a man in a gorgeous uniform who strutted up and down, working himself into a fury and barking streams of orders which were completely ignored. At long last, the train slowly pulled away into the night, and we discovered that we were six grown men squashed into one compartment while the compartments on either side of us were empty. As it was stuffy and getting warmer every minute, I moved into an empty compartment and waited nervously; fiddling with my passport and trying to remember any Portuguese words I had picked up on my travels. Soon I heard the sliding of doors and the chilling sounds of "Passports please." When my door shot open, I handed over my passport with a creditable display of nonchalance and said, "Transit to Blantyre." The official glanced at the photo, said, "Blantyre. Good," stamped a page, and, with a crash of doors, was gone.

The compartment contained two long seats covered in fake leather and two let-down bunks covered in the same smooth material. Apart from a tiny metal washbasin with a tap that produced a trickle of warm, brownish water, there was nothing else. Even though it was nearly midnight, it was getting warmer by the minute as the train worked its way slowly down from the mountains to sea level. Opening the window didn't help. It merely allowed in a swarm of insects and a constant shower of ash from the old wood-burning engine, so I quickly slammed it shut and lay down in just my khaki shorts.

Day 4

I awoke sticky and uncomfortable. We were obviously at sea level, and the air was hot and humid, in complete contrast to the dry air of Rhodesia. At a tiny station located in the thick bush, two Portuguese officials came into my compartment. They spoke no English, and the odd looks they gave me when I tried to communicate showed that my Spanish was not as good as I thought it was. So I gave up and went next door, where my companions swore that their dreams had been disturbed by visions of me rotting in chains in some dismal dungeon.

The train made its slow way through a region of rivers, swamps, and thick forest. There was hardly any cultivation or sign of civilization. Here and there, squatters had built hovels of sticks and mud on the railway embankment, which seemed to be the only dry land. They survived on fishing. As we rattled over the numerous bridges, we could see stick traps and nets set in the reeds. At the frequent stops, they crowded about the train, selling fish skewered five or six at a time on peeled sticks. The two other coaches of the three-coach train were third class coaches and full of black men returning home after working in Rhodesia. They had money in their pockets and the fish sellers did a good business.

As we were crossing one particularly wide expanse of muddy water, one of the Rhodesians said, "See that? That's the Pungwe River. It's washed out over twelve miles of the road." He laughed at me and said, "That's the road you were thinking about hitchhiking on. It will take them months to fix it." The others agreed and pointed out the obvious fact that this lonely, mosquito infested swamp was no place to get stranded in.

Building that railway through the swamps of Mozambique and over the mountains to Mashonaland, as this part of Rhodesia was then called, is one of the many unrecorded epics of the late 19th century. Cecil Rhodes had quickly realized that crude wagon trails from far away British South Africa could never keep his little colony supplied and fed, especially during the rainy season. A wagon road to Beira not only proved to be almost impossible to build, but it was also quite useless when tsetse fly attacked the oxen, so he ordered a railway to be built. It took five years. Five long years of mosquitoes and lions, of heatstroke and foul water. Africans refused to work on the line, so Indians were imported, and of the five hundred Indians, only a tiny handful survived. Nearly 400 European engineers and administrators also died, making tombstones a regular part of each shipment. One major problem was keeping the coffins from float-ing to the surface in the waterlogged cemeteries. But the rail line was built and proved immediately to be vital when Mashonaland was cut off from the Cape during the Boer War.

We arrived at Beira only two hours late. I walked through the crowds and over a bridge across the tidal flats to the nearest store, where I changed Rhodesian currency for local money. The heat reflected from the ground in solid waves, a humid and heavy heat that slowed me down to a lethargic stroll. I found the hotel that the Rhodesians had recommended and was fortunate enough to get a tiny room high up in the annex. It overlooked the sea and was de-lightfully cool. There was a louvered door that gave onto a veranda. Out to sea an Italian liner lay at anchor, streamlined, white, and gleaming on the flat blue Indian Ocean.

After lunch, I went back to the train station to book my return, and then I found the post office, which was in a pleasant, spotless marble hall, I bought a set of stamps and sent off a postcard. By the time I got back to the hotel, the stamps had stuck together into a sweaty lump, and I was in need of another shower and a com-plete change of clothing. Noel Coward's song about mad dogs and Englishmen going out in the midday sun was running through my head. There was a slight breeze on the veranda, so I sat and watched two new ships arrive. I guessed that the English civil servants I'd met would soon board one of them and have a pleasant voyage back to England. Would they go around the Cape or through the Suez Canal? Below me, some fishermen, up to their knees in mud, slowly and patiently dragged their nets in a wide half circle through the shallows and onto the beach where a handful of tiny fish gleamed in the mesh.

At sunset, I went down to dinner wearing an open necked shirt and cool slacks. As I entered the dining room, however, my way was blocked by a large black figure in formal evening wear. It was still very hot, but there was not a bead of perspiration on his face. He was the head waiter. He informed me in perfect English that I had to have a jacket and tie. I travel light, so when I told him that I had neither jacket nor tie, he winced, then snapped his fingers. A figure bearing a green silk tie appeared. I put it on. The head waiter looked me over. Satisfied, he ushered me to a table with the dignity of the standard bearer of a Roman legion. My table companion was one of the Rhodesians from the train. "This hotel was owned by a British company," he explained. "They owned the railway, too. There was none of this twaddle about dressing up for dinner in those days." He laughed. "Now that's a real turnabout."

We ate with our eyes on the door, watching The Admiral, as we called him, ambushing the guests and laughing at the expressions on the guests' faces as they were made respectable with an endless supply of perfectly hideous ties.

After dinner, my friend and I went upstairs to the lounge, where there was a dance. Finding a table well hidden behind another huge palm, we settled down to a cool glass. But The Admiral found us. What was good enough for the dining room was certainly not good enough for the dance floor. I had no jacket, and it was too hot to argue, so I got up to leave. A man nearby offered me a spare jacket he had in his room. It turned out to be a double-breasted business suit in blue pin-stripes and was much too big for me. It also clashed horribly with my khaki slacks. I felt like a clown but, in The Admiral's eyes, it was pure Saville Row white tie and tails, and so he gave me an approving smile.

The only women at the dance were some elderly tourists and a few extremely attractive Portuguese girls who were so heavily guarded by male relatives that asking for a dance was obviously out of the question. So my friends and I went for a stroll along the harbor wall. It was a perfect tropical night with a gentle breeze from the ocean. We gazed at the reflections of the brilliantly lit ocean liners lying at anchor and also watched a small boy fishing by the light of a huge yellow moon. I was back in my room before I realized that I still had the stranger's jacket and The Admiral's tie and I spent at least an hour tracking them both down to return their gifts.

Day 5

My fifth day was Easter Sunday. I had no trouble finding a church. I just followed the crowds. The inside of the church I entered was all gilt and enamel in a bright and cheerful décor that matched the congregation. After an overly long service, I stood and watched the people coming out in large family groups, loitering and chatting in a festive mood. There were Portuguese and Africans, Indians and other Asians and Europeans, every mixture from three continents, all in their holiday best. It was a kaleidoscope of color pouring down the steps and along the road.

In theory, there was no color bar in the Portuguese colonies at that time. In the eyes of the law, a black African was as good as a white African or a brown African. But it was obvious who held the top positions and where the money was. Real integration was mostly at the bottom, even though people of every race and every economic level appeared to intermingle quite casually in public.

Beira is not an ancient city. When the daring Portuguese mariners rounded the Cape nearly 500 years ago, they immediately clashed with the Arab traders who monopolized the route to India. In a series of battles, the Portuguese wrested a number of important seaports from the Arabs and then drove deep into the African interior. Portuguese trading posts and missions were established in Mashonaland centuries before Cecil Rhodes was born, and Portuguese explorer-merchants had crossed from coast to coast between Angola and Mozambique, a hundred years before the famous Dr. David Livingstone awakened English interest in the dark continent. One of the most important sea ports was fabled Sofala in Mozambique, where iron and copper were shipped to India and legends claim the oxen had golden collars. The metals that were exported came from Mashonaland, along with ivory and slaves, and the town became an important jumping-off point for expeditions into the interior of Africa. Sadly, when the railway builders arrived in the 19th century, they chose a spot some miles north of Sofala, where the river mouth offered better anchorage and today the ancient city is quite forgotten.

The Beira I saw was a sleepy port of low buildings on the mud flats at the wide mouth of the Pungwe River. There was little of interest in the newer part of the city except for a few colonial public buildings, slowly decaying in the humidity, and streets of low roofed shops with their wide open doors and dark interiors. The older part was more fascinating. Most of the houses were raised off the ground on six foot pillars to catch the breeze. There were wide balconies covered in shutters that were propped up on long sticks, the gardens were tangles of vegetation with great patches of hibiscus and banana trees, and all the roofs were red corrugated iron. Small children of every color played on the long wooden steps, and I could smell lunch cooking on wood burning stoves.

The sea wall was crowded with holiday fishermen, mostly old men and small boys. They were actually catching fish. The muddy water must have been teeming with fish, for as I watched, an old man lifted a great monster about two feet long and showed it to me. It was a squat brute with too many fins, and I didn't recognize it. At first, it was brilliantly colored in blues and greens, but it quickly turned black in the sun. The old man tied it to his bike and pedaled off with his Easter Sunday dinner. Years later, I read an article about the coelacanth, a famous prehistoric fish. It was discovered in the Indian Ocean very near Beira.

When I went for a walk after lunch, looking for a place to take a swim, I came upon a path that headed towards the sea. It led across a wild salt swamp, where the mosquito-infested, stagnant waters stank in the heat. Near the path stood the concrete skeleton of a large building and a weather-worn sign boasting that it was destined to be the finest resort hotel on the coast…when completed. When I climbed over the sea wall, I saw that the long walk had been worth it. Beyond some low dunes lay a majestic curve of silver sand and a limitless blue sea edged with gentle white surf. There were no people, and as far as the eye could see, no sign of civilization except for the picturesque wreck of a small boat half buried in the sand. The picture was framed by tall palm trees leaning into the soft breeze.

It was pleasant to sit for a while in the shade of the wreck, listen to the silence, and watch the incoming tide swirl gently across the sand. When I changed, I left my clothes on the wrecked boat and walked in my shoes across sand that was too hot for bare feet. I left my shoes well above the high tide mark and spent a delightful hour in the warm water. But when I came out, my shoes were gone. My clothes were still there, but the tide had come in higher than I had expected. I ran up and down the beach, searching in the flotsam and worrying about returning barefoot to the hotel where, fortunately, I had a spare pair of shoes. Once I caught a brief glimpse of my shoes, still tied together by the laces, but a wave splashed sandy water on my glasses and I lost them. For another half hour, I scrabbled about in the shallows, but I eventually had to give up. I hobbled across the hot sand and through the swampy area to where I had seen a bus stop. The sympathetic bus driver let me off at the hotel, which was crowded with extremely well dressed guests and I tip-toed up the steps…only to run into my Rhodesian friends, who had a good laugh at my expense. I escaped them and slid, barefoot and extremely the worse for wear, into the crowded lobby, where there seemed to be a cocktail party going on. The Admiral was nowhere in sight, so I assumed what I thought was a nonchalant attitude and walked casually up the grand staircase, ignoring the horrified stares and the giggles behind me. At dinner that evening, The Admiral handed me a tie without a word, then deliberately glanced down at my feet to see that I was properly shod.

Later, I stood on the little balcony and waited. The sky was heavy with clouds and the air was still, much too still. Soon large rain drops began to plop into the dust and bell boys ran around winding up the windows of parked cars. The air was filled with that special smell of rain on hot dust, and I stood and watched as the drumming of rain on the roof turned into a dull roar.

Day 6

By morning, when the refreshing rain had turned into a dismal downpour, I splashed towards the main part of town. The rain gave me the excuse to shelter almost anywhere, so I stopped at every door with a little roof over it and poked around rickety little stores with the oddest collections of trade goods. Sewing machines and blankets kept company with bush knives and bundles of dried fish, gaudy plastic necklaces hung from kerosene lamps, and swaths of bright cloth sat on cases of sweetened condensed milk. Here and there a small black baby wearing only a shirt splashed happily in a puddle while East Indians were visible though the open doors of their little tailor shops. Ignoring the rain, they were industriously pedaling their sewing machines and running up bright shirts and khaki shorts.

In the Chinese part of town, I spent my time trying to decipher the labels on curious little tins in dimly lit shops. One place boasted an enormous shark fin on the wall, while another was festooned with dried octopus. I found the various smells of strange spices intoxicating. Thinking I must be the only person out in such a downpour, I bought a few postcards and headed back to the hotel. But then I turned a corner and came across a soldier in full dress uniform and a long bayonet. He was standing perfectly still in the pouring rain guarding a public building. His uniform was soaked and the rain dripped down his face and down his rifle, too, but he stood stiffly at attention, staring straight ahead as the tropical deluge lapped around his ankles.

It was uncanny how my hotel bill exactly matched the money I had in my pocket, right down to the last centime. The rain stopped while I was packing, and by the time I reached the station, the roads were dry and the sun was blazing down again. After checking on my compartment on the train, I sat on a packing case on the platform and watched the crowds of passengers hurrying about as if the train were due to start while at the same time the railway officials strolled around as if it had not yet arrived. Vendors were doing a brisk trade in sickly-sweet colored drinks and shaved ice cones, and huge quantities of food and wine were being passed through the windows of the compartments.

I was soon joined in my people-watching on the platform by another passenger, an elderly farmer from Umtali who was returning to Rhodesia. When I told him what I was doing, he said, "I wish I had the time to travel. It's such a fascinating part of the world." He pointed to the train behind ours. "See that train over there?" he asked me. "That one goes north to Nyasaland."

The train stood there, quietly waiting, half a dozen old, weather worn coaches pulled by a huge black monster. "I've lived in Umtali all my life," my new friend said, "and I have never had a reason to go up to Blantyre." He then added, "But I sure wouldn't go on that thing."

I disagreed with him and said that if I had known there was a rail line up to Nyasaland, I would have planned to go that way.

"Well," he replied, "if you have all the time in the world, take lots of food with you, and don't mind mosquitoes, I guess it could be interesting. The line goes through pretty wild country, most of it swamp, and I hear that the tracks are overgrown and either flooded or washed away most of the time. There's a bridge over the Zambezi, if these damn fools haven't let it fall down. Over two miles long. Supposed to have been the longest railway bridge in the world, when it was built." He smiled and shook his head with wonder. "That must have been something," he added, "building the world's longest bridge in the middle of that miserable country." He had the highland farmer's contempt for the wet and humid lowlands.

"So then the railway goes up into Nyasaland. That's quite a climb." I said. "They say that Nyasaland is very beautiful. Maybe I can get there."

He laughed, "Not by hitchhiking, you won't!"

Our discussion was suddenly cut short as the train began to move. We had been so sure that it would not leave on time and that the engineer would give at least one blast on his whistle that, for a second or two, we just sat and stared in astonishment. Then we made a mad dash for the nearest open door and leapt aboard.

Thanks to a clerical error, two women had been assigned to our compartment. The train was quite full, and there seemed to be little we could do about it, but the women had other ideas and went off to find the conductor. They returned with their victim and gave him the sharp edges of their tongues in very rapid Portuguese. He soon staggered off with their suitcases, leaving me and three Rhodesians to enjoy the extra space. Darkness fell with tropical swiftness, and the compartment was soon filled with flying insects of every shape and size, but mostly mosquitoes. After ten minutes swatting at them, somebody had the bright idea of turning out the lights and opening the passage door. The insects immediately flew into the lighted passageway and we slammed the door shut behind them before they realized that they had been tricked out of their supper. My companions had all been fishing along the coast, and so our conversation turned to the merits of surf fishing as compared to renting a boat. When I asked about river and lake fishing in Rhodesia, however, they lost interest. Part of the fun for the inhabitants of a land-locked country was to go to the seaside.

When my compartment-mates pulled down the bunks and prepared to go to bed, I went out and stood on the open platform at the rear of the passenger cars. The air was warm and smelled damp, but it was better than the stuffy compartment. There was little to see in the pitch dark, but now and then a giant beetle would crash noisily into the wall of the coach behind ours or the train would rumble over a bridge. The croaks of giant bullfrogs added another note to the insect chorus that forms the background of any tropical night. Just a few weeks earlier, I had been freezing in England because (thanks to post-war rationing) there had been no fuel for the barracks heater, and we had spent a week clearing the road of six-foot snow drifts. Those had been days when I had wondered if I would ever be warm again. Now, remembering the freezing cold and feeling grateful for the tropical heat, I stretched my face out into the warm night air...and was rudely awakened from my reverie by a shower of stinging ash from the engine.

This portion of western Mozambique, consisting of Manica-land and Gasaland, was a major source of contention between the British South Africa Company and the Portuguese. Yearning for access to the sea for his land-locked colony, Cecil Rhodes had tried to lay claim to the land and, late in the 19th century, made a number of treaties and agreements with various tribal chiefs in the area. The Portuguese prince consort appealed to London, and armed forces were prepared on both sides of the border. Acting quickly, a small police force under a Captain Forbes hurried to the coast, claiming the land and arresting some Portuguese officials. Forbes was less than two days' march from the ocean when a message reached him, ordering him back immediately. London had decided in favor of the Portuguese, preferring to stand behind the 500-year-old treaty of friendship with Portugal rather than add yet another bit of use-less real estate to an already huge and unwieldy empire.

The train stopped many times at points in the bush. There were no stations, just clearings near the track where an acetylene flare would illuminate one or two figures, somebody would clamber off the train, someone would climb aboard, a figure would help with the luggage, and the train would pull away. Sometimes the delay was a trifle longer, and I spotted the shadows of unlit buildings in the background. Children often appeared out of the dark to sell fish and do a brisk trade with the Africans in the rear passenger cars as other ragged urchins selling cigarettes and biscuits concentrated on the first-class passenger car at the end of the train. Despite their young age, these vendors were quite capable hagglers and switched from Portuguese to English or Afrikaans as the need arose. They usually got the price they asked.

Late in the night, we left the lowlands and the train started the long climb up to Umtali. The symphony of frogs faded slightly, it became noticeably less humid, and the bush near the track became less dense.

Chapter Three: Umtali to Salisbury

Day 7

We were awakened by the Portuguese customs at exactly 3 a.m. as, with sadistic glee, they slammed the doors of each compartment open and switched on all the lights. After shouting a few unnecessary questions to which they received barely civil replies, they left our compartment to repeat the process next door. Hardly had we resumed the horizontal when the doors were again slammed open and the lights came on again. This time, passports were requested. After the third interruption, this time by the conductor, we gave up any attempt to sleep and got up and dressed, washed, shaved. Then we sat and swore at the Mozambique civil service. We soon got the opportunity to swear at the Rhodesian civil service as the whole process was repeated at exactly 6 a.m.

We reached Umtali two hours later. The town was still asleep, so I returned to my seat in the park and waited for the post office to open. I had arranged for money to be forwarded to me at Umtali and couldn't go anywhere until I had some cash in my pocket. When the post office doors opened, I found that there was no letter, but the clerk said that the mail from Salisbury was due in at ten. I went back to the park. Long distance travelers usually leave early, so a hitchhiker has to be an early bird. I sat there in frustration, watching the traffic gradually thin out. At ten there was still no letter, so I threw a tantrum and demanded to see the supervisor and insisted that they look again for my letter. Sure enough, it was there.

The road out of town was deserted by that time, but I was tired of just sitting in the park, so I walked slowly up the hill. I was almost at the foot of the pass before I got a lift. The driver, a Scots engineer working in the copper mines in Northern Rhodesia, assured me that if I ever got that far I could tour a mine. He was on holiday in Inyanga (now *Nyanga),* another popular resort town at about 5,000 feet up in the hills.

"When my pal and I first got here, Inyanga was nothing," he told me. "Just a few shacks in the bush and a road that was useless when it rained. Talk about isolated! And game? There was all kind of wildlife, including lions. It took us a few years, but we got a nice little business going and built nice houses. And we're still young enough to enjoy it." He paused, then added proudly, "And we didn't get any government subsidies or take any hand-outs from anybody. Did it all ourselves."

Everywhere I went in Rhodesia, I heard the same story. Anybody who wanted to work hard and take a chance or two could attain their heart's desire. Nothing was impossible. The future was wide open. Whether they were recent immigrants from the British Isles or descendants of the original settlers, they all seemed to be cut from the same bolt of cloth and shared a marked disdain for all bureaucracy, a contempt for social and class distinctions, and a firm belief in rugged independence.

The Scot and I made good time over the pass, and I bought him a drink at Rusape in Manicaland, where he turned north. It was a hot day, but after the humidity of the coast, the dry air was quite refreshing. Just past the immaculate police station I found a convenient milestone under a tree. I waited there, and soon a battered truck bounced to a stop, and the driver, a stocky man of about fifty wearing a dusty felt hat, called to me to jump in.

"Only five miles or so," he said, "but every little helps." I agreed. "Who are you and where are you going?" he then asked, and when I described my travels, he said that I would join him for lunch. It was more of a command than a request.

He soon turned off down a rough farm track where the grass stood taller than the truck's window. I could see nothing for the next few miles until we stopped in front of a large, white, thatched-roofed cottage nestled in the shade of a huge tree. Here the driver gave some rapid instructions to a group of African farmhands. Then he turned to introduce himself.

"I'm Mister Dee and I grow tobacco," he said as he led the way into the house. It had thick adobe walls, a stone floor, and half walls that allowed the air to circulate freely through the open rafters. It was delightfully cool. We were joined for lunch by a boy of about seventeen, who was Mr. Dee's managing assistant and the only other white man on the farm. The boy dominated the table conversation with talk about cars and racing when it was clear that his boss would have preferred to talk about tobacco.

Later, as he guided me proudly around his farm, he complained, "I'd be happier if he spent as much energy worrying about the crop as he does about his damn cars. One of the problems in this business is getting reliable managers. They have to be bloody conscientious." He frowned, then said, "But if they're any good, they either get their own plantation or they're off to Salisbury. Got to take what I can get," he added.

"Can't you train Africans?" I asked.

"Oh sure. They can be trained to do the job. In fact, I couldn't run this plantation without properly trained labor. But they are so unreliable. Even my best men take a day off when they bloody well feel like it." He shook his head, "No, a black would never do as a manager."

Tobacco farming was completely new to me, and Mr. Dee proved to be an excellent guide. We started at a field where the tobacco plants stood five feet high and some of the large green bottom leaves had already been picked. This part of the country was subject to rare but disastrous hail storms, I learned, but Mr. Dee's farm had never been struck, so he gambled on not insuring his crop. But hail was the least of his worries. Tobacco is a greedy crop, and after the virgin land has been cleared, it will give two years of tobacco. Then it has to be turned over to other crops, such as maize. This means breaking new ground all the time, and even then, large amounts of fertilizer are needed and, of course, insecticides. We moved from the field to some large sheds where teams of farm workers were fastening the leaves to long poles to be hung in the drying ovens. They worked quickly, their hands flying along the poles, attaching two or three leaves at a time, and the huge baskets were emptied almost as quickly as the truck brought them in from the fields. My host showed me how to feel the oil content of the leaf with the tips of my fingers. Next, we went into the drying barns where the poles are hung in huge ovens. Warm air circulates around each leaf and the temperature is slowly increased until the leaf is dry but not baked. This is the most important part of the operation.

"The slightest change in temperature could ruin hundreds of pounds of leaf," Mr. Dee said. "The boy and I take turns sleeping on that cot over there. Have to check the thermometers every hour or so. We don't get a decent night's sleep until the whole lot is safely dried and baled."

I climbed into an oven and looked up to see the men balancing the sticks in higher and higher layers, carefully arranging them so that no leaves touched each other. The large thermometer hung in the middle of the oven. The fuel for the dryers was the bush that had been torn up during the previous year's land clearing.

"It's getting harder and harder to find new land," Mr. Dee said. "I have fields scattered all over the place. I can use more fertilizer, but what the hell will I burn?" he asked.

Rhodesia has coal mines, but no oil or gas had been discovered, and heating with electricity would be too expensive. Wood, usually the tough gnarled roots of the thorn trees, is the main source of fuel for many of the whites and for almost all the blacks.

As we walked over to yet another large shed, we passed a work gang coming in from the fields. "How many blacks do you employ?" I asked.

"A couple of hundred in the busy season," he said, "but I'm always recruiting. They come and go so much that I pay an agent to bring them in by the truckload. I suspect they mostly come from across the border, from Mozambique." He pointed to some thatched roofs. "I have to provide houses for them. And food, too. It's the law." His voice rose. "And the relatives! My god, you should see the wives and children and parents they have. One of my biggest expenses is feeding them all."

The staple food in that part of Africa is "mealie," known to Americans as corn and to Europeans as maize. It is never eaten corn-on-the-cob style, but is usually ground up and served as a form of porridge, a tasteless and extremely dull porridge, but highly nutritious. Mealie porridge is supplemented with meat or vegetables when they are available, but often it is breakfast, lunch, and supper for weeks on end. Since it lacks protein, all employers have to provide their workers a ration of meat; the amount is set by law. Sometimes mealie is also made into a type of flat bread.

After all the tobacco leaves are properly dried, they are stored in a shed to allow them to absorb some of the moisture in the atmosphere. I climbed to the top of one of the stacks. It was an aromatic mountain of tobacco, with huge slabs of lead on top to compress it. Then my host showed me how the experts hold the leaf to the light to judge the quality, although a real expert, he said, can tell just by feel. Mr. Dee's tobacco seemed, at least to me, to be a beautiful golden yellow with very few spots or blemishes. It was flexible and oily and had a delicious smell. Later, the leaves would be sorted by skilled workers and baled for the auction rooms in Salisbury.

As it was now late afternoon, my host suggested that I stay the night. We sat on the patio with a pot of tea and he told me about the period after the war when the Europeans couldn't afford to buy tobacco and the price had hit rock bottom. The late 1940s had also been a time of drought and vicious hail storms. Tobacco disease and bush fires had swept through the area, and many of the young, eager immigrants who had invested everything in their farms were wiped out. A hard core of old timers managed to hang on, however, and now the industry was booming and the price was higher than anybody had ever dreamed.

"After all those bloody miserable years," he said, "I deserve every penny of it! Let's go have supper."

As it was Mr. Dee's turn to sleep in the drying sheds, his young assistant and I drove to Rusape. He wanted to show off his 1930s sports car, which, he proudly claimed, was the only one in Africa. It was as big as a battleship and almost as heavy, but it lacked a few parts, including one headlight and a license plate. We roared off for a hair-raising ride down the rough farm road with me crouched down behind the tiny windshield and praying that no game would suddenly appear in the light of the single headlight. But the monster car broke down after a mile, and we spent part of the cool evening poking about under the hood. After we located the problem, we limped into Rusape to a friend's house, where they went off to test the car while I sat on the veranda listening to the insect chorus and drinking the friend's beer.

The cooler was empty when they eventually returned and explained sadly that the local policeman, who had been trying to catch them for months, had at last got lucky.

"He threw the book at me!" my friend complained. "He stood there for half an hour finding things to write up."

"Well at least he didn't do what my girl did," said his friend, and he led us around behind his house to see the sad remains of his car. It had once been a beautiful thing of chrome and bright red paint, "Silly cat didn't tell me she never passed her driving test," he muttered.

Mr. Dee's employee and I drove back to his farm in silence. As we pulled into the yard, we caught a glimpse of Mr. Dee on his rounds, keeping a sharp eye on his precious crop.

Day 8

The next morning, Mr. Dee and I drove to the mill in Rusape with some sacks of maize to be ground into mealie for his workers. Then we went on to his other farm, which was on high ground not usually used for growing tobacco. His manager, a Greek immigrant with years of experience, had had a couple of good years and expected another. We stayed only long enough to drink a cup of sweet, black coffee, then dashed off to another farm to return some sacks of mealie and catch up on local gossip. After an early lunch and a quick check of the thermometers, we drove all the way back to Umtali.

I didn't mind returning to the lovely mountain town because my host said that after a brief visit to his lawyer, he was going to drive to Salisbury. He leased a great deal of land, he explained, but the lease limited the amount of land he could clear every year. He had cleared more than he should last year, and the owner was making problems.

"He's what you call an absentee landlord," Mr. Dee complained. "Lives in England and has never set foot in Rhodesia. Silly fool hasn't any idea of what's needed to farm in Africa."

I sat in the truck while he talked with the lawyer, and when they came out, the lawyer persuaded us both to stay for supper.

It was a lovely big house in the best part of town, surrounded by an immense garden with a variety of trees and shrubs. The interior was dark and cool, the walls hung with weapons and trophies, and there was an overweight Persian cat asleep on the settee. The lawyer, a large, hearty man who was deeply involved in national and regional politics, talked continuously and enthusiastically about federation.

At that time, Southern Rhodesia was a self-governing colony, not quite as independent and self-governing as Canada or Australia, but not a mere colony ruled from England, either. Immigration from England was encouraged, and as the economy grew and the white population increased, control over Rhodesian affairs by London was gradually relaxed so that the country was almost completely self-governing. It had its own coinage, stamps, police, military, and even a minuscule air force. Northern Rhodesia and Nyasaland were native protectorates with local governments, but they were essentially ruled from England. There was no unrestricted white settlement, and all foreign investment and economic activity were carefully controlled by London. By the early 1950s, there was a movement to join the three countries in a federation. Everybody seemed to think it was an excellent idea and that such a union would create a country as rich and economically powerful as the Union of South Africa.

After supper, we went downtown to a meeting in the hotel ballroom. It was supposed to be a pro and con meeting where both sides of the federation issue would be discussed. I looked forward to hearing the other side of the issue. It transpired that almost everybody in the cheerful crowd that had gathered was for federation, and only a tiny handful were against the idea. These unfortunates were surrounded by proponents.

"Don't you see, man?" the conversation—argument—went. "We could combine the copper in Northern Rhodesia and the coal in Southern Rhodesia with all the industry and commerce that we already have to make one helluva country. We could dam the Zambezi for hydroelectric power, we could extend the railways. We already grow enough food to export. And we have all kinds of minerals. What's wrong with that?"

When one dissenter asked about the black African role in this planning, the atmosphere changed. A large blonde man in khaki shorts and a starched white shirt stepped forward and said in a strong South African accent, "How long have you been here? A couple of months? The Africans had this land for a thousand years, and what did they do with it? Nothing!" His voice began to rise.

"They did nothing but kill each other or sell their neighbors to the Arab slavers or die of starvation. My grandparents came here the hard way, and they built something for themselves. We work hard and make something of this bloody country, and the blacks get the benefit." There were murmurs of agreement in the crowd. "We give them work and money and schools, we give them houses and hospitals, and they don't pay a shilling in taxes." He paused. "Hell, man, we even have to feed them!"

Another man added, "They pour across the border from Mozambique just looking for work. There are people in England who say we are robbing the Africans. Well, they should just come out here and take a good look for themselves."

Almost everybody seemed to be in agreement that federation promised a great future. Everybody except for our lawyer friend, who wondered quietly who would pay for it all. "I have a feeling that I would end up paying higher taxes," he grumbled.

We left soon after, and it was late when we got back to the tobacco farm, but Mr. Dee would not go to bed until he had taken one last look at the thermometers.

Day 9

We were up before dawn, and just as we reached the main road, we saw the great yellow sun rising over the distant hills. It was a beautiful morning, cool and bright and fresh, and we sped along the strips at top speed, bouncing through the detours and admiring the huge, dust-covered, road-building machines. On the new stretches of road we roared along as fast as the old truck could go, and my host yelled, "When I came up from the Union, over twenty years ago, it took a week to get to Salisbury. Two if it was wet. Now look. We get there in one morning." He paused, then added, "That's why my wife is not at the farm. Too lonely. She lives in Salisbury. Has her job and an apartment. Won't even visit the farm." A while later he said, somewhat sadly, "That's the real problem in farming out here. The women can't take the loneliness. They have to have company." He shrugged and changed the subject. "Look at these roads. Aren't they beautiful? It's roads that tie a country together. The Romans knew that."

As we neared Salisbury, our conversation switched to tobacco again as Mr. Dee explained that he had leaf all baled and ready for sale at the start of the season, but, acting on a tip from a friend, had held it back until the price went up. Instead, the price had dropped slightly, and now he was threatening to "tear tickets." If the grower is not happy with the auction price, he explained, he simply tears the corner off the buyer's label, and the bale is put back for auction. He is gambling, of course, that the price doesn't drop even further. After the mandatory stop in Marandelas to wash down the dust, we headed straight to the tobacco auction sheds in Salisbury.

The auction was held in a huge warehouse with a refreshment counter at one end and the rest of the space taken up by neat rows of bales with the tops open and a handful of leaves lying on top of each bale. We soon found Mr. Dee's bales, which were the first bales of this season's crop. Each bale was bid for separately, and he was silent with anxiety, looking suspiciously at the sample leaves and examining the bales around his. All the other growers were doing the same things, feeling, sniffing, walking about nervously and holding random leaves up to the light. A large group of wives in their festive best and in a holiday mood were clustered near the refreshment counter, gossiping and renewing friendships, while another group of men in business suits quietly discussed fertilizer or pretended to read the government bulletins.

The auction itself was fascinating. First came the lead actor, a tall, thin man wearing a hat on the back of his head, who appeared to be strolling casually but actually moved very quickly. This was the auctioneer, an American with a strong Southern accent. Right behind him came his clerk, a little man carrying a large clipboard and scribbling rapidly all the time and flinging the tickets down onto the bales. Next came the buyers, some in business suits, others dressed casually. They were very solemn and never spoke or smiled, but quickly picked up a leaf or two, squeezed them, and threw them down as if in disgust.

Mr. Dee pointed out one buyer in the crowd. "That's the Imperial Tobacco man," he said. "Right now, I'd say Rhodesia is providing almost all the tobacco smoked in England."

Each buyer was bidding with prearranged, secret signals. Crowding behind the buyers came the growers, pretending mightily to be uninterested, but actually bursting with impatience to snatch up the tickets and see what their bales had brought. A whole year's hard work depended on that little bit of paper.

I learned later that tobacco auctioneers were highly paid professionals who traveled the world from auction to auction. Each auctioneer has his own particular "gabble," which he chants or sings non-stop as he takes the bids. It is so fast and so laced with nonsense rhymes and pure gibberish that it seems that the only person who understands him is his clerk. But the buyers knew what this auctioneer was saying. They were bidding with signals like a nod, a wink, a shrug, or any type of signal the other buyers would not recognize. In the seconds that they spent at each bale, the buyers had to estimate the quality and the value while also keeping their employer's requirements in mind. Like the auctioneers, the buyers also traveled the world in search of the precious weed. After a few rows, a second auctioneer took over while the first man stood and sipped from a soft drink. The second man was a gravel-voiced veteran, another American, with a face as wrinkled as the leaves he was auctioning. I followed the crowd, fascinated and amused by the performance as auctioneer, clerk, farmers, and buyers made their way up and down the rows of bales. Between them, the two auctioneers had soon covered the entire warehouse. Then a small army of laborers hustled the old bales away and replaced them with fresh bales for another auction in the afternoon.

Mr. Dee told me that prices had been good and he had only torn one ticket. He was relaxed and smiled a little as he celebrated over a cup of coffee. Even I could see that his leaf was of finer quality than other bales, but his happiness was slightly dulled when he found that even inferior leaf had brought good prices.

"It's those bloody filter cigarettes," he said, "In the old days, the leaf was stripped and the woody part was dumped, but now they use everything. Even the sweepings off the floor!" Then he smiled. "Well, let's not worry about that now. I'm going to buy the biggest refrigerator in this whole town. A present for the wife."

When I asked what he would do when the last leaf was picked and sold, he threw back his head and roared, "Going fishing! I'm going to Beira and get a boat and not tell anybody where I'm going and I'm going to sit and fish as long as I bloody well want to."

Chapter Four: Salisbury to Tete

Day 9 (continued)

Before he went shopping for the refrigerator for his wife, Mr. Dee dropped me off under a huge jacaranda on the road north at the outskirts of the city. The road went through Mozambique, across the Zambezi, and would eventually get me to Nyasaland. It had been a pleasant few days, and I was sorry to see him drive off, but I was also eager to get moving again. After a while, a very large car driven by a very British Englishman stopped. Despite the heat, he wore a Harris tweed jacket and his old school tie was firmly knotted. He was very *pukha* (starchy) indeed, and he spoke with the appropriate upper-class accent. I had made it a rule always to shave and appear as respectable as possible, but alongside this man I felt like a tramp. I kept trying to peer into the mirror to see if my hair was combed. He did not engage me in conversation.

When we stopped at a private school to pick up his daughter, it was midday. The car was an oven, and the genuine leather seat was scorching. Perspiration ran down my face and between my shoulder blades, even when I put my head out of the window to catch the faint breeze. My host, however, sat quietly in his jacket and tie, listening to the radio with hardly a bead of sweat on his forehead until the daughter arrived. Then we drove through a beautiful residential area and, after a formal handshake, he dropped me off at a likely crossroads, where I quickly got a lift from a young farm machinery salesman from South Africa. This fellow was overly enthusiastic about the ability of his machines to tear out trees and deep-plow the virgin land, and we were soon involved in a heated discussion about the disastrous erosion that would result from the work his machine might do.

When we came to my crossroads, there was plenty of traffic on the other road, but my road to Nyasaland stood long, hot, and empty. After an hour, I got a lift from a recent immigrant from London, a lady who was house hunting for something closer to town.

"I'm just plain fed up with driving twenty miles each way to take the children to school and my husband to work and to get my letters at the post office and do a bit of shopping," she said. "And the road is so bad. Horrible when it rains." She made it clear that she much preferred living in the city to living out in the countryside.

As this ride ended and the lady's car disappeared in a cloud of dust down a side road, I suddenly became very lonely. Up until then, I had been traveling on major roads through the busy heart of the country. Now I was on a second-class road leading north into a very thinly populated region. My map showed a town called Mtoko in Mashonaland, then a town called Tete in Mozambique, then the major city of Blantyre in Nyasaland. But there was practically nothing in between and no hint as to the sizes of these towns. Well, I told myself, where there's a road, there will be cars and trucks.

It was a long wait. I sat at the side of a dusty road in a wide expanse of rolling grassland and thorn trees. There were no fence posts, and I saw only a thin line of phone poles tilting under the weight of two or three wires. A few cows dozed in the shade of the thorn trees, but nothing moved in the heat except three women coming up the road and balancing blanket-wrapped umbrellas on their heads. They walked silently in single file, and little clouds of dust rose with each step they took. No insects whispered and no birds sang as I sat and watched the women vanish into the distant grey-green haze.

It was late afternoon before a car appeared. It sped right past me, but then stopped and reversed. The driver and his wife had strong American accents, and they cheerfully squeezed me into the back seat along with their two children and a pile of luggage. I took them to be tourists, but they turned out to be tea planters from Nyasaland.

"We've been down to the Union on holiday," the wife explained. "We've been promising ourselves this trip ever since we came to Africa from the States ten years ago." She looked out at the dry and dusty scenery and added, "It's been fun, but we'll be so glad to get home." The children agreed.

"We must have put over 5,000 miles on this old car and practically no trouble," her husband said. "I've got my fingers crossed, because the worst stretch is right ahead."

After this ominous statement, they changed subjects and for the next hour they described their corner of Nyasaland with its rolling hills, all green with neatly clipped tea bushes and with white-washed planters' houses standing out in the clear air and the cool breeze that arrived every evening from the blue mountains to the west. It sounded wonderful.

As we drove, the bush became thicker and crowded greedily onto the narrow road. The land became rougher, with dark granite hills looming over the trees. The road snaked around huge rocks and across dried-up rivers, their beds choked with fallen trees.

Many of the rivers had deep holes dug in the sand where natives and unlucky motorists had searched for water. The little boy had fallen asleep on my lap, and the sun was low in the sky long before we reached Mtoko.

The border between Mozambique and Rhodesia is sixty miles further north, but as there is no town there, the combined police, customs, and immigration post is at Mtoko. For some reason, the post was south of the town so that we had to cross the border, with all its petty formalities, before we could go into town. It would be hard to imagine a British police post without white-wash and shining brass, and this was no exception. The floor gleamed. The door knobs gleamed. The flag pole gleamed. Even the road barrier gleamed. Every path was edged with white-washed rocks, and, of course, the hedge was trimmed with mathematical precision. As the American family had a huge pile of luggage to go through, I thanked them for the ride and walked down the hill to the town.

What I found were a store, one petrol pump, a very simple hotel, and a pile of logs. The road looked suspiciously unused, except for small groups of Africans returning home from work in the bush. They looked curiously at the stranger. The very old and the very young raised their hats and said, "Morning, Boss," as they passed me, but the others stared and the women giggled. It seemed that "Good morning" was the accepted form of greeting, so I said the same, even though the sun was clearly setting.

I checked the license plates of the cars I saw near the hotel and saw that, except for the family that had given me a lift, they were all local. The only signs of life came from the bar, so I went in and hoisted myself onto a stool and listened to a heated argument about federation. It was clear that everybody here was in favor, but that did not stop a good argument. The barman, an elderly man with a strong Afrikaans accent, was leading the conversation by sheer force of lung power. One of the customers was a young policeman, and another was a colorful character with a sun-burned face, a red bandana tucked into a checked shirt, and well-worn miner's boots. He said little, but spat with great accuracy into the trash can whenever he disagreed with a statement. I later learned that he was a prospector.

The barman was also the innkeeper, but I didn't have to drag him away from his argument because an African servant came in and took me to a room. He found it by the simple process of pushing open every door until he found a room that was not occupied. The hotel consisted of half a dozen separate buildings scattered under the trees, and I found the dining room by following the sound of dishes through the dark. The only other diners were the family I'd ridden in with. They were busy feeding the children. I was tempted to ask them for a lift to Nyasaland, but it was a very long way, the car was hot and crowded, and I decided that one good turn was enough. Had I known what lay ahead I would gladly have ridden on the roof of their car.

Later, when I was standing on the veranda listening to the night insects, an elderly gentleman came up and started talking. After brief introductions, he told me that he had a car and a small house trailer, his "caravan," he called it, and he was spending his retirement touring southern Africa.

"When I come to a place I like," he said, "I stop for a day or two, or sometimes a month or two."

He was a walking encyclopedia and knew every place from Mombasa, in Kenya, to Cape Town, near the southern tip of the continent. It sounded fascinating, but I got the impression that his was actually a lonely life. When I asked him about this, he replied, "There's a big difference between being alone and being lonely. You can be very lonely in London or New York." Then he quickly changed the subject and cheered me up by saying that I could wait for days for a lift on this road, but when it did come it would be straight through to Nyasaland because there was nothing in the 300 miles in between.

Groping my way back to my room in the dark, I bumped into a young man. "Care to make a fourth for a few rounds of poker?" he asked.

His room was a small arsenal of rifles and shotguns, with boxes of cartridges and cleaning equipment covering the bed and table, so we took the game outside to the veranda. The hunter was the customs officer who spent most of his considerable spare time hunting leopards. Another player was the mailman, and the third was a policeman straight out from England and loving every minute of Africa. We were all young and enthusiastic, and we argued about hunting and played cards energetically if not well, until the gasoline powered generator was switched off at midnight and the light went out.

Leopard hunting was a popular sport in those days, and the Rhodesians had bred a dog called a Rhodesian Ridgeback especially for the sport. It looks rather like a stocky German shepherd, but the hair along the ridge of the spine grows in the opposite direction, hence the name ridgeback. Some of them can be very large.

Leopards, I was told, are vicious, bad tempered, and intelligent and even a small scratch from one claw can result in a festering wound. They are thus a major nuisance to the natives and to livestock, but their favorite meal is the dog-faced baboon. The baboons travel in large family groups, and half a dozen big males can rip a leopard to shreds, so the natural balance is maintained. With the steady extermination of the leopard, however, baboons became more than a mere nuisance. A large group of them can wreak havoc in a maize field. More than one village has awakened to find that the result of months of intense labor has gone into the stomachs of marauding baboons. Unfortunately, baboon hunting did not have the Hemingwayesque aura of the leopard hunt, and the black farmers, who were not allowed to own rifles, were the ones who suffered.

As we were finishing the poker game by candlelight, a car drove up and a man appeared out of the night, dusty, travel-weary, and in no mood for conversation. "Got a room that's empty?" he asked.

"Sure," one of us replied and pointed. "Over that way. Just take the first one you find. Here, take the candle."

Day 10

Next morning I awoke late to find all the cars gone. When I went to pay my bill and sign the register, the innkeeper asked me how I was traveling. When I told him I was hitchhiking he was horrified. "That's bloody dangerous!" he said. Then he looked concerned, "You don't have to pay if you can't afford it, man." I was pleasantly surprised, but assured him that I had money. Then, when he heard that I was in the RAF, he was even more reluctant to accept my money. I did eventually force him to make out a bill, but I am still sure that he undercharged me.

Back on the road, I sat on a log and watched a carpenter planing a large plank. Nothing else moved, no cars passed either way, and nobody came to the store. All I could see was just the narrow, dusty, very empty road and the top of a hill, bald and black through the thick bush. After two hours, the plank was reduced to a pile of shavings around the carpenter's bare feet, and some large flies had found that white man tastes just as good as black. I walked up the road to the combination customs house and police station.

A crowd of Africans were squatting in a rough circle in the shade of a large tree. They were holding a meeting presided over by two chiefs, who wore their official badges of authority, brass plates embossed with the British crown, around their necks. As added sign of prestige and wealth, they also wore, despite the intense heat, old army greatcoats. I had been standing and watching for only a few minutes when a shy young man brought me a wooden chair and hurried away before I could thank him. Half an hour later, a very smartly dressed African constable marched over from the post and invited me to sit in the shade of the veranda. It was much cooler on the highly polished tiles, and I soon settled back to read a book I had brought along for such times as this.

The morning dragged on, the sun rose higher, and the road remained empty. The conference under the tree hardly moved. Even the flies went to sleep. After a while, the young white policeman stuck his head around the door and cheerfully asked, "Care for a cup of tea, old chap?" I sat for the rest of the morning in the corner of his office and watched the police at work.

"That bunch under the tree is a native court," one of the constables explained. "They take care of all tribal disputes. We only get the really serious stuff. Or what they can't settle themselves."

As I slowly sipped my tea, I had the opportunity to see "white man's justice" in action. There was the smart African constable, his shorts creased razor sharp and his puttees wound geometrically perfectly. He stood stiff and erect, stamped his boots on the tiled floor, and said, "Sah!" to everything. On a bench near the open window sat a woman and an interpreter. The white policeman asked a question and it made its way through the black policeman to the interpreter and then to the woman. It was obvious that the wording changed a little during the process, and either the black policeman or the interpreter sometimes rattled off a question of his own. The woman grunted a few words and the constable launched into a lengthy reply.

The woman was claiming that a man had stolen a calf from her son while he was out tending the herd in the bush. The man claimed that he had bought the calf. Naturally, there were no receipts and there was no witness. As he had not been formally charged, the man was not present. I felt as I listened, that he never would be charged, as the woman contradicted herself at every turn. At one point, when she was asked the age of "this little boy" (her son), the woman, who could not count beyond ten, made some calculations and decided that he was 30. The calf, she reluctantly admitted, was two seasons old. The white officer patiently recorded the facts without comment and informed me that the case could go on for days.

"One skinny cow doesn't seem like much," he said, "but it's a very valuable investment to these people, a small fortune on the hoof." He spoke to the constable then said, "Can't settle things like this too quickly. Neither party would feel they were getting their money's worth." Eventually, he put down his pen and said to me, "Let's go have lunch."

We walked down a neat garden path to a spotless bungalow with a wide, overhanging roof. The walls of the large cool room inside were hung with trophy horns and old muskets. The meal was excellent. Over coffee, the serious, elderly gentleman who was the officer in charge depressed me by telling me that days often went by without any vehicles passing in either direction. Some of the old photos on the wall dated from the days of the British South Africa Police, who were more soldier than policeman, and the danger from a native spear or an animal's claw was real. "Hitchhiking in Africa," the elderly officer said, "damn foolish!" It struck me that in 1952 there was more danger trying to cross Piccadilly during the rush hour, but I didn't argue with him.

Back on the veranda, I was just falling asleep when a truck pulled up. It was big and well worn and fully-loaded with boxes under a tarp, plus eight or nine men perched on the cargo. It was also facing the wrong way so I ignored it until my friend the constable called through the window, "I say. You're in luck. This chap's going to Tete. I've arranged a lift for you." I dashed around, thanking everybody, and scrambled into the cab. In seconds we were off down the road in a cloud of dust.

I thought that the road from Salisbury had been bad, but past Mtoko, it became something special. If it were not for the line marked on the map, it would be easy to doubt that this road even existed. The kindest description would be a narrow riverbed in the dry season. We jolted with spine-jarring crashes over ruts, roots, and rocks as branches struck at the cab from both sides and I was soon wondering how anything short of a tank could survive 10 miles, let alone the 150 that we had to go on this awful road.

The driver (and owner) of the truck was a small, wiry Portuguese, born and raised in Tete. He spoke a cheerful smattering of English, and we got on quite well. He explained that this was his route, from the Zambezi River to the Rhodesian border, and he carried anything and everything that would make a profit. He knew every river and creek and pretty well everybody who lived along the road. And he loved his job.

The heavy vegetation around us obscured the view much of the time, but now and then we passed a village of round mud huts with pointed thatch roofs where children played in the dust with the goats and the chickens, and the women stood in the shade grinding mealie in wooden mortars with giant wooden pestles. Now and then we also crossed small rivers that were crudely bridged with a truckload of rocks. Sometimes we ground slowly up steep hills on a track just wide enough for one vehicle. I asked what would happen if we actually met a vehicle going the other way. With his limited English, the driver found it hard to explain, but I gathered that the downhill driver had the right of way. "Maybe his brakes are not so good," my driver said cheerfully. One or two wide rivers had low-level bridges where we stopped for a breath of air, but not once did I see a river with water in it. The beds of most of the rivers were pitted with soak holes, some as deep as a tall man. My host told me the name of each river and gleefully told me how many days he had been stuck in them the last time they were in flood.

Not long after we left Mtoko, we came to the tsetse barrier. It was just a large barn built across the road. The truck was driven inside, and the African inspector closed both the doors of the barn and carefully sprayed the wheels and underside of the truck with DDT. This took only a few minutes, and there was no need to get out. But I have always been curious, so I asked to see the dreaded tsetse fly. I was shown a test tube containing what looked like a large horse fly. It was an ugly brute, and the inspector carefully pointed out various features and explained that the fly didn't put you to sleep. "No, sir," he asserted. "It's the sickness that makes you so weak that you spend your time resting and sleeping." Spraying complete, he opened the barn doors, wished us a safe trip, and added, "You keep a sharp eye out for these little buggers."

Just beyond the barrier, the bush had been cleared back for hundreds of feet in a great open swath that stretched off into the distance on both sides of the road along the edge of the fly area. Since the animals that carry the sickness will not cross such a wide-open space, they are kept out of the clear area without the expense or problems of a wire fence. This Rhodesian tsetse post was well maintained, but, alas, I could not say the same for the one on the Mozambique side. When we arrived the doors were wide open. It was obviously deserted and the bush was reclaiming the cleared strip.

Crossing the border from Southern Rhodesia to Mozambique was an interesting experience. The road had been gradually getting worse, if possible; and, as we churned up the sandy bank of a river, there in front of us was a sight to behold—a brand new road. The gravel was newly graded and wide and the surface was as smooth as a billiard table. There were neatly white-washed stones along the edge, plus drainage ditches, and the bush was cut well back. Precisely on the border, surrounded by gleaming white stones, was a great stone Portuguese cross. My host smiled and said, "Pretty good, eh?"

I agreed, but I was suspicious. My suspicions proved correct. Hardly two miles further on, the road reverted to normal and we were back on the second rate imitation of a riverbed. I have often wondered what Mittyesque civil servant back in far-off Lisbon had the bright idea of building one or two kilometers of expensive road in the heart of Africa merely to impress the very occasional tourist.

At sunset, we stopped at a lonely Indian store on the crest of a hill. It was a plain, tin-roofed building with a flight of wooden steps leading up to a wide veranda on which I saw a group of children and the inevitable sewing machine. I saw this type of store everywhere in Africa, and every one seemed to be exactly the same. The inside was crowded with boxes and sacks and all kinds of merchandise. Rolls of cloth filled many shelves, sacks of rice and maize were stacked against the walls, and there were bright combs and plastic bracelets for the women and bicycle tires for the men. Jars of candy stood on the well-worn counter next to the brass scales, and near the door were cans of kerosene and DDT and sometimes even gasoline. Although there was no refrigerator, there were always bottles of soft drinks and, with luck, beer. My host had his own supply of beer and produced a couple of bottles from behind his seat. Not surprisingly, when we opened these much-shaken bottles, much of the beer came out in a geyser of foam, but the rest was relished down to the last warm drop as we watched the storekeeper's helpers loading and unloading various boxes from the truck.

It grew very quiet as I leaned against the tailgate of the truck and took in the view. The road we had traveled lay twisted and yellow through the forest below, while above it the sky turned orange and purple shadows raced across the ground, eager to swallow the land in darkness. Little lights flickered and brightened as fires were lit to cook the evening meal and ward off things that feed by night. Great starry diamonds appeared in the sky and, on the north horizon a brush fire blazed its golden trail of destruction. After the bumpy road, it was serene and peaceful.

I gathered that a couple of the men on the back of the truck were the trucker's paid helpers and the others were paying passengers. There was no bus service on that road, so people were given rides on trucks. As it grew dark they huddled into blankets and old army greatcoats, all the while smoking large green cheroots of locally grown tobacco. I had tried one once. Once had been enough.

Curious about the cargo, I looked under the canvas and, as it was dark, struck a match. With a gasp, I quickly flung the match to the ground and stared at the men smoking their cigars and flicking the ash everywhere. At least half the cargo was boxes of dynamite! Within minutes, another shock was in store for me. The truck was parked directly in the middle of the road, and as I stood there, open-mouthed, I heard another truck coming. The truck's lights were not on, and the driver was in the store, so I climbed into the cab and fumbled around for the light switch. As luck would have it, the make was foreign to me and had a left-hand drive. The thought of what was in the back didn't help much as I pushed, pulled, and turned every knob and button I could find. The oncoming truck was barely a hundred yards away when I found the right switch and turned on the lights. With an angry blast of the horn and a flashing of headlights the great black monster swerved by in a fog of dust and gravel and disappeared down the hill, eager to reach the border before midnight.

We were well on our way again before I cautiously asked about the cargo of dynamite. "Oh, dinameet," the driver replied. "That go to the mines. Very safe. I never have any trouble with dinameet for many years. No. No trouble."

I was supposed to be a military armourer and know all about such things, so I thought hard and suddenly remembered that modern dynamite is indeed harmless and can be roughly handled safely because it needs a detonating cap to set it off. Still, it had been quite a shock to read the labels on those wooden boxes, and for the next little while I couldn't resist a slight shudder every time we bounced over a particularly nasty rock.

The darkness and the roar of the motor eventually lulled me to sleep, but I awoke when we stopped in the center of a long, low-level bridge. All around I could hear the rush of water. When I looked out, it was black and oily in the starlight. This was the first water we had seen all day and, surprisingly refreshed by the cool, damp air, we soon arrived at the Portuguese customs post in Changara in western Mozambique.

The post was dark and silent, and the barrier was firmly chained and padlocked, but a long blast on the horn soon brought the customs official out. He was a short, overweight man accompanied by three huge dogs, one of which was a beautiful ridgeback with a broad leather collar studded with sharp spikes that must have been two inches long. The two men knew each other well, and they rapidly filled in all the forms by the light of a hissing yellow hurricane lamp. Then the customs official turned to me and said, "Visa, please." I was astonished and said that I was in transit to Blantyre in Nyasaland. He was not convinced, so I tried saying that I was a serviceman returning to my unit, but that failed, too. Next I lied and told him that his consul in Salisbury had assured me that a visa was not necessary, but that didn't move him, either. Finally, I showed him the stamp in my passport that I'd gotten on the train to Beira. This impressed him a little, but not enough.

My host, the truck owner, had been watching and listening silently, and when the government official and I reached this impasse he spoke up, and, in rapid Portuguese that I could barely understand, pointed out that I could not possibly be turned back now, in the middle of the night, on foot, to go all the way back to Salisbury for a bit of paper. Ignoring me, they discussed this conundrum for a while. I more or less understood that my friend was hinting broadly that the official would be stuck with an unwanted guest for God knows how many days if I were not permitted to pass. This seemed to do the trick. The official reluctantly shoved some forms and a pen at me. I signed my name, he gave a great sigh, and then, after a long pause, he stamped my passport.

With the formalities over, we were ushered into the dining room behind the office and introduced to the lady of the house, a short, fat woman dressed entirely in black who smiled a lot and said very little. She bustled about with plates of rice and fish, *bacalhau* imported from Portugal, all marvelously flavored with garlic. There were plates of crisp, fresh bread and a dish of huge black olives gleamed in the yellow lamp light. With the aid of a bottle of good wine, it all vanished under the approving eyes of the lady. Then, over coffee, the two men talked business in Portuguese, with an occasional question to me in English, more out of politeness than curiosity. I was quite sure of one thing: if it had been daytime and I had not been with that particular driver, I would never have crossed that border.

When it was time to go, there were handshakes all around, and the official himself unlocked and lifted the barrier to allow the truck to go through.

The headlights picked out a deserted street of dusty buildings with doors firmly locked and shutters on every window. I had been told that the town boasted a hotel, but if there was indeed a hotel, it did not tempt me, and in minutes we were back in the bush. After the hearty midnight meal, I dozed off, but now and then I was awakened by the sound of the horn. This usually meant that a pair of diamonds glowing in the dark had evolved into a huge brown owl sitting in the center of the road. They always waited until the very last second before unfolding enormous wings and gliding a few feet to safety.

"I don't kill animals," my friend said. "They don't kill me. I don't kill them." Then he told me that the customs official had, only a few days ago, shot an enormous leopard quite near the road. He had been hunting with the big ridgeback with the spiked collar, and it had treed the leopard. "So it was very big," the driver said. "So why kill it?" he asked rhetorically, and I gathered that he did not think highly of hunting as a sport.

At one point, we stopped for no apparent reason and waited silently in the dark. In a minute, the faint yellow flicker of a lamp appeared through the trees and into the headlights stepped a woman and two pot-bellied children. A man clambered off the truck with his bundle and disappeared with his family into the darkness. My friend explained that the man was his assistant and he would pick him up on the return trip. What he could not explain was how he knew exactly where to stop in the pitch dark. There was a solid wall of bush on each side broken only by a skinny telephone pole leaning drunkenly out over the road. There was no clearing or side road. It was just a point along many miles of identical road. We discussed this for a while until it dawned on me that to him, it was not all identical. Where I saw only the forest, he saw the trees, and every mile of the road had its own character and landmarks. I thought that if our roles were reversed and we were in London, he would be just as confused if I were to drive him through the endless suburbs of the great city.

It had gradually been getting hotter as we dropped down to Tete on the Zambezi, almost at sea level, and the night air was now thick and liquid and warm. In the dark, the city appeared to be much bigger than I expected, with tall buildings and street lights. The streets were wide but deserted, with the shops all tightly shuttered and houses hidden behind high walls. Our passengers were dropped off at various corners, and then we drove up a hill past silent houses until we came to one with the lights on and a woman with three or four children standing on the veranda. It was a small stone house, weathered and comfortable in a garden of flowering shrubs, and I stood on the steps in the hot night air, my shirt sticking to my back, in a circle of small white faces while introductions were made. The driver's wife, a pretty woman, had the flat white complexion of a European who has been too long in an unhealthy part of the tropics. She spoke no English, but one of the children was learning English at school. Unfortunately, he was too shy to talk. The lady refused to allow me to go to a hotel and sent the children off to find a camp bed, which they set up in the front parlor. I was extremely tired and very grateful to her so, as soon as it was decently possible, I got a quick wash and went to bed.

The front parlor was obviously rarely used. Faded brown portraits of ancestors decorated the walls and lacy drapes covered the furniture. It was musty and hot, and the windows were hidden behind heavy curtains and I soon found that not only were they locked on the inside, but there were also locked shutters on the outside. It had been a long day, and I was exhausted enough to sleep anywhere, but every few minutes a member of the family would look in to see that I was comfortable. I was offered a glass of water, some biscuits, an extra pillow, even an extra blanket until everybody had had a turn being kind to me. When I eventually lay down to sleep, the thin sheet felt like a sheepskin rug. I lay there, gasping like a fish out of water, until I fell asleep.

Chapter Five: Tete

Day 11

Tete is an ancient city that was an Arab trading post long before the Portuguese arrived in the 16th century. A few miles above the city, the wide Zambezi is blocked by the Kebrabasa Rapids, so that all waterborne traffic must portage at Tete. It was from here that the Portuguese set off to explore the interior of the continent, and it was to Tete that much of the gold and ivory of Rhodesia was sent. David Livingstone knew the city well, for he came here after discovering the Victoria Falls and returned a number of times on his many travels west into the Rhodesias and north to Nyasaland.

I awoke early and after a cool wash felt like a new man again. I congratulated myself on my good luck and marveled at how far I had come in just ten days without getting stuck. Before they would let me go, the truck driver's family insisted that I eat a hearty breakfast of steak, eggs and potatoes, and then, after many handshakes and farewells, I walked down to the river. In the bright light of day, the city seemed smaller than I had first thought, less than half the size of Beira and with little of the bustle and energy of that sea port city. It was dry and dusty with yellow buildings shimmering in the heat, their stuccoed walls flaking, their tall window shutters unpainted. All in all, the town had a general air of sleepy stagnation. There were very few vendors on the streets and the few shoppers appeared listless. Most of the population seemed to be gathered at the river wall where a slight breeze drifted in from the water.

Because there was so little of interest in the town, I ended up sitting on the river wall, watching the mighty Zambezi swirl past on its long journey to the sea. Perhaps Livingstone, the great missionary and explorer, had sat in this very spot a hundred years ago, watching his porters unload the long canoes or, in later years, loading wood onto the little steamboat named for his wife, the brave woman who lies buried and forgotten under a baobab tree near the mouth of the great river.

I estimated the river to be about half a mile wide. The far shore looked like little more than a green haze. The ferry across the river was merely a low pontoon pulled by a motor boat that held it unsteadily in place at a ramp in the wall. It took over an hour to cross the river, and there seemed to be no fixed schedule. When it was loaded, it left. If there was not much cargo, it waited for more. When the pontoon was loaded, it was towed upstream, hugging the bank, for about half a mile, at which point it headed out into the river. It was swept across to the other side and had to be towed up to the opposite bank. I wondered what happened when the river was in flood. There were two or three fishing boats with high bows and triangular Arab sails on the river, but there was hardly enough wind to move them against the current, and so they eventually dropped anchor.

As the sun crossed the sky, I followed the shadow of a tree along the wall and soon found myself in the company of some African soldiers dressed in faded, mud-colored uniforms. These were a marked contrast to the bright, starched uniforms of the

Rhodesian soldiers, but these men were a cheerful bunch and, after an exchange of cigarettes, we were soon engaged in conversation. Most of them spoke English and had lived and worked in Rhodesia. They told me that in the hot season everybody who could afford to, left for cooler districts up in Nyasaland or down on the coast. The town was virtually deserted, they assured me, and there would be very little traffic north. This worried me, and I began to question every driver I found standing nervously watching his vehicle being manhandled onto the pontoon ferry. It was all local traffic.

After lunch I spotted a small truck loaded with boxes and spoke to the driver. He was a chemist working at the tsetse fly laboratory, across the river. It wasn't very far, but I was fed up with waiting and impatient to move even across the river, so I went with him. The crossing was safer than it looked and, on the other side, there was a rough road for about a mile which took us to a smaller branch of the river. There the ferry was an open-ended scow, and the motor consisted of two rows of men with long bamboo poles. They were short men but the muscles on their backs and arms rippled hugely in the sun. After they had poled us smoothly and swiftly across this smaller river, they stood back and disdainfully allowed common laborers to push our truck up the bank. Here the road was split bamboo thrown across the sand, and getting the vehicle out of the ferry was a major operation accompanied by lots of shouting and the spinning of wheels. I noticed that one of the laborers wore the jacket of an RAF sergeant, complete with shiny buttons, and wondered how it had managed to find its way into the wilds of Mozambique.

The chemist turned north along the river bank, the ferry was poled back across the river, and I was left standing in a wilderness of hot sand and reedy marshes. The nearest trees were about five miles away, and there was not even the shade of a large bush. I realized that, thanks to my impatience, I was now in a dangerous position. About 200 yards ahead there was a truck pulled to the side of the trail. When I reached it, I saw that it was only a local truck and the door was locked. A couple of men were sheltering themselves from the sun under the truck. I looked for another vehicle. About half a mile away, behind a sand dune, there was another truck. When I pointed to it, the men under the truck exclaimed, "Blantyre! Good! Blantyre!" I set off for that truck.

The sand was soft and fine and filled my shoes as the sweat ran down my face and stung my eyes, but there seemed to be some activity by the distant truck, so I hurried as fast as I could. When I arrived, I found two African men cooking mealie porridge over a fire. They were surly and answered my questions with grunts between mouthfuls of porridge. They insisted they were not going any further that day, but I became suspicious, especially when they said that the border was closed on the weekend. I knew they were lying, but, as there was nothing I could do about it, I made my slow way back to the first truck, where the company was a bit more agreeable. The sun was directly overhead by now, and the tips of my ears were beginning to burn. The sweat no longer trickled down my back but simply evaporated as soon as it appeared. One of the men called to me to crawl under the truck with them for shade. It seemed a sensible idea. I thus spent the afternoon watching the distant trees shimmering in the blazing heat. Those were certainly the hottest hours that I have ever spent, and to this day I wonder how any man, black or white, could do a day's work in such heavy, paralyzing heat. To add insult to injury, the other truck suddenly started up, but before I could scramble to my feet, it roared off up the road. Yes, the men had been lying.

Hours later, an African man appeared out of nowhere. Without a word, he unlocked the door of the truck above me and started the engine. As my two companions climbed aboard, I slipped into the cab, and soon we were all happily inhaling the warm breeze as the truck raced up the road towards the distant trees. The ride didn't last long. Just inside the forest, the driver stopped at a store that was under the trees and many degrees cooler than the baking sand.

I went inside, where it was even cooler and smelled of spices and salt cod. The Portuguese owner, who spoke some English, explained that the store, along with the little cluster of buildings nearby, was the town of Moatise. It was the end of the rail line.

"But I thought the line from Beira went all the way to Blantyre," I said.

He shrugged and said, "Oh, yes! That line goes to Blantyre, but this is only a branch line. We get maybe one train a month."

When I asked him how I could get to the junction and catch the passenger train to Nyasaland, he had to consult with some other men in the store. About 200 miles down the river, was the consensus, or maybe only 100. "But the road is bad," the store owner said, "and nobody goes that way." It was obvious that I would not be going by train.

I drank a warm lemonade and sat on the veranda and watched the road, but the few vehicles that appeared always turned off at the store. Once a large truck pulled up and started to unload cases of imported goods, including grapes and peaches. It was obviously an important occasion and suddenly, almost magically, the little store was filled with people, and the luxuries of civilization vanished as quickly as they were unpacked. There were bottles of wine in the shipment, some of which were opened immediately, and, as a result of this, I saw the only case of white brutality that I personally witnessed in all my tour of Africa. A black man was standing in the way as a particularly large white man came out of the store. He immediately slapped the black man across the face and then laughed while the black man just stood there and grinned foolishly. A few minutes later, a servant staggered out with a heavy box, and the same Portuguese man gave him a healthy kick to help him on his way, followed by another loud laugh. Some of the customers looked up, but then they quickly turned away, and nobody said a word.

Just as it was growing dark, I got word that an Indian storekeeper would be driving to Blantyre at ten that evening. I found the Indian driver working on his truck and inquired. He agreed that *if* he went—and it was a big *if*—he would give me a lift, so I walked back to the store, prepared to wait a few more hours. The frustrating day and the unaccustomed heat had made me very tired, and I must have dozed off because I was awakened about nine o'clock by the arrival of a water tank truck. Two men got out and went into the store, then came back out and said something to me in Portuguese. I gathered that they had a place for me to sleep, as there was no hotel in Moatise. I tried to explain about the Indian driver and his truck, but the conversation got too complicated and I was so tired that I gave up and climbed into their truck.

As the truck crawled up a steep hill for a few miles, all I could think of was a soft bed in a comfortable room with, perhaps, a bath or at least a shower. A surprise awaited me. We stopped in the dark, stumbled down a bushy trail, and came to a smallish thatch-roofed building made of sticks plastered with mud. It was an African trading store. By the weak light of a lamp, I could see rolls and sacks and boxes of trade goods inside. Behind the counter, stripped to the waist, was a mulatto man doing the accounts with a pencil and a small notebook. The light reflected weirdly off his golden skin as he sat there. The truck driver spoke to him in Portuguese for a long time as he continued his laborious writing and never once looked up. At last, after a long silence, he spoke a few words and the others drove off. By that time, I was so tired that I could have slept on the mud floor itself, but I sat down on a sack and forced my eyes to stay open. Eventually, the mulatto closed his book and addressed me. He explained that the others had elected him to take charge of me because he spoke a little English. It was indeed only a little, and when I tried to explain about the Indian driving his truck to Blantyre, this man didn't understand. I gave up.

He led the way by lantern light around to the back of the store, where I hoped to find a bed or even a hammock. Instead, I found a table and chairs set out under the night sky. Hardly had my body settled into one of the comfortable cane chairs than an overwhelming sleepiness crept over me. I found it almost impossible to keep my eyes open, so out of politeness to my host I forced myself to sit bolt upright on the edge of the chair. I also had to keep pinching myself to stay awake. Suddenly, my new friend clapped his hands, and out of the dark appeared an African woman in a long, bright dress bearing a bowl of eggs. He showed the eggs to me and asked, "You like?" I nodded that I liked eggs and wondered how long it took to cook one. But then the woman, who had disappeared, came back with a bowl of potatoes. I admitted that I also liked potatoes before I remembered how long it would take to cook them.

It seemed like forever as I talked incessantly about anything that came to mind in my attempt to stay awake. After what seemed like an eternity, the woman returned with a giant potato omelet. My host gave me the lion's share, and I steadily worked my way through it. But twice my face came dangerously close to the plate, and just as we were finishing, he finally guessed my problem.

"You want to sleep." Stating the obvious, he led me immediately to a small room that contained a bed and a chair. He pulled back the cover to show me the clean sheets, patted the pillow, and said, "You need anything, you say." I said no thank you to all his offerings of water or more blankets, and he soon left. Within seconds, all the mosquitoes and tsetse flies in Mozambique could not have awakened me.

Day 12

When I woke the next morning, fully refreshed, I was able to take a look at my surroundings. The walls were almost transparent where the mud had fallen away from the sticks, and the morning sun blazed through. The floor was packed clay but swept clean, and the roof was very thinly thatched, with daylight showing through in many places. The sheets were spotless, however, and although the mattress was packed with straw, it had felt like goose down to me.

My host offered me a basin of hot water to wash and shave in and a cup of tea with sugar. I thanked him for his hospitality and we talked for a while, or rather, he asked questions that I deciphered then tried to answer using basic English and what little Spanish I knew. I quickly learned that Spanish and Portuguese are completely different languages. We got along fine, however, with the aid of a great deal of pantomime.

When I said that it was time for me to get on the road, he explained that any vehicles going north would be heard long before they reached us because of the steep hill. Meanwhile, I could sit in a comfortable chair in the shade and relax. I relaxed for four hours until my behind began to ache from the relaxing. About noon, I walked up the track to the road, where the dust lay soft and completely undisturbed. When I got back I found lunch waiting. We dined on rice and *bacalhau* with mayonnaise potatoes, and he opened a bottle of port that had been on the store shelf for years. "Native people not drink this wine," he told me. It was a very quiet Sunday afternoon, and we dozed in the cane chairs.

When it got really hot, I decided to take a shower. At the edge of the small clearing were a woven grass screen, some buckets, and a step ladder. The woman filled the buckets, then climbed the ladder and poured the water over my head. While I soaped myself, she went off and got more water, climbed the ladder again, and again poured the water over my head. The screen was wide open to anybody coming down the trail, but luckily there were no customers just then.

Finally refreshed and eager to be off, I rolled an empty oil drum to the edge of the road and perched there to wait. I waited for hours, but not a vehicle passed, and I finally strolled back to the store. As soon as I did so, I heard the sound of an engine and raced back to the road just in time to glimpse a large, powerful car with Rhodesian license plates vanish over the crest of the hill. My host was very sympathetic. He clapped his hands like an Indian prince, and a little black boy appeared. He was perched on the drum with strict orders to stop all vehicles going north, even at the risk of his life.

Back at the store, some customers had arrived. These were mostly old women in long skirts who were obviously chaperoning a young girl and her boyfriend. They had walked all day through the bush and intended to enjoy themselves. They took a long time inspecting all the brightly colored cloth and the gaudy plastic jewelry, discussing every item in great detail and in soft voices. When they spoke to the storekeeper, he answered them in their own language. The girl wheedled her boyfriend into buying her a green plastic comb, then also persuaded him to buy her a red bracelet to add to the dozen she already wore. When she stepped out to show off her prizes to the old women sitting in the shade, the boy stood by, smiling foolishly, broke, but happy. All afternoon, customers came and went, some to buy, but most of them to squat in the dust, where they talked to friends and smoked their homemade cigars. Since they all wore fairly drab clothing, mostly European cast-offs, there was no way for me to tell one tribe from another except when I heard them speaking. But the storekeeper knew his customers and spoke to them all in their own dialects. Since everybody took so long to decide everything, it was not a very exciting afternoon.

At sunset everybody left, and we devoured another huge supper of potato omelet, after which we sat and talked in the warm night while insects buzzed the lamp and cast grotesque shadows on the wall.

"Tomorrow Monday," my host said. "My boss come. He Indian. Maybe he go to Blantyre. Boss rich man," he further informed me. "Has many stores in bush, Nyasaland, also."

This was good news indeed. He predicted that the Indian owner of the store would arrive about six in the morning, so I went to bed happy. After such a highly relaxed day, however, sleep was impossible. Hardly had I found a good position than I heard a rustling sound. My hair stood on end as I thought of rats and snakes. Of the two creatures, it was snakes that I disliked more, so, logically, I persuaded myself that it was a rat and banged my shoe on the floor. This only served to let the mosquitoes know where I was. I spent the rest of the night suffocating under the sheet with only my nose poking out.

Day 13

Six o'clock found me washed and shaved and wearing a clean shirt. Eight o'clock came, then nine. At ten we had breakfast and told each other that the Indian had been delayed at the ferry. At noon we decided that he had stopped somewhere for lunch but would arrive any time soon. While we were convincing ourselves of this, a large fly landed on my neck and bit me. I swatted it, and my host picked it up, looked at it. "Tsetse," he said. "Very bad thing." I agreed and made a mental note to see the medic when I got back to camp. By three o'clock, I was beginning to despair when the sound of engines came clearly up the hill. We both dashed to the road where the small boy was standing on the oil drum and waving his arms. There, in a halo of dust, was a whole fleet of brand new trucks. One after the other they raced by and it took all three of us, waving our arms and leaping like madmen in the middle of the road, before one of them stopped. I shouted a thank-you and a goodbye, yanked open the door, and clambered in.

The African driver was most unhappy at my dramatic entrance. "I'm not allowed to give anybody a lift," he said, in perfect English as he raced to catch up with the other trucks. "The boss will kill me."

It took a while for me to calm him down and explain that I was not a hijacker. I promised to explain my situation to his boss at the very first stop we made. The driver told me that the convoy of new vehicles was from Port Elizabeth in the Union and was bound for Blantyre, a trip of about 2,000 miles. About an hour later, we came upon the rest of the fleet parked outside a store. I waited near the trucks until the last vehicle arrived. This was a large car. Two white men stepped out of it and stood staring at me. It was obvious that they couldn't quite work out what I was doing in the middle of the wilderness, and when I began to offer a hurried explanation, the older man said, "Good God! Hitchhiking in Africa. Now I've heard everything." They told me I could finish the trip, at least as far as Blantyre, in their car and instructed me to toss my bag into the car. When I asked them not to yell at the truck driver who had stopped for me, one of them said, "Forget about it. He did the right thing. Let's have a beer."

When the convoy was under way again and I told the two men where I had spent the last two nights, they were horrified. "Without any mosquito net?" one asked. Then they told me that they had intended to spend the night at the hotel in Tete. "We didn't expect luxury," one said, "and it wasn't exactly the Ritz, but when the bloody chickens wandered into the room, we just up and left." And the other added, "We slept in the car. Most uncomfortable."

As for the ferry, they were still fuming. While they were loading a truck that was carrying a car, a plank had shifted. The whole lot was saved from a trip to the bottom of the Zambezi River by one iron rail. It had taken a lot of time, perspiration, and bad temper to right the vehicles. "Man," the younger man said, "I really thought we were going to lose both the truck and the car in that damn river."

"Then," the other man said, "on that island bit in the middle, we saw a man who had his leg chewed on by a leopard last night. Nasty mess! And he was washing it in that dirty water. Probably get gangrene."

I thought about the sounds I had heard the previous night.

It was a long, slow climb out of the river valley and into the highlands, and we passed the time discussing anything that came to mind. The driver, who was about thirty, was the supervisor. The older man was the big boss from Cape Town and had come along to see conditions for himself. There were thirty vehicles in the convoy, some carried piggy-back, and when I suggested sending them by rail, the older man said in deep disgust, "The last shipment we sent weeks ago is still sitting on the docks in Beira. It'll probably still be there when we get home." They talked of convoys of a hundred vehicles or more that they had sent nearly 3,000 miles to the copper mines in Northern Rhodesia over roads as bad as the one we were on. They also talked of freak accidents and outlandish insurance and the problem of carrying their own petrol and getting the drivers home afterwards. When I asked what shape the cars were in when they arrived, the younger man shrugged. "Hey, man," he said, "the trip does no harm. Just tighten up a few nuts and bolts and they're as good as new." The older man grunted, "Probably better."

The conversation drifted, inevitably, to hunting, and the older man recounted tales of old Boer hunters he had known or heard about in his youth, of mad Englishmen, of fools who had injured themselves, and of the rich and wasteful foreigners who had slaughtered the game. I thought of the family who had given me a lift to Mtoko. They had complained that they saw almost no game on their long trip, and what they did see was in game reserves. I myself had seen nothing in nearly two weeks of travel.

Back in the 19th century, the older man said, such great white hunters as Swartz, Viljoen, and Selous had set astonishing records. A dozen elephants a day was not unknown, and Viljoen once returned with 10,000 pounds of ivory. Slaughtering elephants was not the hunters' only occupation; they were traders, too, and Selous later turned to collecting wildlife specimens for the zoos of the world. "You'll never guess what his specialty was." My host laughed. "Butterflies!"

It was dark when we reached the Mozambique customs office, where all the engine numbers were checked and a mountain of forms was filled in, papers were stamped, and carefully counted carbon copies changed hands. Then came my turn. The South Africans and their drivers had no trouble, but when the customs official came to me, he was horrified. "How did you get into Mozambique without a visa?"

As I tried to explain, he became more and more agitated. He didn't care a fig about the stamps in my passport or all the forms that I had filled in, and soon it looked as if he were going to send me all the way back to Salisbury. I pointed out that I was leaving, not trying to get into his territory. The South Africans pointed out that I had no form of transport.

"I suppose that would make you responsible for delivering him back to Changara," one of them said in a calm and courteous voice.

The official sat silently for a while. Then, obviously deciding that the dreadful deed was done and could not be undone, he waved his hand in dismissal. We were free to leave. From there, it was only a short run to the Nyasaland post, where a strong Irish accent greeted us from out of the dark. This cheerful official merely made me sign a form that said I could not seek employment in Nyasaland nor stay longer than thirty days. That done, he recommended a hotel a few miles up the road.

It was a charming place, and we hurried to get the drivers settled down. Most of them preferred to sleep in their trucks, so the only question was where they could light the fires to heat their food. One of the vehicles carried a load of firewood for this purpose, just as others carried jerry cans of drinking water along with emergency petrol, oil, and transmission fluid. After a week or two on the road, they had it all down to a smooth routine, and the mealie was cooking before we had even sat down to our own delicious supper in the hotel. I could hardly wait to climb into a steaming hot bath, soon after which a snowy white mosquito net hung around me in a real bed in a modern hotel with walls thick enough to dissuade any rat or snake.

Chapter Six: Blantyre to Lilongwe

Day 14

After breakfast, the long line of vehicles started on the last lap of its journey. We in the car brought up the rear, well behind the worst of the dust. The land had been getting hillier as we left the Zambezi valley, and now the air was much lighter and definitely cooler. The forest was greener, too, and we crossed little streams running across the road.

After about twenty miles, we came to the bridge over the Shire River, where we stopped to admire the view of the gorge and the rapids. There was a restaurant on the riverbank near the rapids, and a narrow track through the trees led to a heap of huge, water-polished rocks and a superb view of the rushing, tumbling waters as the overflow from Lake Nyasa rushed to join the mighty Zambezi River. It was this series of rapids that had so frustrated Livingstone in his attempts to bring his little wood-burning steam ship—and European civilization, up to Lake Nyasa, which, during Victoria's reign, was infested with slave traders, both Arab and African. The noise of the rapids drowned out our attempts at conversation, and so I sat quietly on a cool, damp rock and watched the spray and mist being flung high against the walls of the gorge The black and white of the water contrasted with the clear blue sky above, and here and there a plant somehow clinging to the sheer rock added a tiny dash of brilliant green. Much too soon, a hand on my shoulder reminded me that we had to be off and once again raise the dust of the long road.

As we traveled, we began to see signs of civilization again—a store, and then some houses, and then more and more people. Where the road widened, we found the rest of the convoy parked near a river. The drivers were busy washing the dust of the long journey off the trucks they were driving. They were doing a thorough job and had even taken out all the seats and moveable fittings, and I marveled at how the fine dust had seeped into everything, even the ash tray of the car that was riding on a truck. One truck was particularly dusty, and the driver explained, "When we left the Union, the boss said to fill her up with sand, for ballast." He ran his finger through the dust, "Not much left now."

When the men had finished, the vehicles gleamed in the sun, factory fresh, unscratched, and showing no sign that they had been driven so far over such terrible roads. I took a look at the odometer on one of the trucks to see how many miles it had traveled, but it read under 20.

"We unhooked them before we left," the senior manager said, adding, "Well, we are supposed to be delivering brand new cars, aren't we?" As he leaned over I saw that he had a pistol in a holster under his jacket. He patted it and said, "Just in case."

A few miles further on, we reached a surfaced road and passed an airport. At the next crossroads, I said goodbye to my good friends, and they wished me luck.

I was now on the outskirts of Blantyre, the town that I had struggled so hard to reach. It was early afternoon. Although I had lost some time and my pass was good for a little more than thirty days, I began arguing with myself. It was just another town. I had come to see the country and the people, not just more buildings. So I decided to push on north to Zomba, the old capital of Nyasaland (now Malawi).

I soon got a lift to Limbe, a small untidy town, where I stood outside a mission and watched the people while I waited for my next lift. There were hundreds of them, some on foot, some on bicycles (many of which were brand new), and most of them appeared to be healthy, cheerful, and well dressed. Quite a few carried a string of fish for their supper. After the emptiness of Mozambique and the widely spread out population of Rhodesia, the crowds here were quite a shock and took a little getting used to. At the time, Nyasaland had a native population of between two and three million, with only about 4,000 Europeans, most of them civil servants. Compared to the rest of the continent, tiny Nyasaland was very heavily populated.

One of the reasons that David Livingstone spent so much time and energy on Nyasaland was the slave trade, which he hated intensely. When he arrived in about 1860, he was astounded by the number of burned-out villages and the overcrowded slave stockades he saw along the lake shore. This, the most beautiful land he had ever seen, had been virtually depopulated by African slavers in the west and Arab slavers in the east. Dhows crowded with human misery regularly crossed the broad waters of Lake Nyasa, and the highlands of Nyasaland were as empty of people as the Sahara. Livingstone blazed a trail for later missionaries who came with Bible and gun. As the slave trade declined in the 19th century, the land was quickly re-populated by Africans, who poured in from surrounding lands, attracted by the climate and the soil as well as the trade schools and the stores of the mission stations. In a few generations, the unpopulated land became an overpopulated land.

My next lift was forty miles to Zomba. The driver who picked me up was an older man in casual business clothes who had lived in Nyasaland for many years and proudly pointed out interesting features as we drove along. Essentially, what I saw was the chain of mountains along the west side of Lake Nyasa. But these mountains are quite unlike those in Rhodesia and more like the mountains of Scotland. The soil and the climate in Nyasaland are ideal for growing trees, and the well maintained road led now and then through small forests of evergreens and blue gums. The vegetation seemed softer here, with a greater variety of bushes and shrubs, and the dry season did not seem as dry as in other parts of southern and eastern Africa. He pulled up at a view point on a hill to point out the dark blue bulk of Mt. Mulanje, the sacred mountain.

"She's nearly ten thousand feet high," he said. "Over forty miles away from here, yet she doesn't look more than ten miles away. God, this air is clean!"

I admired the view and stood there filling my lungs with the sparkling air. "Where are the tea plantations I've heard so much about?" I asked.

He pointed to the mountain again and said, "Right there! That blue look is tea. All the tea plantations are on the sides of Mulanje. That's where the soil is best and they get just the right rainfall. Lovely country. Pity you don't have time to see it."

There were so few Europeans in Nyasaland that everybody seemed to know everybody else. On the rare occasions that we passed another car, the drivers nodded and smiled at each other and my driver told me who it was and made an educated guess as to where he was going and why. In sharp contrast to Rhodesia and Mozambique, the roads were full of Africans and the countryside was dotted with villages. I envied anybody who lived in such a beautiful country.

The hotel in Zomba claimed to be at 3,000 feet on the slopes of Mt. Zomba. It was airy and cool, with tiled floors and wide rooms. The manageress watched me sign the register and commented, "RAF, are you? Based at Heany, near Bulawayo?" Surprised, I admitted that I was, and she flipped back through the book.

"Here we are," she said. "Jefferson. Do you know a J. Jefferson?"

I laughed. "Everybody knows Jeff. He's the station postal clerk. I hope he paid his bill."

She smiled. "Oh, yes. He was such a nice boy. I have never met a person who has traveled so much, he must have seen every inch of this country."

The man she was talking about was one of those naturally friendly people that everybody instinctively likes. He was a born salesman and, since he had to drive into Bulawayo every day to pick up the mail, he shopped for anybody on the base who needed anything and made a small profit on everything. He had an assistant in the post office, which gave him time to go off exploring Rhodesia and even got into Bechuanaland (now Botswana). How he got as far north as Nyasaland puzzled me until I later learned that he had made friends with a businessman who owned a small plane and often flew to Blantyre. What amused me most as I spoke about him was that I had never seen a leave application with his name on it cross my desk.

The small, friendly group in the bar were very English. They were civil servants who had worked in Nyasaland for years, sometimes a lifetime. But they did not think of themselves as Nyasalanders as the Rhodesians thought of themselves as Rhodesians. They were Europeans who came to work and often stayed on after retirement. They loved Nyasaland and were proud of it and of their work, but they still said, "Back home," by which they meant Britain. After supper, we had a game of darts and drank beer out of pint glasses. Except for the pleasantly warm night air and the sound of the night insects drifting in through the open windows, we could have been in any pub "back home."

Later in the evening, we heard noise in the kitchen, and then one of the cooks dashed in, obviously frightened and yelling something in the local language. Everybody ran into the kitchen. As the manageress called to a pair of huge dogs, somebody flung open the back door and yelled, "Get 'em, boys!" and the dogs ran out, barking fiercely.

I caught a glimpse of figures clambering over the garden wall and heard one of the guests complaining, "Oh damn! I knew I should have brought my rifle." It was all over in a minute and we slowly returned to the bar. It seemed that some African nationalists had come to the kitchen window and threatened the staff because they were working for the white men. The manager went off to arrange transport home for his staff for the next few days "just in case."

I thought this episode was very sad. Here was a beautiful country with an apparently happy people, better fed and in much better health than Africans in many African countries. Education and health care were free. European immigration was strictly limited, and yet violent nationalism and perhaps terrorism had already begun. I gathered that this was not an isolated incident and that many white men had begun to carry guns. The population, I suspected, was evenly divided between those who hoped the whole business would blow over and those who slept with a gun under the pillow.

From my bedroom window I could see the mist slowly creeping down the mountain side, silvery white in the starlight. For the first time since I had come to Africa, I slept that night under two blankets.

Day 15

Zomba, which proved to be quite a small town, was clean and bright in the morning sun. After the mist vanished, I strolled along to the crossroads, where there was a large public school. Within minutes, I found myself waist-deep in a tide of noisy, well-scrubbed school children. The boys wore white shirts and khaki shorts, and the girls wore the traditional blue gym slip of English schoolgirls the world over. The only difference between England and Africa was their bare feet. Most of them had shoes tied by the laces and hanging around their necks. They put them on just before they entered the school yard. The children were fascinated by this white man standing on the corner, and they cheerfully asked me a stream of questions in excellent English.

Quite fittingly, my next lift was from a family so very British that it was comical. Father was a portly, red-faced Colonel Blimp type wearing a heavy tweed jacket, and Mother wore a fox stole. The teenage daughter wore a huge, white, garden-party hat, which was just too awkward for the little English car into which we were all squeezed. In this very formal atmosphere, my attempts at conversation soon fizzled out. I was sure that they had picked me up from a firm belief that it was unseemly for a white man to be seen standing on a corner chatting with a swarm of native children. Father was a civil servant, newly arrived from England. I fervently hoped that a few months with the charming people I had met so far would thaw him out. They dropped me at the ferry across the Shire River, near where the road forked.

One road led to Fort Johnston at the southern tip of Lake Nyasa. I was sorely tempted to go that way and spend a day or two swimming and fishing, but half my leave had already been used up and I still had a long way to go. With deep regret, therefore, I took the road north to Lilongwe (now the capital of Malawi) and crossed the Lilongwe River on the pontoon ferry. I watched the ferry, which was mostly loaded with people and bicycles, but now and then a car or truck going down to the lake or into town, make its way back and forth for awhile. Almost everybody was chewing sugar cane, and the road was littered with bits of spent cane.

It was a fine day, and I soon began to stroll up the road. In about an hour, a car screeched to a stop next to me and the driver called out the window in a rather anxious tone, "What's wrong?" When I told him that I was hitchhiking, he burst out laughing and threw open the door. Only the previous week he had read of a Scotsman who was hitchhiking from London to Cape Town, and he had argued with his friends that it was "a bloody fool thing for a white man to do."

We drove to the garage where he had arranged to sell his rather large car. The prospective buyer, a Scotsman, arrived in a small pickup truck, and after a while they decided to simply exchange vehicles. They each took a trial run, then signed the papers and sealed the bargain over a bottle of beer. I continued my journey in the same car with the new owner and his wife.

Now we entered a region of open plains punctuated by bare hills. Our first stop was at an old fort that had been turned into a charming restaurant. The ivy-covered stone building was set in wide lawns fringed by tall blue gum trees and filled with luxurious rhododendrons and majestic pine trees. From the courtyard there was a magnificent view eastward towards the lake. We had tea and biscuits in the cool, oak-paneled hall, its walls hung with trophies and old muskets. I learned that the lovely climate and the mountains and lakes had attracted many Scotsmen to the country, and Scottish names could be found everywhere. "Aye, now," said my host, "we don't call them mountains. They're highlands. We always call them highlands."

He worked for the Forestry Commission and pointed out areas where the government was busy planting trees and trying to reforest the bare hills. Unfortunately, the huge population was using firewood at an alarming rate, and the young trees had to be fenced in and guarded. Also, herds of goats that eat anything, including young trees, were learning to climb the fences. "The curse of Africa isn't the tsetse fly," he said. "It's the damn goats!" He insisted that overgrazing, especially by goats, had caused the great deserts of Africa, including the Sahara, and he snorted angrily whenever we passed a flock on the road.

At one point we drove a little way off the road to the top of a hill where there was a fine view. Behind us was a level plateau of yellowing maize, but in front of us the land dropped away in a long sweep to Lake Nyasa, blue in the sunlight. The clear air reduced the fifty miles to ten, and I could see the southern tip of the lake, while, to the right, Lake Shirwa in Mozambique glistened like a silver blanket. The land between us was a deep gold with patches of green, and the distant mountains were steel blue. Over everything hung a fine haze, not enough to affect the view but enough to give it all the delicate unreality of a Japanese painting.

It was a long drive to Dedza, but my hosts were eager to talk. When I commented on how overpopulated Nyasaland was, compared to other countries nearby, my host let loose a flood of angry words. "Oh, yes, it's badly overpopulated," he said, "but they're not all born and raised here. This country is a magnet. Strangers come here by the thousands. They pour across the borders. Some of them come from as far as the Congo." He paused, then continued, "The locals don't like it, and sometimes there's trouble. But nobody does anything about it."

I asked him what the attraction was.

"Easy living, that's what!" he exclaimed with a snort. "Free schools. Free health care. Electricity and water and plenty of cheap food. All paid for by the British taxpayers back home. Natives don't pay taxes worth a damn. And what do we get for it? Nothing! Absolutely nothing." He was silent for a mile or two, then he added,

"We have tea plantations and tobacco farms, but we are not allowed to expand. We pay enormous taxes, but not enough to pay for the engineers and civil servants who actually run the country." Like a good Scotsman, he considered the cost. "There's a bunch who want independence. I say let them have it. But who's going to pay the bills? It costs money to run a country, and Nyasaland doesn't have any." He went on to explain that over-farming and the ruinous practices of the African farmers were rapidly wasting the land, and while the scientist produced better and better grains, the natives let the top soil blow away or let erosion make gullies in the hillsides. "While the commission is planting trees on one side of the mountain," he said, "the natives and their goats are uprooting the seedlings on the other." Thousands of tons of mealie had to be imported every year, mostly from Rhodesia, "and the population keeps on increasing."

To show me the difference between British protection and old-fashioned, exploitive colonialism, he drove off the road to a low hill, where we got out of the car.

"What do you notice?" he asked.

It was a particularly lonely stretch of road. Suddenly it dawned on me. "There are no villages. Where are the kraals? There are no people."

He smiled grimly. "This bit of road, about fifteen miles of it, is technically in Mozambique. It curves a lot, and the border isn't marked, but the blacks all know." He waved his hand, "In Nyasaland, a nice level bit of land like this would have a kraal every few miles. You'd see the roofs poking through the bush everywhere. But not here."

When I asked why, he said, "Why? Because the Portuguese make them work at least six months out of every year, and they pay taxes." He laughed bitterly. "So they all come over here to Nyasaland to live the easy life under the British." Looking west across the empty countryside, he added, "You could go twenty miles through there and not find a single soul."

Later, back in the car, his wife changed the subject and told me some things about the lake that I had never heard before. Lake Nyasa is part of the Great African Rift Valley, she said. The Great Rift Valley has mountains on both sides and is over 350 miles long and up to 50 miles wide in places. The beauty of the lake is deceiving, she said, and its placid waters can be whipped by furious storms. In 1946, a brand new steamer was capsized with the loss of 150 lives. The lake is over 2,000 feet deep in parts and rises and falls over the years as much as 25 feet. It covers more than 10,000 square miles, which makes it bigger than either Lake Erie or Lake Ontario in North America, and it is stocked with a wide variety of fish. The first steamers to plow the deep blue waters of Lake Nyasa were carried there piece by piece past the Murchison Falls on the Shire River and assembled on the lake shore. In the 1890s there were also three tiny gunboats there to show the British flag to the covetous Germans and Portuguese. The African Lakes Company (founded by Scotsmen) ran a regular steamer service on the lake at the turn of the 20th century and, before silting blocked the Shire River, ran paddle steamers down it from just below the falls to the mouth of the Zambezi. The wars in Europe had echoes in Africa. During the First World War, the German gunboat *Hermann Von Wissmann* was sunk by one of the little British gunboats, which had the impossible name of *HMS Gwendolyn*. This naval battle was ignored by historians, but not by Hollywood. In 1951, this incident became the basis for *The African Queen*, starring Katharine Hepburn and Humphrey Bogart. Alas, not only were the facts made almost unrecognizable, but the location was changed from Lake Nyasa to Lake Victoria.

My Scottish family and I spent the next few miles following a set of tire tracks in the dust. By estimating the size and type of vehicle and the way it was driven, my host and his wife gradually eliminated all the residents of the area until they decided who the driver was and where he was going in the middle of the week. When they saw that person's car parked outside the hotel, which proved them correct, the wife turned to me and said, "When there are so few people, you get to know each other pretty well." We shook hands, and she said, "Goodbye and good luck."

The Highlands Hotel in Dedsa was very pretty. Built like a hunting lodge, it was tucked under tall trees, where the pine scent and the rhododendrons gave it a very Scottish atmosphere. The town of Dedsa itself nestled at the foot of a glowering mountain whose lower slopes were covered in new fir trees. Near the summit clung the tiny forestry hut, which must have had a superb view.

Day 16

Eight o'clock in the morning found me standing outside the gates of the hotel and gazing eagerly down the road. Five-thirty in the afternoon found me sitting about one hundred yards up the road, bored stiff and with a crick in my neck from looking down the road. A hundred yards past the hotel, the road forked and both the roads led to Lilongwe. For fear of missing any traffic that might take the road I didn't take, I stopped at the fork and waited. I spent my time testing the strength of ants by placing pebbles in their nests and watching them drag them out. There were ants of every size and color on that short stretch of road, but my scientific experiments were, alas, neither interesting nor very scientific. A bus passed once, but it was so terribly overcrowded, with heads sticking out of every window and the roof covered in bicycles and trussed chickens, that I didn't even think of boarding it. A large truck also passed, but it was going only as far as a quarry and it soon returned. Late in the day, a young couple going in the opposite direction stopped and told me that a policeman would be going to Lilongwe next morning, and if I phoned the station he would pick me up at the hotel. This cheered me up, and I went back to the hotel to phone the police station.

As I dropped my bag in the lobby, the lady behind the desk gave me a sympathetic smile as I said the obvious. "Well, that's it for today. Nobody seems to be going to Lilongwe."

Suddenly a voice behind me said, "Want a lift to Lilongwe, old chap?" I turned to see a man in a suit sitting in the lounge and half hidden behind a newspaper. "I've finished in Dedsa," he said, lowering the paper, "and was just wondering whether to drive to Lilongwe now or go in the morning. As soon as I've finished this cup of tea, I'll drop you off there."

The setting sun painted the sky a gorgeous flamingo pink—just for my benefit—as we twisted and turned along the narrow road at high speed. The fifty miles were soon covered. A rugby team had arrived in town that evening, so I was lucky to get a room at the hotel. Actually, all the rooms were taken, but one guest was away hunting for a few days, so I was given his room on the condition that the rightful owner could have his bed back if he turned up in the middle of the night. I prayed that he would have good hunting…at least until dawn.

Chapter Seven: Nyasaland to Lusaka

Day 17

After a steak and eggs breakfast, I went in search of postcards to mail to family and friends. Lilongwe was a small town with few major buildings and appeared to be the administrative center as well as the regional agricultural center. Since there was no color bar in Nyasaland, I lined up at the post office with Africans and Indians and thought nothing of it. Strangely enough, my presence worried the Africans, who stepped aside and insisted that I go first. All of them, that is, except for one young man who very ostentatiously pushed in ahead of me. I pretended not to notice, but he had also pushed in ahead of his elders, and there was an ominous quiet while we were being served. As soon as I stepped out the door, I heard the old men, and the old women, too, giving him the sharp edges of their tongues.

My first lift of the day came from a very large and well dressed African man who was accompanied by an even better dressed Indian. They took me to the bus station, but all the buses had gone, so I walked down the road to a crossroads. My glimpse of the rickety, overcrowded bus yesterday was still fresh in my mind, and I was rather glad that they were all gone. The country was quite open here. The wide fields were planted with maize and native tobacco and acres of tall, green sugar cane that whispered in the light breeze. There was a small airfield nearby. I was astonished at how that little field with its tattered windsock changed everything. The isolation and the loneliness vanished, the huge distances became practically unimportant, and the major cities with all the blessings of civilization seemed just minutes away.

A lady soon stopped for me, and after I got into her car, I explained what I was doing. She immediately insisted that I stop for a cup of tea, but I persuaded her that I really had to get moving, so we settled on a promise that if I didn't get another lift that day, I would stay overnight at her farm. I hoped that I would not have to make use of her generosity, especially as her farm was about five miles off the main road. My next lift was from an Indian who took me as far as an Indian village. Every town has its Indian store, sometimes two or three of them, but this entire village consisted of a long line of Indian stores strung out down one side of a dusty road. They were all more or less the same, with the inevitable Italian-made sewing machine on the veranda and the cool, spice-scented interior crammed with every conceivable item. I wondered how they did any business. There were also children everywhere, plus people who had to come out to look at me. Shy, sari-clad women peeked at me from behind the wide doors. Near the middle of the village, I stepped into a store for a lemonade, and treated myself to a shoe shine by a cheeky imp who had obviously just borrowed his mother's dusting cloth. He did a nice job but my shoes were dusty again before I reached the end of the village.

At the bottom of the hill was a river where I leaned on the railing of the bridge and watched the women washing clothes in the murky water. Squatting on the rocks and close enough to gossip, they rolled the clothes into tight, wet bundles, then pounded them with heavy wooden paddles in the ancient, unchanging way. I had

been standing for only a few minutes when a car pulled up and the
driver offered me a lift to Fort Manning (now Mchinji) in Malawi.
He was an engineer on his way to Dar es Salaam on the coast of
Tanganyika (now Tanzania), just south of Zanzibar, and was quite
willing to give me a lift all the way there. I was very tempted, but
when I looked at his map and worked out that it was close to a
thousand miles, I knew there was no hope whatsoever that I could
get back to camp on time. I had to very reluctantly decline his offer.

Fort Manning consisted of a small store, a small customs
post, and a striped pole across the road to mark the border with
Northern Rhodesia. The number of forts in both the Rhodesias and
Nyasaland is a relic of the 19th century, when the forts, actually little
more than trading posts, were a clear symbol of British sovereignty
to Portuguese, Germans, Belgians, and the Boer. More often than
not, they were built by the British South Africa Company under
instructions from Cecil Rhodes, and later they were officially but
reluctantly sanctioned by the British government. Rhodes was
extremely interested in Nyasaland, and the British South Africa
Company, which he controlled, spent much time and money in
the region. But settlement and trade were never very great, and
the company's holdings were eventually bought out by the British
government. In the 1940s, the British government also bought out
most of the farms owned by Europeans and returned them to the
Africans, so that today less than five percent of the land is held by
Europeans.

At the border between Nyasaland and Northern Rhodesia,
the African customs official stamped my passport and offered me
a chair so that I could sit in comfort in the shade. After a while, I

strolled over to the store and bought a packet of English biscuits as my emergency rations. Every travel book reminds the reader to have rations for three days and to always have a full water bottle. Up until then, I had had no trouble quenching my thirst or hunger and had grown careless. Now I didn't even have a water bottle. The next couple of days were going to remind me that Africa was not quite as tame as I thought and had some nasty surprises for the careless.

Back at the border post, the official now offered me a cup of tea. While I was enjoying it, a truck arrived from the wrong direction. When it reversed at the barrier, I saw a Rhodesian license plate. I finished the tea with one gulp and ran out to look for the driver, but the customs official stopped me. "No hurry, sir. The driver says you are welcome to a lift to Fort Jameson." Five minutes later we were off into the gathering darkness.

My new host, an Indian man, chatted all the way to Fort Jameson. "It is a big town, Fort Jimmie," he said "Two hotels." He paused and laughed. "Well only one now. Last week one burned down. But I know the boss of the other." He flashed very white teeth. "Don't worry. I'll see you get a room."

True to his word, he dashed into the bar as soon as we arrived and reappeared with a house boy who escorted me to a very large, odd shaped room with two beds. It was obvious that the room had been recently converted, and while I was trying to work out what it had been, a man came in and explained that, as the hotel was full, he had been given the other bed. I didn't mind, and after dinner we sat talking in the bar until quite late. We returned to discover that the light was on, but there was no light switch. We looked everywhere that it should logically have been, then in the illogical places. We even tried balancing a chair on the bed and trying to unscrew the bulb, but it was too high up, so I went in search of the house boy. But the hotel was silent and asleep, so after one last futile search, we went to sleep with the light on.

Day 18

When the house boy brought in the morning tea, he went directly to some massive curtains hanging in the bay window and, reaching behind them, switched off the light. To this day, I remember Fort Jimmie as the place with the light switch so cleverly hidden that two grown men could not find it. Fort Jameson (now Chipata) was the service center for a large part of Northern Rhodesia, and although it wasn't very big, it was crowded and lively with Saturday shoppers. I walked from the center of town through a comfortable residential area with shade trees and a nice view of the distant hills and decided that, although nobody was ostentatiously rich, it was clear that many people were doing quite well in this remote corner of Africa. Around the town, the crops were varied. I recognized peanuts among the fields of maize and tobacco. Somebody at the hotel said that there was a coffee-growing region further up in the hills.

The cool of the morning had long vanished when two white men stopped. They were road maintenance workers, and they gave me a lift to their bulldozer and grader, about ten miles out of town. Even the best laid gravel roads need constant attention, and the plague of African roads is corrugation where the surface is packed into ridges like corrugated iron sheeting. Sometimes these ridges are six to eight inches high and eighteen inches apart, but just as often they are lower and closer together. Drivers have only two choices when faced with miles of corrugation. They can drive at full speed and skim along the top or go slowly, which more or less protects the vehicle, and suffer every bump. The men argued about what caused corrugation. One insisted that it was wind from the speed of vehicles that packed the dirt into these strange ridges, whereas the other was sure that it was the bouncing of the wheels of the vehicles that caused the ridges. I got the impression that they had been arguing this point for years.

When the great machines had dropped me off and lumbered away, I felt very much alone. The yellow road appeared out of the dark hills in the east and cut straight as a ruler through the bush to disappear over the low horizon in the west. There was not a soul on the road, neither on foot nor on a bicycle, not a building to be seen nor a wisp of smoke from some cooking fire. Even that symbol of civilization that had watched over me for many hundreds of miles, the tall, crooked, skinny, and always drunkenly leaning telephone pole, had abandoned me.

After about an hour, I saw a cloud of dust appear. Gradually it stretched itself comet-like towards me. As it roared past me, I saw that it was a bus crowded to overflowing, with its roof piled high with widely assorted goods, included a huge stem of bananas and the inevitable net of live chickens. The bearded Sikh driver, his turban immaculate, gripped his wheel tightly as he squeezed the last ounce of energy from his sadly aged and even more sadly battered, but brightly painted, vehicle. In the dust cloud behind the bus there was a heavily loaded truck trying desperately to pass. The racers were gone in seconds, but the dust cloud hung over the road for an hour.

Some time later, a large truck appeared and, to my great relief, stopped. The driver was African, but next to him sat a white man with a sun-reddened face who was obviously the boss. "Climb up on top," the boss yelled. "You'll find it's cooler." I did so. It was a big diesel truck loaded with sacks and boxes. There were two or three helpers asleep on the cargo, and an empty trailer bounced along behind.

I made myself comfortable on a sack of rice, facing into the breeze, and within minutes my hair was a tangled mass of sweat and dust and the sun was burning my face. But the breeze was delicious. I took it for granted that the truck was going to Lusaka, the capital of Zambia, because the map showed nothing but wide-open space for over 400 miles.

We soon left the hills behind and entered a vast bush veldt that was mile upon mile of level ground and fairly dense bush broken now and then by a meadow of long grass. At rare intervals, there was a domed, bald hill of granite gleaming in the sun or covered in tall cactus. Some of the cacti were in bloom, with clusters of pale pink blossoms adding a splash of color to the monotonous green and grey. At even rarer intervals, a tiny native village showed its thatched roofs through the trees.

When we stopped at a store, where the men unloaded boxes and sacks and my host, the truck owner, visited one of the small houses nearby, I stretched my legs. The Indian owner spoke to me about life in the bush and told me that his loneliness had been intense at first, but slowly his eagerness to get back to the city had faded. "And now," he concluded, "I wouldn't leave it for anything."

Also in the store was a young woman buying a length of cloth. The storekeeper explained that there was a set ritual about such things. Feeling the cloth and comparing it with other samples can take hours, perhaps days. "Time has no value to somebody who cannot count," he said. "This lady has walked days to get to this store. It is very bad manners to rush a customer." Then he added, "Also very bad for business. She is quite ready to walk another day or two to another store." He laughed. "She might even wait until I die so that she can be served by my successor."

A blast on the horn, and I climbed up to my perch again. An hour later, we stopped at another store, where the owner was waiting for us with a pot of tea. When I asked him how he knew we were coming, he just shrugged his shoulders and smiled. Seated comfortably in the cool gloom of his back parlor, we sipped excellent tea out of good china and discussed cricket. "You know," he said, "it is very difficult to put together a good team nowadays."

"From what I see," I blurted out, "I think it would be difficult to get any kind of a team together out here."

"Oh, no, sir," he replied. "We're not so isolated as you might think. It looks lonely, but actually there are quite a few ranchers and tobacco farmers sprinkled about."

My host, the truck owner, agreed and said that I had probably not noticed the tracks leading off into the bush, but we had passed quite a few homesteads during the last few hours. I could only wonder at the strength and independence of anybody who would homestead in that wilderness.

While we were talking, I learned that my host was a partner in a transport company. He had come to the Rhodesias after the Second World War and put his small savings into a truck. Less than a decade later, and after a great deal of hard work and sweat, he had a fine company in sound condition. "I wouldn't change this life for a million pounds," he declared. He hired Africans to drive the trucks over the terrible roads. "I drove some pretty rough roads in North Africa and Italy during the war," he said, "but these are twice as bad, especially during the rains. I don't do much driving anymore." Then he added with a laugh, "When I do, I have to rest a couple of days just to recuperate."

While we were talking, a huge mail truck went by. The thought of having to breathe his dust for the next hundred miles was not pleasant, so we hurriedly gave chase. The helpers had bought a chicken for supper, and it was perched on the cargo. As soon as the truck was moving, the wise bird took off over the side amid shouts from the men and screams of glee from the women hanging around the store. About a mile ahead, a dust cloud marked the location of the mail truck, and, sure enough, we were soon coughing and choking behind it. The other driver knew his business and skillfully blocked the narrow road until my host wrapped a bandana around his face, leaned out of the window, and roared a few choice phrases in the local dialect. Grudgingly, we were allowed to pass. We emerged into the bright sunlight and the mail truck slowed down to let us get well ahead.

Late in the afternoon, we stopped at a government rest house. This was a simple, white-washed building with a place to sleep and a servant to cook any food you might have brought with you. It was at this point that I was forced to admit to my host that I was not equipped for camping out. "I have always reached a hotel by nightfall," I explained, "or almost always."

"Not very wise out here," he said. "There's no hotel between Jameson and Lusaka. Still, we should reach the next guest house before dark. I don't think we'll be camping out tonight."

We had a pot of tea then set off again but were soon engulfed in a cloud of dust. The mail truck was still behind us, so it must have been the bus that had passed me that morning.

Overtaking the bus proved to be quite a challenge. The bus had open spaces where windows would be, but no actual windows, and if his passengers had to breathe our dust for the next hundred miles, the unlucky Sikh driver would surely feel the edge of their tongues. We managed to pull alongside at a bend in the road, but the Sikh would let us go no further, and so we raced neck and neck for the next three miles down the narrow twisting road. The air was unbelievably thick with dust and rent by the blasting of horns. The drivers yelled at each other, and the bus passengers added their own shrill accompaniment. Trying to breathe, I clung desperately to my perch on the rice sack. As luck would have it, we were approaching a tiny village with its usual litter of goats, chickens, and children scattered across the road. As the bus slowed down, our driver darted ahead with a Grand Prix flourish and we were out in the fresh air again.

As evening approached, the land became more rugged, but the bush remained as thick as ever. We sped on and on in the setting sun, our dust trailing behind like a pink cloak until it slowly settled and added another layer to the roadside trees that stood grey and ghost-like in the gloom.

When the sun went down, it grew chilly on my high perch, and by the time we reached the next guest house, I was stiff with cold. The drop in temperature had been a sudden surprise for which I was quite unprepared. Dismounting, I stamped around for a minute to work some life into my bones. In the starlight, I could see a striped pole barrier across the road and a small but rugged pickup truck parked near the guest house. The owner of this truck was a tall, blonde, young man on his way to Nyasaland. When we all introduced ourselves, he turned out to be one of those travelers who go well prepared for everything, with a sleeping bag and a mosquito net, enough food and water for a week, a case of whiskey, and a large carton of toilet paper. When he found out that I had absolutely nothing, he was horrified.

"God, man! You're not going for a stroll in Hyde Park," he shouted. "This is Africa. You've got to plan ahead." He shook his head at my carelessness. "You don't have a mosquito net or even a bloody water bottle."

I explained that when I'd set out, I had not had the slightest idea just how long and empty this stretch of road was. He shrugged and said, "Don't worry, man. I have enough to feed an army." He went out to his truck, and when he returned, the guest house servant took an armful of cans and packages and soon reappeared with a delicious stew, which we quickly polished off, followed by cheese and biscuits. There was a small fee for the servant's services, hardly more than a tip. I paid it as my share.

After supper, we relaxed on the veranda under a kerosene lamp with a glass of the best quality. The mosquitoes had not yet appeared and the night was cool and clean, though the night insects were already making a loud racket in the bush. The flame in the lamp flickered, and, if I tilted my chair back, I could feel the heat of the day still in the wall.

The young blonde driver explained the barrier across the road. "This stretch of road is called 'the escarpment,' and for about one hundred miles the road is so bad that big trucks can only go through at certain times. For a couple hours a day, the traffic is west to east, then for a few hours at night it goes east to west."

My host added a detail. "If you're driving a car, you can try it any time you like, but you have to give way to the oncoming traffic." He paused, then added, "I wouldn't do it myself. I'd rather sit and wait."

As the conversation centered on "the road," I sat enthralled, listening to tales of accidents they had been in, of trucks that had jack-knifed or stripped their gears or gone over cliffs, of run-away trucks, of the reliability of drivers. Both men had employed experienced drivers who had gone home for a day or two while making a delivery. My host told us about one of his drivers who left a fully-loaded truck at the side of the road and went off to court a second bride. A search found the truck, but the new groom didn't turn up again for weeks. Another man told us how he had been stuck in the mud for ten days last rainy season. He and his crew had unloaded nearly nine tons of cargo, but the truck still would not budge, so they had made camp and waited for the road to dry out.

From the road, the topic switched to hunting, and now I listened to tales of leopards sniffing around trucks under which the men were sleeping. They spoke of snakes and pondered whether wild dogs were actually hyenas. They then moved on to the obvious fact that game was getting much harder to find every year. When the bottle was empty and the lamp was almost out, I borrowed a blanket and slipped under the mosquito net.

Day 19

It seemed that I had hardly closed my eyes when I was shaken awake. "Time to go. The gate will be open in five minutes," said a voice. My watch said it was three in the morning.

I had quite forgotten that westbound traffic went over the escarpment at night. While we had been relaxing over supper, the bus and the mail truck had arrived and taken up positions near the barrier ahead of us. There were no other vehicles, so, rather than race with them, we let them get a good start before moving off into the dark.

I took up my customary seat high on the sacks of rice, but as soon as we began moving, I realized my mistake. It was cold. Very cold. And the wind drove right through my thin shirt. Trying to keep warm, I huddled down between some boxes. Now I could appreciate just why the Africans were so fond of discarded army great coats. Those heavy, pure-wool coats that hung down past their knees must have been martyrdom during the day, but a wonderful blessing at night. The truck's exhaust pipe stuck up behind the cab, and given the choice of freezing to death or asphyxiation from the fumes, I chose the latter and hunched down as close to it as possible.

After about an hour, we were stopped by an African man who stood outside the cab door and spoke rapidly. My host, the owner of the truck we were riding in, sounded very angry, and within minutes some of the helpers on the back of the truck joined in and began shouting at the stranger. Eventually, he climbed up onto the cargo and sat alone. I learned later that he was a very good driver, intelligent and educated. But one day, in the middle of a trip, he had stopped his truck, stepped into the bush, and vanished. Today, weeks later, he had suddenly turned up and asked for his job back. He had no excuse except that he'd had a pocket full of money and had been passing a kraal where he was well known.

We drove on, and in the half light that precedes the dawn, I was able to see that the land was becoming more and more mountainous. A wild and lonely land with its thin covering of thorn and cactus, it looked like some forgotten world. I was wondering just how far away the nearest human beings might be when we rounded a bend and skidded to a halt, our empty trailer skewing drunkenly across the road. We were in what is called a cutting, high-banked and sloping steeply downward. In front of us were the bus, the mail truck, and the cause of the blockage. A large diesel truck coming up in the opposite direction had run back down the hill and its tail had plowed six feet into the muddy bank. This had swung the whole vehicle across the road, blocking all movement in either direction. The truck was stuck as tight as a cork in a wine bottle. The African driver was sitting in the cab unhurt but the gear lever waggled loosely in his hand.

As we stood on the road, looking at tons of trouble, the sun rose with tropical suddenness, flooding the sky with pink that turned to gold, then yellow, and gradually faded into the pale blue of another scorching day. As the bus passengers came awake, the mass of huddled figures disentangled itself and poured out, stretching and yawning. Some walked ahead to stare at the wreck, others lit fires, and women headed off with tin cans and bottles to find water. It was obvious that they were prepared to settle down and wait a day or two for somebody to do something.

"Messed up his transmission," my host declared.

There was a long silence.

"What happens now?" I asked.

"Well," said my host, "nobody can get past, so the next car that comes from Lusaka will just have to turn around and bloody well go back to Lusaka. Looks like it's going to need a mechanic and spare parts."

I began to get worried and said, "That's going to take some time."

He shrugged philosophically. "Yep. Could be we're stuck here for the next two or three days."

My heart sank. Not only did I not have a scrap of food, but I had no sleeping bag nor even a blanket, and no mosquito net, either. Also, my leave was beginning to run out.

We had just walked back to our own truck and were standing in the shade, staring glumly at the disabled truck, when a small van appeared from the other direction. It stopped by the wreck. By the time we got to it, the driver had explained the problem. By some extraordinary stroke of luck, the van driver, a mulatto, was a mechanic from the same truck company. In a few minutes, he was on his back under the truck. Soon a small mound of pieces began to appear. Since he didn't need any help from me, I spent the next two hours nervously wandering around. Wondering about our good luck, I squatted down where the mechanic was working and found out that a car that had been a little way behind the wrecked truck had indeed "turned right around and bloody well gone back to Lusaka" and reported the wreck and the blocked road.

By now, the bus passengers had fires going and were heating mealie and making tea. Some were barbecuing little bits of meat for breakfast.

At the foot of the slope, a few feet beyond where the truck had stopped, I discovered a very deep gully that was quite overgrown by leafy bushes. If the truck had slid into this gully, we might have passed without seeing any sign of the accident. Both vehicle and driver would have vanished, perhaps not to be found for months.

About nine o'clock the mechanic tried to move the truck, but after grinding forward a foot, it stopped again. We were deeply disappointed, but my host had an idea and got every man he could find to help unload the truck. Reluctantly at first, but then cheerfully, the men (and some women) swarmed over the truck, and in less than an hour over ten tons of assorted cargo was stacked alongside the road. The mechanic started the engine again. With a horrible grinding noise, the truck crawled to the side of the road. I felt like cheering, but everybody else was clambering into their vehicles. In the rush to get away, our driver managed to nose out both the mail truck and the bus, which was hampered by lost passengers.

With high spirits and no dust in front of us, we headed off again for Lusaka.

There had been some shade in the cutting, but out on the open road again, I was glad to resume my seat on the rice sack. As the road became worse and worse, I found that a sack of rice is not the best of cushions. At times, I was more comfortable standing up, but I was also glad of the breeze.

To make up lost time, our driver raced at top speed down the hills and blasted the horn at every bend as he slithered the truck around. Blind with our own dust, we tore through narrow gullies and bounced across rickety bridges, the trailer swinging wildly. Behind us was always that long plume of dust, and as we climbed higher, I could see it floating above the road for miles. None of the rivers we had crossed had water in them, but suddenly I caught a glimpse of water ahead. We turned a corner and rumbled out onto a large modern bridge that looked out of place in the wilderness. Far below ran the waters of the Luangwa River, a major tributary of the Zambezi. Up and down this lonely river had traveled many a trader and explorer. The Portuguese had built a fort at its junction with the Zambezi, a hundred miles to the south, and Livingstone had crossed it at least twice, perhaps at this very spot. But now it was a forgotten river, mere inches deep and shrunken to a wide shadow in the sands, perhaps dreaming of the next rains.

On the other side of the Luangwa, the road climbed still higher until it became little more than a track along the edge of the mountain, a very narrow track with a crumbling rock wall on one side and a long, ugly drop on the other. Our driver took it very cautiously. There was almost no vegetation, and it got extremely hot. Every now and then, my host took pity on me and passed the water bag out the cab window. These canvas water bags were an essential part of life in Africa. Every car seemed to have one hanging on the front bumper where the air and evaporation would keep the contents delightfully cool. I was glad that we carried not one but two of them.

About thirty miles past the Luangwa, we crested a hill where there was a magnificent view. Before us, the road twisted downhill and out onto a great, flat plain which disappeared into the distant haze. There was a dry river in the distance, and the plain was dotted with trees and one or two lonely villages, the irregular circles of huts almost blending into the dry yellow grass.

Suddenly my daydreams were interrupted by a shout and another emergency stop. We were at a sharp bend, with the cliff on one side and a sheer drop on the other, and in front of us was a small car. I climbed down to listen, but there was no argument. For the car driver, a young white man; it was simply a case of "get by or go back." He walked up and down the road, but there was no place wide enough to pass. Then he studied the road surface, testing it with his foot while carefully avoiding looking over the edge. The surface was loose and very crumbly.

"If you could pull her a little closer to the side," he said, pointing to the cliff, "I think I'll try passing."

My host nodded, climbed back into the cab, and the driver climbed back into the cab and cautiously moved the truck until it was touching the cliff. Very carefully and very, very slowly, the other driver drove to the edge of the road. Nobody spoke as he inched past. Stones slid from under the outside wheels of his car and dropped hundreds of feet onto the rocks below. I honestly thought I was watching a stubborn man committing suicide. My host, the truck owner, must have thought so too, because he turned his back on the scene and stood staring away into the distance with no expression on his face, prepared for the worst. Miraculously, the young man squeezed past our truck and trailer. There were audible sighs of relief all around.

"Nice job." said my host.

"Yes, it was a bit tricky there for a bit," the stranger replied. "Well. Thanks a lot. Got to go. In a hurry, you know." And he drove off.

When we came down from the mountain we found the road stretching wide, straight, and inviting across the plain. In a few minutes, we were at the western barrier of the one-way stretch of road, where there was a guest house. There were no vehicles there. We stopped for a cup of tea before starting the last leg of the trip. Sitting in the shade on the veranda, sipping the hot tea, I felt again the heavy, humid heat of low-lying country. I washed my face, but it made no difference, and my shirt seemed permanently stuck to my back with sweat and dust. Any movement brought a mist over my glasses and sweat dribbling down the sides of my nose. I was not sorry to climb back on the truck. Soon we had crossed the wide valley and were climbing up to higher land.

About five o'clock that afternoon, we reached the surfaced road outside Lusaka, then the capital of Northern Rhodesia, now the capital of Zambia. The bush had suddenly become rolling farmland, with neat farms and fields of maize rustling in the breeze and water pumps standing like lonely palm trees and lonely palm trees standing like water pumps in the green fields. We stopped at a major crossroads, where I jumped stiffly down. My host pointed out my road, then they were gone.

After a short wait at the crossroads, I got a lift to a residential area of the city, where the houses were all brand new and brightly clean with still bare gardens. From there, I walked on to the center of the city. On one side of the road ran the rail lines, and on the other there was a row of shops, bars, and offices. Lusaka may have been a capital city, but I was disappointed because it didn't look like a very big town.

I was also wondering why the shops were all closed and everybody was soberly dressed, and then I suddenly realized that it was Sunday. I hurried to the hotel, where a very stuffy white clerk warned me that I might have to share a room. I didn't mind, I said, just as long as it had a bath and hot water. I soaked most of the dust away, shaved, and found a clean shirt in my pack. Feeling much more civilized, I then went down to dinner. I was stopped at the dining room by the head waiter, who was short, white, and ridiculously pompous, but not as impressive as the Admiral in Beira. What was worse, he had no supply of ties. I tried to explain, but he would not listen, so I went to the desk clerk. He was not interested, either, and his superior attitude made me very angry, so I said. "If you won't let me eat in the dining room, I'll eat in the kitchen!"

He almost choked in his starched collar. "You can't do that," he spluttered.

"Well, send my supper up to my room," I countered.

"We don't have room service," he said disdainfully, as if room service was something only lower class hotels had.

By that time, I was very angry. Pointing out that I had not had a decent meal in two days, I exclaimed that I intended to eat, "even if it's off the lobby floor!" I stalked off to my room.

Half an hour later, I sent the bell boy down to find out where my supper was. He did not return. Another half an hour passed with no food. By this time I was both famished and angry, so I marched back down to the lobby, where the smell of food drove me crazy, and slammed my hand on the desk, demanding in a very loud voice to see the manager. The lobby was crowded with Sunday guests. The snotty clerk wriggled in his stiff shirt and assured me that my supper would be sent up straight away.

"At once!" I roared and went back upstairs, feeling justified but very foolish.

Before I could close the door, a servant appeared with a huge brass tray loaded with food, including two desserts.

Chapter Eight: Lusaka to Mufalira

Day 20

The road from Lusaka to the Copperbelt Province is the main artery of Northern Rhodesia. It runs parallel to the rail line across the heart of the country. I expected to see dozens of vehicles traveling in each direction, but it was not so. I got a short lift from an African civil servant in a government vehicle, then a lift to Broken Hill in a big truck driven by an African who had his small son with him. For safety, he had tied the passenger door closed with string, so I had to climb through the window. For 70 miles, the little boy sat staring at me as if I had two heads. No amount of persuasion or humorous coaxing could get a word out of him.

The road was well graded and quite wide. There were farms and houses spread out along the side of the rail line, and the high plateau was sprinkled with trees. In a little while, we came to the lead and zinc mining town of Broken Hill (now Kabwe). The ores being mined were discovered many years ago, and serious production has continued since the railway crossed the Zambezi. But the ground has given up more than just minerals. In 1921, a landmark archeological discovery was made when the mine yielded up a well-preserved Neanderthal skull.

The driver let me off at the location where he lived. The word "location" was widely used and usually referred to the black African part of town, although it sometimes also referred to tribal lands. In this case, the location was a large tract of houses built by the mining company for its workers. What I saw were rows and rows of huts made of stone and concrete with latrines and wash houses evenly spaced between them. There were a few trees, but the ground was clean and bare, and all around there was a high wire fence. Crowds of Africans were everywhere, coming from work, going to work, or just hanging around. Almost all of them were men. The only black women I saw were shopping in town. This clean, bare, efficient, but quite soulless place was home for the hundreds of workers who came in from the bush to work in the mines where the pay was (for them) very good. A few of the men brought their wives but the majority did not, and quite often their hard earned money was squandered away on beer and boredom. The alternative would be for the mine owners to allow slums and shanty towns to grow up around the mining towns. Not only would this be unpleasant and dangerous, however, but it would also encourage more migration from the countryside to the cities. To dissuade the men from leaving their villages permanently, they were allowed to work for only two years, then they were forced to return to their homes.

Broken Hill was a fairly large town, but it was clearly a mining town, untidy and unplanned, with a line of stores and businesses strung out along the rail line. I would have liked to see the mining operation, but suddenly and with very little warning, the skies opened and it began to rain. I cautiously worked my way from one store veranda to the next until I ran out of buildings. There I stopped and waited. It was a long time since I had seen rain, and I knew it was needed, but I soon became impatient and set off again. The rain continued just long enough to soak me thoroughly.

About a mile up the road, I was picked up by an old Afrikaner in a car that had seen better days. He was a tall, thin, older man with a narrow, white, pointed Jan Smuts beard. (This style of beard was very popular with old-time South Africans because Smuts was a very well-liked prime minister of South Africa.)

"Just heading back home to Ndola from a trip to Wankie [now Hwange, Zimbabwe]," he told me. "Haven't stopped at a hotel or restaurant all the way. My wife made up sandwiches for me, and I just stop to fill my thermos with coffee." He jerked his thumb at the rear seat and said, "When I get sleepy, I just take a nap. Have to stick my feet out of the window, though." He had covered a thousand miles in record time this way, but he drove at a steady 45 miles per hour, no matter how good or bad the road. "Forty-five is the most economical speed for this old girl," he assured me.

We talked cars for a while, and it was soon clear to me that his car was a friend and companion, not just a machine and he admitted that he had not been on a train or a bus for many a long year. As for air travel, he despised it as unnatural and called it "no fit way to get from one place to another." When he went on holiday, he drove to Durban in South Africa and loved every minute of the trip.

At a fork in the road at a lonely spot 40 miles north of Broken Hill, he stopped the car. "Would you believe that road leads to Tanganyika and Kenya?" He sighed wistfully. "Probably get you to Egypt, if you follow it far enough." The road looked little used, and he smiled when he said, "Its official title is the Great North Road." I asked if he had ever driven up it, but he shook his head, "I've never had a reason. But maybe…one day…."

I looked at my road map and saw that, about sixty miles up the Great North Road, there was a tiny speck of a place called Piccadilly Circus. I wondered what was there and who gave it that name.

As he drove, the man told me his story. He had come up north from Johannesburg many years ago, both out of curiosity and for the high wages they were paying at the mines. He had fallen in love with the country and the way of life, had married a local girl, and had put off going home countless times, although he still retained his South African citizenship. Home today was Northern Rhodesia, and the Union of South Africa was just a nice place to visit.

As we drove north, the land became more thickly wooded but not tall trees, just short, twisted things fit only for firewood; in fact they were reserved for that very purpose, as there is no other form of fuel for the natives, The road was badly corrugated in places but I was an old hand at bad roads by this time and did not bother to grit my teeth as we bounced along at a constant 45 miles per hour. We reached The Copper Belt in the late afternoon, but there was nothing to indicate that beneath us lay the richest seam of copper in the world. I saw only the same dry bush and fairly level land, wild and empty under a clear sky.

Ndola, the main town in Zambia's Copperbelt Region and the largest of the half dozen mining towns scattered across the belt, was a fairly large town, alive and busy with people everywhere. Groups of Africans, mostly men, were standing about talking and enjoying themselves. Most of them were loudly dressed, and they all sported flashy wristwatches and heavy rings. My Afrikaner companion was firmly of the opinion that the black miners earned too much money too quickly.

"Look at them," he said. "A few months ago, they were living in the bush, where they never even saw a pound note, Now they don't know what to do with their money. They just chuck it away!" Since the mining companies provided housing and food as well as work clothes, he was also of the opinion that "all that money is just pocket money to them." He dropped me off at a hotel and chugged off down the road.

I got a room on the usual condition that I might have to share it. In fact, I was lucky to get any room at all because there had been a rail breakdown and an airline mixup, and there were a lot of stranded passengers. I had a drink before dinner and had the bad luck to get stuck with an engineer who was newly arrived from Nigeria. As we talked about Nigeria, it soon became obvious that he was a believer in the natural superiority of the white man. But things had changed in Nigeria, and he found that not only could he no longer insult his African workers anymore, but he was shocked to discover that his new superior was an African whom he had trained. It had all been too much, and he had taken the next plane to Rhodesia, where, he hoped, he could treat Africans like Africans. Luckily for me, he met an old timer who sympathized with him and they sympathized together until the early hours of the morning. I went for a walk.

There were crowds of people taking in the cool night air, looking into the brightly lit shops, or just standing and talking under the trees. Plenty of noise came from the numerous bars, and a group of Africans passed by strumming a tune on tiny guitars. It was, without doubt, the liveliest town I had been in so far.

As I was preparing for bed, my roommate came in. He was a cheerful Cockney salesman from Johannesburg, and as we chatted I mentioned that it really would be exciting to get as far as Elizabethville (now Lubumbashi), which is nearly at the southern tip of the Belgian Congo, before I had to hurry back to camp. He gave me a long string of tips about traffic and visas and mentioned that he himself was going to Elizabethville sometime later in the week. He sold brushes and other household goods and, for the next half hour, I lay in the dark while he spun hilarious yarns about selling brushes in Africa. He had a very poor opinion of the road into the Belgian Congo and doubted there would be much traffic.

"It would be better if you could wait a few days and go with me," he said, but I could not afford to waste even one day, so we promised to meet at the King Leopold Hotel if I was in the Congo next Sunday, although I hoped to have been to be there and back by then.

Day 21

After breakfast, I strolled through a comfortable Ndolan residential district of tidy bungalows that did not look like company housing and soon got a lift from a couple of elderly gents. They were third-generation Rhodesians, born in Bulawayo, and they swapped yarns about that city in the early days, when it was little more than a trading station with half a dozen stores and a hotel. In those days the trip out to the Matobo Hills took a whole weekend, with the women and children in a lumbering ox-drawn wagon and the men riding alongside, ever on the look-out for leopards. They took enough food for a week in case a river rose and stranded them, and a whole army of "boys" was needed to pitch the tents and set up camp. Today, they said, it was a Sunday afternoon drive.

Then the older man described in detail how he had shot his first lion from his own back porch. "That was the same lion that killed an African one night," he said, "right behind the hotel. Couldn't have been more than fifty yards from the bar, which was packed. They were singing and shouting like crazy. Damn lion just ignored them and grabbed a *kaffir* for his supper." I took his description of an elephant "happily uprooting every tree in his back yard" with a grain of salt, but a week after I returned to camp, I heard that a man in Umtali had been forced to shoot an elephant when he caught it pulling the pillars off his back porch.

All too soon, we were in Mufalira, and I had to leave these gents and their marvelous stories. We had been driving through thick scrub in a land that had not changed for thousands of years, but, suddenly, we found ourselves in a modern oasis. Mufalira was a well laid out town with paved roads, street lights, and shade trees. The shops, banks, and hotel looked new and gleamed white in the brilliant sunshine. On one corner was a public market made of brick and tiles, all glistening wet from the morning wash, while behind the business district lay rows of neat bungalows. There was also a very smart police station, and in the distance I could see the top of a diving board. Everything was so clean and tidy I felt as if I should wipe my shoes before walking through the town.

Just beyond Mufalira lay the copper mine, a fascinating jumble of odd-shaped buildings with black smoke pouring out of tall chimneys. Towering over everything were the great wheels of the elevators. Every now and then, the wheels turned rapidly and then stopped as a cargo of humans was plunged deep into the earth or a load of ore was lifted to the surface. Here was the wealth of the Rhodesias.

This was too good an opportunity to miss. I was determined to see as much of the mine as I could. The problem was, just how does a wandering stranger get permission to visit a copper mine? Since I didn't know the answer, I took the direct approach. There were some huge gates standing wide open and nobody was about, so I walked across a tangle of rail lines and dodged around some very large trucks until I reached an office. There was one man in the office. I walked up to him, smiled, and said, "Good morning. May I go down your mine?"

He looked up and replied, with a very straight face, "Certainly. Here, fill out this form, please."

A little dazed at my success, I quickly signed a form releasing the company from any liability. He told me to come back on Thursday evening, in time for the late shift.

Back at the hotel, I reserved a room for Thursday night and decided that, with luck, I could get to Elizabethville and back in 36 hours. At the police station, where I went to check on permits and visas, the civilian clerk was quite against hitchhiking in the Congo.

"It just is not done!" he insisted. "It's dangerous and foolish." He brought up various arguments and ended by stating flatly that it was quite impossible to enter the Congo without a special pass. I didn't believe a word he said, so I smiled politely and hitched a lift to the frontier, which was only ten miles away.

The border consisted of the usual striped pole and a very small office in which I found an African soldier. I had been nervously rehearsing what I hoped were convincing arguments in my limited French. Now, taking a deep breath, I said, "Bonjour, Monsieur." To which he replied, "Good morning, sir." This rather took the wind out of my sails, so I blurted out, "I'm going to Elizabethville." To which he replied, "Yes, sir."

I looked at him, then slid my passport across the table. He slid it back to me. I had been lucky so far, but this was too easy. Anyway, I like collecting stamps in my passport, so I said, "Please stamp it." But he did not want to stamp it for the simple reason that he had never stamped a passport and didn't even know if he had a stamp. We searched through the desk until we found one that looked nicely official. Since he had no ink pad, I breathed on it a while to moisten it and then stamped my own passport.

My map claimed that the sorry collection of buildings sitting in the blistering sun was called *Makombo*. It was little more than a store and two bars, but there was a car parked outside one of the bars, so I went in. The only customer was an elderly, sun-burned, white man nursing a beer. "Elizabethville?" he said. "Not me, I'm going north to Fort Rosebery [now Mansa, Zambia]. You know, there's not much traffic to Elizabethville, but if anything does come along, they'll stop here. There isn't another bar for a hundred miles."

When he left there was nothing for me to do but sit on the steps and stare down the road. It had not been graded for many months, and the grass down the middle was thick. The bush was dense, but through the trees I could see the local gendarmerie with the Belgian flag hanging listlessly in the sun. *Makombo* was absolutely silent and deserted, with not even a stray dog or a chicken in the road. I sat reading a magazine I had brought. When I found myself reading the advertisements, I wandered into the bar and had a sandwich, which I paid for with Rhodesian money. When I asked the African barman how the town could support one bar, let alone two, he shrugged and smiled and had no answer.

I stared up the road that led to Fort Rosebery. Somewhere, two or three hundred miles up that lonely road, the traveler will come to a small town, hardly more than a village, in the unhealthy swamps south of Lake Bengweulu. It was there, in Chief Chitambo's village at Ilala, that David Livingstone died. His heart lies buried there in the wilderness of Central Africa, while his body lies in Westminster Abbey.

The sun was low in the sky by now, and I decided to call it a day. I reluctantly walked back to the hotel in Mufalira, where I found that my luck had really run out. A large party had arrived, and there was not a bed in the place, nor in any part of town. There was nothing to do but go back to *Makombo,* where the bar had claimed it was also a hotel. Since there were homes scattered through the bush almost to the border, it was easy to get a lift back, and I was soon crossing the "impassable" border. Back at the bar, I got fixed up with a room, which turned out to be clean and tidy. The supper was good, too. The elderly Belgian lady who owned the place was eager to talk, as I was the first guest she had seen in a week. She told me she was having problems with her staff, who took advantage of her age, stole from her, and were insolent. They worked when they felt like it and did as little as possible, and they didn't stay long.

"It would take very little for me to just pack up and leave," she said, "But where would I go? All the Congo is just as bad." She thought for a while, then added, "Belgium? I have no relatives left. No connections anymore. Anyway, what would I do in Belgium?"

Day 22

The next day, taking no chances that any traffic would get past me, I stationed myself very early in a carefully planned strategic position on the road. By noon, the day's traffic had added up to two vehicles. One was a small truck going out to get a load of firewood; the other, a lumbering bullock cart with automobile wheels. The situation was hopeless, and I knew if I persisted I might miss out on my visit to the mine, so back across the border I went again. I checked in at the hotel, where I was lucky to get a room. I spent the rest of the day on the veranda watching the flow of cheerful, well dressed, and well fed humanity, Such a contrast it was to the Belgian side of the border. The manager, a woman newly out from the British Isles, was surprised to find that there was an RAF base in Rhodesia. She was from Cardiff, and, after the grey skies and constant rain of south Wales, she was settling down quite happily in Africa.

After supper, I went for a quiet moonlit stroll in the garden, but the watchdogs were not impressed by the color of my skin, and I beat them to the safety of the hotel only by the length of one tooth. It had not been a very successful day

Day 23

In the cheerful light of a new day, my confidence returned, and I decided that I still had time to go to Elizabethville, but only after I had toured the copper mine. The route through *Makombo* was obviously hopeless, but there was another route through Tshinsenda in Katanga Province near the Copperbelt town of Chingola. A guest at the hotel warned me that I would need a visa, as there was a white gendarme on duty at that crossing. It had been many months since the guest had crossed, but I decided to play it safe and get a visa, so back to the police station I went. The civil servant there told me I had to get the visa in Ndola. Even when I explained that I had been across and back twice before, this made no difference. I would have to go back thirty miles to Ndola to get permission to go forward 100 miles and come back.

Feeling frustrated, I sat in a neat little park and wondered whether it was worth it. Finally, I decided that I would go to Ndola and get the damn visa after I had toured the mine. Then, if I had any time left, I would make one last attempt to reach the elusive city of Elizabethville. Bored with sitting around, I strolled out of town and did not have to go far from the business district to be back in the timeless bush, A mile from the chrome and plate glass of the business district, the tall anthills stood like twisted fingers pointing at the blue heavens, as they had stood for ages before men discovered the fabulous wealth beneath the dry ground.

Chatting with strangers in the hotels, I had learned a lot about the Copperbelt. Surface deposits of copper had been mined in this region for hundreds of years, but the geologists had insisted that nothing of value lay below. Despite this "expert" opinion, deep drilling was carried out during the 1920s, and immense deposits were discovered. The financing came from South Africa, England, and the United States, and, naturally, the huge profits left the country along with the copper. Little of the wealth stayed behind in the land that produced it, which led to great bitterness on the part of the permanent residents, both white and black.

The Copperbelt Province of the Belgian Congo lies in a finger-like extension of Katanga Province that juts into Northern Rhodesia, and the history of this odd-shaped but valuable piece of land makes sad reading. During the mad scramble to partition Africa, Cecil Rhodes rightly guessed at the future importance of the region and sent representatives of the British South Africa Company to make treaties with all the chiefs in the region. One of the chiefs, Msidi of the Katanga, refused to sign any agreement with any foreign power, preferring to remain independent. The British left him to think it over for a few months, but before the second emissary from Rhodes could get back to Msidi, a Belgian force arrived. Trapped between the two European powers, the chief decided to sign with the British. But it was too late. The Belgians shot him and annexed Katanga to the Belgian Congo.

As appointed, at seven-thirty, Thursday evening I made my way to the copper mine, where I met three people—a tall South African mining student, a short woman with glasses who looked like a school teacher, and a slight girl of about nineteen. We were all given overalls, boots, helmets, and lamps with batteries that clipped to our belts. We were also advised to wear as little as possible underneath the overalls. Fully equipped, we thumped our way in the awkward boots across to the pit head. It was a dramatic sight in the moonlight. The great mass of steel towered over our heads; pipes and rails lay under our feet, we could hear the rattle, hiss and rumble of heavy machinery all around us, and silhouetted against the night sky before us stood the great wheel. Our guide was a large young man wearing a sheepskin jacket and his helmet tilted to the back of his head. He took us first to the conveyor belts, where skilled workers removed extraneous material from the ore. While we watched, he rattled off statistics on quantity, percentage of ore, and world prices, which all seemed very high. Then he led the way to the cage.

It looked like a very large service elevator with an upper level and a lower level. There was a wide ramp over our heads, and up it hurried scores of African miners, chatting and laughing as they squeezed in, their eyes gleaming in the light of many safety lamps. We went into the second section, along with about a dozen white miners who all carried sheepskin jackets, not because it was cold down below (quite the opposite), but because it would be cold when they came out. "Since there is no gas, there is no danger of explosion," said our guide. "Our biggest fear is catching a cold!"

Although the elevator dropped hundreds of feet in seconds as it plunged into the earth, there was almost no sensation of movement. The cage stopped at several levels, and when it was our turn to exit, we stepped out into a very large, brightly lit tunnel. It was clean and impressively quiet. Our guide told us how far down we were, warned us to watch out for vehicles, and cautioned us to keep close to him. With whole tunnels devoted just to ventilation, the air was as fresh as "up top." Other tunnels had double rail lines, and we squeezed into little alcoves whenever the loaded cars rumbled by.

At one point, the ore vanished into an open pit in the tunnel floor. My first impression was that the whole business was as mechanized as humanly possible. Most of the main tunnels were whitewashed and, our guide said, every week the roof was tested for cracks. We walked along numerous tunnels, dodging into an alcove whenever we heard the whistle of the ore train. Then we went down some wooden steps to the next level.

Our guide moved quickly, though it took us visitors a while to get used to the clumsy boots and the dangling wires of the safety lamps. For three hours, we scrambled down dozens of steps, always going deeper and deeper into the mine. We were taken along narrow, winding passages where the mud came nearly to the top of our boots, through great unlit chambers where the light of our lamps could not reach the walls, down more and yet more ladders so steep our helmets banged on the roof. We slithered on wet floors. All the time, we got hotter and hotter, The cool, whitewashed tunnels were far above. Now we were in the real working heart of the mine. At one stage, the young girl gave up and returned to the lift in care of another miner, but the school teacher was as game as ever. While the South African and I were busy squirming our six foot lengths over piles of rock, panting like marathon runners, she was trotting after our guide asking a steady stream of highly technical questions that sometimes surprised him.

Everywhere there was something of interest to see. The time flew by. At one point, they were blasting. For the benefit of us tourists, the miners omitted the warning whistle. The noise of the blast wasn't very loud, but the solid wall of compressed air that roared out of the tunnel hit us with astonishing force and almost bowled us over. We were worried until we saw the grins on the African miners' faces. Gangs of men, stripped to the waist and shiny with sweat, were fighting the clumsy, roaring drills while others, wearing safety chains anchored to the rock, were forcing the ore down open holes.

The whole mine seemed to work on gravity. A seam of copper was undermined and allowed to fall, then it was dragged by machines to holes through which it fell into trucks, which dropped it down yet more holes to a central shaft. There the ore was lifted to a crusher and then conveyed to the surface. When we reached the central shaft, we stood on a small ledge and held on to safety chains and gazed open mouthed at a scene worthy of Dante. The shaft was so big that our combined head lamps could not reach the other side of it. Into it rumbled a continuous stream of rock, raising great clouds of gloomy dust that were sucked up into the darkness above. We stood there in awe, watching this fantastic Niagara as the tons of rock and copper plunged down in a never-ending stream and the noise pounded on our eardrums.

Since we were such a small group, our guide decided to show us something special. He took us to a broad chamber, about thirty feet wide but only four feet high, where we wriggled over the rubble and squatted in the very center. Here our guide pointed out the streaks of green in the roof. The ore did not come in nice tidy seams like coal, he said, but was spread throughout the rock. This was why a seam was undermined and left to collapse of its own weight. A few feet of rubble were left to cushion the shock. I ran my fingers over the copper ore and wondered where it would end up…perhaps in a phone line in Chicago or as a fake antique in Sydney, but I was startled back to reality when the guide said, "Don't go poking at the roof. This section has been undercut and we're just waiting for it to drop."

We crawled out fairly quickly.

Our next stop was the pumping station. This was a huge room, bright and spotless, with half a dozen large generators humming quietly. It looked like any other power station, except that it was hundreds of feet below the ground. Except for one concrete wall, it was carved out of the rock. After the engineer had proudly shown us his machines and told us how much power they produced, we climbed up an iron ladder and peered through a small opening at the top of the wall. My lamp reflected off the surface of a great, dark underground lake. Behind the concrete wall lay millions of gallons of ice-cold, sparkling clear water. Our guide told us that when they were digging the mine, they had come across an underground river and had been forced to dam it. There was enough water there to use in the mine and in the smelter and even enough to supply the town. The generators below us were even powered by this water. I stared again at the dark underground lake and thought of the parched land above and wondered just where such huge quantities of water had come from originally.

From the room next to the lake, we went to the crusher, which was on another level of the mine. This monster was as tall as a three-story house. Its operator claimed that it was the biggest in Africa. From a high catwalk, we stared into its gaping mouth, where, at the touch of a small button, a huge lid opened to reveal a wedge shaped blade that moved about a foot back and forth. A stream of rocks, some of them over six feet square, fell from a chute into the crusher. Slowly, effortlessly, and relentlessly, they were broken into small bits, after which they disappeared. The place was filled with the slow thump of the behemoth and the roar of tons of falling rock, and it was with ringing ears and sweat-soaked clothing that we at last stepped out of the cage and into the cool midnight air on the surface.

Day 24

The next morning, thinking I had seen the last of Mufalira, I got on the road to Ndola. A lift from two Indians in a huge American car got me to the Belgian consulate, which was little more than a desk in a travel agency. But then the female clerk pointed out that my passport was not good for the Belgian Congo. Sure enough, the small print revealed that some clerk in London had apparently decided that although I could go to Russia or to Cocos Island. I could not go to the Belgian Congo. Fortunately, the woman was sympathetic and sent me to the police station, where I got stamps fixed and things stamped and things signed and stamped. Then I returned to the consulate, where I was given another form to be filled in by my employer or bank manager. I tried to explain my situation, that I was on leave from the RAF, but it was to no avail. Back to the police station I went. This building surrounded a courtyard, and the doors were open to the breeze, so I peered into each office looking for a sympathetic face, preferably somebody who would swear that they had known me for many years and that I was politically sound and had never been to jail. About half way around, I spotted that special type of moustache unique to RAF pilots and walked in.

"Hello!" I said. "I'm in the RAF. Down in Bulawayo. Could you sign this form for me?"

He looked up and smiled. "Certainly, old chap. Pass it over."

I had guessed correctly and he signed it with a laugh as we chatted about military life for a while.

Back at the consulate, I finally got my visa, which was good for only three days. After all that trouble, it was only to be expected that the next day, when I reached the border, the visa was not asked for and, when I showed it to the official, he claimed that he had never seen one before and certainly didn't know what to do with it.

As it was midday, I got on the road to Kitwe and was offered a lift by a couple who, hearing that I was in the RAF, insisted that I stop for lunch at their home. They came from a town in England that was a mere bus ride away from where my parents lived, so over lunch we talked about England, though not with much nostalgia. Nobody that I met in the Rhodesias ever told me they wished they were back in England. On the contrary, many of them seemed to spend their time trying to persuade friends and relatives back home to come out and join them in Africa.

Late that afternoon I got a lift from a very old gentleman who drove at a steady twenty miles per hour and swore violently at everybody who passed him, calling them road hogs and much worse. The amusing part was that he was driving a beautiful, brand-new car with the power to pass anything on the road. He dropped me in Kitwe, a very attractive town, where I crossed the Kafue River and waited. It was dinnertime, and the traffic had dried up. Nobody passed me except Africans on shiny new English bicycles, the new status symbol that had replaced the cow as a sign of wealth and was also a very practical form of transport.

It was dark when I eventually managed to stop a car. We had only gone a few miles when we stopped for another hitchhiker, a young man whose car was in for repairs. He had never walked as much as five miles in his whole life and complained about it all the way to Mufalira.

Day 25

At breakfast in Mufalira, I looked across the room, and there was my Cockney friend, the brush salesman from Johannesburg. He laughed, "I see you haven't got to Elizabethville yet." When I admitted that I certainly hadn't, he said, "Well, if you can wait a bit longer, I'm going tomorrow."

It looked as if my luck had turned. I went with him back to Kitwe to get a permit for his car, Here again there were problems because the car was registered in South Africa, but all the problems were finally solved and we returned to Mufalira for lunch. Afterwards, he went off to contact his customers while I sat in the air conditioned bar and people-watched. There were office workers in sports jackets and businessmen in suits, but the majority were miners dressed in everything from sleeveless shirts to sheepskin jackets, with footwear from sandals to riding boots, and any kind of hat, just as long as it was pushed far back on the head. They talked in a variety of European languages and laughed a lot and put back enormous quantities of beer.

In the late afternoon, my salesman friend and I drove out to the golf course. I didn't play, but it was delightful to take off my shoes and follow the others across the well kept greens and feel the softness of the heavily watered, brilliant green turf on my feet. Like almost everything else in the towns of the Copperbelt, such as swimming pools and cinemas, the golf course was provided by the mining company and almost free. At dinner, we heard that there was a Saturday night film at the social club, which was actually a modern cinema. The parking lot was full, and there were large groups of people chatting as they slowly made their way in. It was obviously a social occasion and an excuse for the women to wear their best dresses and the men to look uncomfortable in their suits. I wore a borrowed tie. The movie was not exactly new, but nobody seemed to mind that, and the interval between the cartoons and the main feature was extended so that everybody could go into the bar and socialize or stand in the cool night air exchanging gossip.

My roommate that night was a very fat, jovial salesman who had, of all things, a banjo. It was past midnight when he arrived, but he insisted on playing a couple of tunes for my benefit while I sat on the edge of the bed, trying to look appreciative but wishing someone would start banging angrily on the wall so I could go to sleep. But nobody complained, and I must say he was a very good banjo player.

Chapter Nine: Getting into the Congo

Day 26

The hotel and the town were so quiet that we both overslept, so it was noon before the salesman and I reached the now familiar border crossing at *Makombo*. Here I got a rude surprise. The African soldier who had allowed me to cross back and forth had suddenly become officious and refused to let us cross. We had to go to the Belgian officer's house, where that gentleman (who we had obviously roused out of bed) gave us the works. There were forms to be filled in and signatures and rubber stamps and dozens of questions about the car, Soon it became clear that he thought we were going to sell the vehicle in Elizabethville.

"The silly bugger thinks we're going to sell the car in Elizabethville and make a fortune," my friend whispered. "How the hell does he think we would get back home without a car?"

It took so long to get all the forms signed that a small line of vehicles had collected at the barrier before he reluctantly let us go. It was probably the busiest day that *Makombo* had seen in many years.

For the first twenty miles, it was possible to go reasonably fast, but after we passed the deserted huts that were, or had been, Tshinsenda, the road dwindled into a track through the forest. It was deeply rutted and hemmed in by trees on either side, and grass also grew down the center so high that it rustled continuously against the underside of the car. We forded the rivers, crawling cautiously down steep banks to bounce across, not knowing whether the muddy waters hid a level surface or giant pot holes. Years ago, somebody had put up road signs, but the termites had made short work of them. We caught glimpses of the remains of signs lying at odd angles in the weeds. We learned later, that the Belgian Congo was so huge that the Europeans traveled by air and the Africans traveled by river boat. There was no road or rail system worth bothering about. Unbelievably, the road seemed to get worse as we approached Elizabethville. It was late afternoon when we entered the city.

The first sign of civilization was a towering slag heap near what was probably a uranium mine. Then the transition from bush to city was almost immediate. After a few miles of driving through suburbs, we found ourselves in an extremely large city. The buildings were tall, solid, and permanent. Many had the little balconies and tall, shuttered windows found in Europe. Unlike the wooden buildings in Rhodesia, they were built of stone and they had a very Continental look about them. The wide avenues were fully paved and gracefully laid out with trees and street lights and, except for the Africans everywhere, it could have been a neighborhood in Brussels or even a district in Paris. It was not what either of us had expected

We soon found the hotel that somebody had recommended and checked in, but the already big building was being enlarged still further and smelled of paint and plaster dust, so rather than eat there, we went in search of a good restaurant. The streets were crowded with people in their Sunday best. We saw both well-dressed and prosperous looking European families and equally well-dressed Africans strolling up and down the boulevards in the cool of the evening. We also found dozens of cafes with tables on the sidewalk, Parisian style, but we could not find a restaurant, so we went back to the hotel for dinner.

The prices were a shock. Choosing very carefully, we each found a meal that we could afford. Dinner was more than delicious. It was superb, and we decided to complement it with a bottle of wine. After a glance at the prices on the wine list, however, we decided to stick with plain water.

"Well," I said, "at least the room includes a breakfast."

The head waiter told us proudly that his chef could produce any dish that a diner might request, and he had received some strange requests. "Everything is flown in from Johannesburg or from Paris," he said. "It is expensive, but it is worth it. Don't you agree?" We agreed.

The whole town seemed to be sampling the cool of the night and sitting at the little sidewalk cafes just long enough to drink a coffee and see what other people were wearing, then strolling to another café and repeating the process. The salesman and I found a little wrought-iron table, too, and sat and watched the crowds, the white women in the latest European fashions, the black women in skirts and shawls of flowered cotton that made a bright show against the grey buildings. Our budgets would not permit more than one beer so, after a sample of the best coffee that I had tasted in years, we returned to the hotel.

Day 27

The bell boy woke us with coffee and croissants, and after this appetizer, we went in search of a real breakfast, only to find that we had eaten it. We were both indignant about starting the day on a mere continental breakfast, so after a loud argument, the head waiter ordered the reluctant chef to cook bacon and eggs "English style." After breakfast, as my friend had work to do, I headed off on my own to the main post office to collect postage stamps. The lobby was decorated with framed sets of beautiful stamps, but the clerk was forced to admit that most of them had not arrived from the printers, and probably never would. Outside the post office was a wide plaza, obviously the traditional marketplace for dealers in curios and souvenirs, Most of the dealers were Muslim Arabs dressed in fezzes and long robes and soft leather slippers, squatting on little prayer carpets, just as if they were in Cairo or Casablanca instead of the southern edge of the Belgian Congo, more than 4,000 miles from home. I later learned that they take months, even years, working their way from market to market, buying and selling as they have done for hundreds of years.

The Arabs were surrounded by carved ivory elephants, leather slippers, inlaid boxes, African masks, Indian brass bells, and countless other fascinating articles and charming curios. I strolled about, looking and wishing but unable to buy, They tried at first to get me to bargain, but some trader instinct soon told them that I had no money and they gave up. The workmanship was exquisite, and I wondered at the long miles the Moroccan leather must have traveled or how they had persuaded some African chief to part with a mask and how long it would be before it was hanging on a wall in Manchester or Milwaukee.

After I had feasted my eyes, I walked down long avenues of modern offices and showrooms full of the latest model American cars and along tree-lined avenues of fine houses which, except for the tropical shrubs, could have been in Paris or Brussels. Almost everybody spoke English, so I had little chance to practice my French. On a side street, I came upon a crowd outside a gunsmith's shop. They were gathered around the body of a very large lioness that was propped up against a box. The blood around the little bullet hole in her neck was still damp, and the corpse was not yet stiff. People were taking photos. She had been a magnificent beast. When I returned to the hotel, I mentioned the lion to my friend. He instantly dragged me out to the car. We raced to the shop, but the lion was gone, and when we asked about the lioness, we were taken around the side and shown the remains. It was not a pretty sight with the skin, teeth, and claws removed. My friend was eager to buy the skin, but I pointed out that an uncured skin would not last long in that heat and it was a long way back to Johannesburg. The store owner showed us on a map where the lion had been shot. It was so close to the city that it was practically in the suburbs. I found it hard to imagine that only a few minutes' drive from the boulevard cafes in this very cosmopolitan city, a citizen had shot a large lioness.

The brush salesman turned out to be an avid souvenir collector. He took me along to watch him haggle with the Arab traders in another market. We waited until prayer time, then he strolled up and down, handling things and attracting the traders' attention. When he found what he wanted, a beautiful little box inlaid with mother-of-pearl and ivory, he pointed out invisible flaws to me and hastily put it down when the Arab suggested a price. He walked away, but in less than three steps, the price was halved. We returned and looked at it again and offered a ridiculously low price. The Arab nearly wept, but he brought his price down a bit. This continued until there was a loud hiss from an elderly bearded Arab nearby who was reading from the Quran and standing by his prayer rug. Our trader also began to say his prayers, but he still kept a sharp eye on us. We waited until he was kneeling, then my friend made another offer. Devoutly, the trader ignored us until his head touched the ground, at which point he whispered a counter offer under his arm. This went on for a few minutes until they were both satisfied. When prayers were over, the Cockney paid for his box and the Arab, speaking good French and bad English, condemned his sacrilegious bargaining system. Meanwhile, some small boys had slid a cigarette butt under the head of an old patriarch when he was praying and laughed when he stood up with the butt stuck to his forehead. Unfortunately for the boys, the Arab was not as old as he looked, and, when prayers were over, he picked up a stick, jumped over his wares, and chased them across the market shouting things in Arabic that never came from the holy book.

That night, we both tossed and turned in the heat and humidity. There was no cooling breeze or air-conditioning, and the traffic noise was too loud for ears accustomed to quiet nights. Even a couple of large bottles of Belgian beer proved to be of little help.

Chapter Ten: From the Congo to Victoria Falls

Day 28

The heat seemed worse at four in the morning. "We're not doing any good here," my friend said. "Let's get going."

I agreed, and after a little bit of trouble with the night watchman, who thought we were sneaking out without paying our bill, we drove out of Elizabethville. Or at least we tried to. Since the town lacked any traffic signs and the streets were deserted, we were soon lost and found ourselves driving in circles until we happened upon two African policemen. Unable to understand their instructions in French, we persuaded one to get into the car and show us the way. He acted as if he thought we were trying to kidnap him, but when he had got us onto the correct road, he was more than pleased when we emptied our pockets and gave him all our Belgian small change.

"What an extraordinary place," my friend said as we drove through the suburbs. "A chunk of Paris in the heart of Africa, and almost no way to get in or out except one rail line to the Rhodesias." Then he added, "That man at the gun shop said there's a rail line to the coast through Angola, but he didn't know anything about it. No wonder everything is so expensive, I bet they have to pay a mint just to get anybody to work in a place where everything must come in by plane."

I was looking at my map. "You know," I said, "if you take

Africa south of the Sahara and find the *very middle*, that's where Elizabethville is."

He laughed. "Well, it was worth a visit. Wasn't it?"

I agreed. We were half way back to Makombo before the shadows vanished and the mists rolled back to reveal the great yellow sun.

At the border we were politely asked to stop at the immigration offices in Mufalira, but we had both had quite enough of useless bureaucracy and sped on to Kitwe for breakfast. At Ndola we filled the tank to the very top and raced off again. The salesman was in a hurry because he had contacted all his customers and had arranged for his wife to fly up and meet him at Victoria Falls for a little holiday. I was in a hurry because my leave pass was good for only thirty days and, unless a miracle happened, I was going to be in deep trouble in two days.

The miles of bush sped by, broken only by meadows of tall, dry grass, ragged and yellow, or barren patches of land where huge ant-hills stood three to six feet high and looked like the ruins of some ancient city. The termite, or the white ant, is the most cordially hated pest in Africa. I heard many a homeowner say, "My place belongs to the bank and to the termites." But the pest has a use. As they build their towers, the termites poison the fine gravel so that nothing will grow on it, resulting in an excellent material for tennis courts. All that is needed are a truck and a couple of brave laborers, and you can have an excellent weed-free tennis court.

By lunch time, we reached Kapiri Mposhi in Zambia, where I had downed a glass with the old Afrikaner. By coincidence, there was another South African at the bar. On hearing that my host was from Jo'burg, he immediately started describing the natural beauty of Cape Town, where he was from, and I soon learned that there was an intense competition between the two great cities of South Africa. By the time we had finished a quick lunch, I was determined to visit both those cities and see for myself. We filled the tank again at Broken Hill, but just as we were leaving town, we heard and felt a heavy thump whenever the car hit a pothole. We stopped the car and looked, but there was nothing obviously loose, so we tried to ignore it. But the noise seemed to get worse. After a few miles, we pulled up in a shady spot. I wriggled underneath the car and he checked out the engine. We soon found the cause of the noise. The wicked jolting that the car was receiving on the rough roads had torn out one of the bolts holding the engine to the chassis and had almost stripped the thread off another. The two remaining bolts were bent but still holding. We continued, but at a greatly reduced speed.

While we were creeping along, my friend told me a rare bit of history involving Northern Rhodesia that he had read somewhere. During the First World War, a tiny German army was formed in Tanganyika, which was then a German colony. Under the command of the extraordinary General von Lettow-Vorbeck, it spent the entire war marching through the wilds of east Africa, crossing borders at will, living off the land, hitting and vanishing and tying up quite a number of British troops who vainly pursued it through the trackless bush. Not only did the tiny army survive, it grew more audacious as the months went by and, in 1918, von Lettow-Vorbeck headed for Broken Hill in an effort to cut the rail line. He would probably have succeeded but for the Armistice and the end of the war in Europe.

It was getting dark by the time we reached Lusaka. We drove slowly up to the hotel, but even the thought of dressing up after such a long, hot day was not to our liking, so we drove on a couple of miles to a motel outside town. It was a pretty little place with one central building and a dozen African huts scattered under the trees. The round, thatched huts had been whitewashed and modernized into sleeping units, and the atmosphere was rustic and casual. The bar was full of salesmen and planters with of bare knees and open-necked shirts.

After we had registered, we went into the bar, where I mentioned the trouble I had experienced at the other hotel the last time I had been in Lusaka.

The manager scowled and spat expertly into the trash can. "Oh. That place," he said scornfully. "Only 'two-year contract people' go there, not real people." He looked at me. "You know the type. Paper pushers from behind some desk in Whitehall. Get sent out for a couple of years and think they're God's gift to the bloody colonials. The place is swarming with them."

A man who had been listening turned and said, "Got to save face in front of the natives, old chap. *What? What? Old boy. Dress for dinner, don't you know. Jolly good show.*" His put-on upper-crust accent started a general discussion of the type of civil servant that London sent to Lusaka. It was not complimentary. What seemed to annoy most of the people here was the way the "toffee nosed bastards" refused to mix with the Rhodesians and formed exclusive clubs, complete with blazer badges and club ties.

In the general discussion that followed, I learned that Northern Rhodesia was not as independent and self-governing as Southern Rhodesia, nor was it as completely closed to Europeans as Nyasaland. It was open to settlement, but it was run by London. All decisions of any importance were made back in Whitehall, and British politics governed everything. Almost all the civil servants were sent out from London, and the locals had very little to say about anything. Since many of these civil servants were political appointees who knew almost nothing about Northern Rhodesia, there was, not surprisingly, quite a bit of resentment.

Before we went to bed we checked the engine bolts in the car. As they seemed no worse, we decided to press on in the morning.

Day 29

After a predawn start, we crossed the Kafue River and reached Mazabuka while the day was still cool. We were making good time, but the noise from the engine was getting worse and worse. Soon we were forced to stop at a little place where a very gloomy mechanic talked very soberly about "a very long job." My host switched to his most persuasive salesman's voice, and soon the mechanic agreed that a couple of sturdy bolts would hold the engine down, at least as far as Bulawayo.

While they were working on the car, I stood on the veranda of the Indian store and watched the proprietor sewing a pair of khaki shorts. The customer, a young African man, stood next to the sewing machine, and whenever a fitting was needed, the tailor held the cloth against him and cut out the shape with a large pair of scissors,

He didn't use a tape measure, and the skill with which he fashioned the garment was amazing. By the time the car was ready to go, he was putting finishing touches to a pair of shorts easily as good as any pair hanging inside the store. When the tailor was finished, my friend, a natural salesman, showed him in his brushes. The Indian was cautiously interested, but he insisted on calling his brother and his father over, and they discussed the possible transaction carefully in Hindi. With the air of men about to purchase the Koh-i-Noor diamond, they eventually settled on an order for two dozen brooms. Considering that there were fewer than a dozen houses in the place, it was a big order.

As we went further south, the country opened out into grass veldt with more cultivation and quite a few farms dotting the landscape. The road zigzagged across the rail lines, and there was water in some of the rivers but there was little else to see. I offered to do some of the driving a number of times, but the salesman liked driving, so my offer was politely refused. During a long lull in the conversation, I dozed off.

I awoke when the car stopped at the top of a hill. As the dust cleared, we saw spread out before us a huge expanse of golden prairie, mile upon mile of open country lightly sprinkled with trees and stretching in a sea of gold and green until it was lost in the shimmering heat. We got out of the car and stood in the tall grass, trying to see the spray from Victoria Falls, which was about twenty-five miles away. And suddenly we saw it—a great column of white mist gleaming in the sun. "'The water that smokes,'" said my friend. "That's what the natives call it." It was not until we were almost in the city of Livingstone that we saw the mist again, towering over the town like the smoke from a great bonfire with the setting sun adding its dash of color.

By the time we checked into the hotel and had dinner, it was quite dark. My friend, who had been to the falls a number of times, had a surprise for me. There was a full moon that night, and, as we drove the mile or two to the falls, we could see the spray. The noise grew from a faint murmur to a thundering roar. We parked and stood on a flat, wet rock where, only a few inches from my feet, the Zambezi River glided quietly until it plunged suddenly into the darkness below. Mist rose in great billows from the gorges below us, swirling over our heads in the light breeze. My friend and I stared in amazement, and then the breeze shifted and moved the mist aside, allowing the moon to shine clear. And then we saw it—a moon rainbow! In the palest tints of green and yellow, the rainbow floated in the mist, one end anchored in the dark river, the other arched over the brink to plunge down into the roaring gorge. I was overcome. Such a delicate thing in the violence and the thunder of the water. For perhaps five minutes we stood there in silence, then the rainbow vanished and we went back to the car.

Day 30

At breakfast, I met my friend's wife, a charming little Scot who had never seen the Victoria Falls before and had come up to meet us. As it was obviously a second honeymoon, I went to the falls by myself and saw them in all their grandeur in the bright light of day, stretching for a mile before disappearing into the mist. Unlike most falls, the Victoria Falls do not simply drop over a cliff. For centuries, the great Zambezi River has eroded a series of parallel gorges so that the water tumbles into a confined space and must rush through a zigzag of half a dozen deep canyons before finding release on the plains below. In the rainy season, when the river is high, the spray from the falls and from the cataracts in the gorges is so intense that viewing is difficult and touring the falls can be a wet experience. Even in the dry season, the size of the river and the volume of water is surprising.

I bought a tour map that showed some steps going down into the first gorge, almost under the falling waters. These steps were overgrown with weeds and looked none too safe, but I went down anyway. As I descended, the steps grew steeper and more unsafe, but the view of the falls was spectacular. As I looked up from the depths of the gorge, the water seemed to be tumbling out of the blue sky directly over my head. The spray dropped like heavy rain and soaked me to my skin. At that point, I decided I had gone far enough.

The great column of rising spray has to come back to earth in the shape of rain. It falls all the time in some places, which makes it possible to walk in mere minutes out of the sun into fairly dense rain forest with tall trees and matted undergrowth. I strolled through one such forested area, under dripping trees and along a very sharp ridge, until I was stopped by a notice forbidding visitors from going any further. Rather than commit suicide, I went to another gorge that was sheltered from the bulk of the mist. It was like the Africa of the old Tarzan movies, with a trail that led steeply down, then meandered through thick jungle where the foliage closed over my head and creepers draped themselves across the path. Where palm trees had poked a hole in the green roof, I could see the thick vegetation on the canyon walls. The path was broken by little rushing streams fed by an eternal rain.

At one point, there is a sharp bend where the entire river is compressed into a narrow gorge. The result is an enormous whirlpool, above which I sat on a rock to enjoy the solitude, the coolness, and the smell of the water. At one point, I watched a huge tree, uprooted somewhere in Angola, swirling slowly round. Then I looked up and saw the bridge, a thin, graceful arch over 650 feet long, leaping the gorge almost directly overhead. I could just see tiny specks moving across it, along with a toy train that tried to add its plume of smoke to the mists from the falls.

A few hours later, when I was sitting in the dry grass looking down into one of the gorges that I had just explored, a workman and a policeman passed, chatting excitedly. They had something on a stick. After studying it intently, they threw it down into the gorge. It was a four-foot-long snake. I immediately scrambled to my feet… and then I remembered that this was the only snake I had seen the whole trip.

It was a long way to the other side of the falls, but it was a beautiful day and I was in no hurry, so I walked across the bridge. Peering over the rail, I could see the Zambezi River flowing 300 feet below, rushing muddy and angry down to Tete and eventually to the Indian Ocean. Livingstone must have crossed the river somewhere near here when he discovered the falls in 1855. My map showed a viewpoint directly in front of the falls, aptly named the Devil's Point, so I headed in that direction.

At that end of the falls, there is a miniature rail line that carries tourists down from a big hotel. When the little trolleys arrive in the rain forest, they are greeted by baboons. The creatures are expert beggars and clever thieves, and I watched one get half a bar of chocolate from a lady, then walk by her side for a hundred yards with one hand outstretched and the other tugging at her skirt until he got the rest of the chocolate. There were notices in the parking lot warning people to lock their cars securely, and I spoke to a man who had caught a baboon busily trying to remove his license plate. When I set off for Devil's Point with a troop of baboons following me, I was astounded at how the gently rising mist could return to earth as such heavy rain. The baboons wisely remained in the shelter of the trees while I slipped and slithered along a trail where only the shortest grass could survive the perpetual rain, which thundered down worse every few yards. I walked until I could not see the trail under my feet. It was too dangerous then, so I slithered back to join the baboons.

Since the area around the falls was free from curio shops and hamburger stands, getting a snack meant a long walk back up to the hotel. There I found a shop with the finest selection of souvenirs I had seen so far. There was every kind of African beast carved from wood and ivory, there were stuffed baby crocodiles, carvings, skins, masks and lion's teeth as well as all kinds of necklaces and rings. But it was not a bazaar and there was no haggling over prices. I think my Cockney friend would have been disappointed there.

That afternoon, I found the statue of David Livingstone, one hand clutching a gun, the other shading his eyes as he peers across the falls, endlessly searching the vast land that he helped open to the car and the plane and the train, and I wondered what he would think of the past one hundred years.

Inspired by the stubborn Scotsman, I tried once again to reach the Devil's Point. This time, without the company of the baboons, I approached it from a different angle and remained in the clear… until the wind changed and I was back in the heart of a deluge. The path was so wet that I took off my shoes and socks and slithered along barefoot, wading deeper into the walls of falling water. The wind refused to blow the rain away, even for a brief moment. The map had clearly warned that the trail ended in a sheer drop of hundreds of feet right into the heart of the falls. Again I retreated.

Thanks to the afternoon sun, my clothes were soon dry, and I walked back across the bridge into town. The road lay past a small game preserve, where I could peer through the fence and see zebra and kudu antelope, but, as I was not in a car, I could not enter. I stood outside and watched a few tourists drive in and wondered what the animals thought of the creatures in the mobile cages that passed through their little forest with windows tightly shut and official labels to show where they came from and whether or not they were licensed.

I thoroughly enjoyed myself at Victoria Falls, even being constantly soaked. That night, I slept like a log.

Day 31

My leave pass was for thirty days, and I was now officially absent without leave. After breakfast, therefore, I searched the hotel for a lift to Bulawayo and found a Polish mining engineer who was going as far as Wankie. My new host was a large man who drove a small English car and had been in the armies of four different nations during the Second World War, Polish, German, Russian, and British, and spoke half a dozen languages. He had come to Rhodesia with nothing and was now an engineer making good money with a family, a house with a swimming pool, and ten acres of land. He had even started a side line as a radio mechanic and had come to Livingstone to pick up spare parts. He was not inclined to talk about Europe. "I'm an African now," he said. "A white African, and I don't give a damn for Europe." Then he added, "I want my boys to grow up in the fresh air with no more killing. No more stupid wars."

There was no trouble at the border between Northern and Southern Rhodesia, and the road was reasonably good. About thirty miles along, we passed the turn off into the Wankie Game Reserve, where we saw a large notice telling us that the road was closed for the rainy season. When I said that we were still in the dry season, my host said, "The rains are due any time now. It won't take much rain to turn all that dust into slippery mud and make some of those roads quite useless. It's a very big place. Nobody would know where you were." So we drove right past one of the best game reserves in Central Africa.

Wankie turned out to be a decidedly ugly town. It was one of the biggest and most important coal mines in southern Africa, and it looked like it. The pit head and loading gear, plus the usual tangle of rail lines dominated the scene, and everything was coated with that layer of grey dust that is the trademark of a coal-mining town anywhere in the world. The clear air of Africa was fouled with smoke and smell, and I promptly walked out of Wankie.

When the rail system was being built from South Africa, Cecil Rhodes wanted the line to go due north to the southern tip of Lake Tanganyika. His dream of an all-British Cape Town to Cairo railway had to be set aside for practical matters. There was coal at Wankie, immense quantities of coal, and there were mines in Africa that needed that coal for power. Before the advent of oil and hydro-electric power, Wankie shipped coal across a very large area of southern Africa and the mine can still sell all the coal it can produce.

As I walked out of Wankie, an expensive car stopped and a youngish man offered me a lift. He was another salesman, big, blond, and oozing complete confidence in his own abilities. He was a second-generation Rhodesian of English parents who cared nothing about England or Europe. Since the topic of federation was on everybody's minds in the early 1950s, our conversation soon turned to politics, and he made it clear that he had a very low opinion of the black African. He was not in favor of the South African system of apartheid; in fact, he was quite scornful of the system's laws and passes, but at the same time, he just could not believe that a black man could ever equal a white man and was quite confident that the present system was the best for all concerned.

"We take care of them," he said. "We give them food, give them schools, hospitals, good jobs, running water. Everything! They have their own part of town to live in. They can go into business if they have the brains, Own their own homes. Hell, man! There are plenty of rich Bantu in Rhodesia."

When I called this attitude paternalism, he shrugged and said, "Well, I suppose it is. But everybody's happy."

As we traveled, we were also keeping an eye open for game. When we passed a large notice that said *Beware of Elephants*, we slowed down to a crawl. The bush was patchy here, but there was enough cover to hide an elephant. For a long time, we saw nothing, then suddenly we heard the unmistakable sound of an elephant trumpeting very close to the road. We stopped and listened, but there was absolute silence. We got out of the car and scanned the area. We must have been peering and listening for about two minutes before we turned to get back into the car. Our sudden movement was reflected in the grass and, as we turned, we saw that the seemingly empty meadow was filled by a herd of deer! Little brown creatures with huge ears had been listening to us and watching us all the time. Suddenly they turned and vanished without a sound. There was no apparent movement. They just vanished. A little way further on, we came across the place where the elephants had crossed the road. If we had not stopped, we probably would have seen them because there were piles of droppings in the road, still steaming in the morning air. We sped up in the hope of catching them, but we had to stop when we found a small felled tree blocking the road..

The elephants had evidently stopped for breakfast. We followed their tracks to a clump of trees close to the road, but, try as we might, we could not make out any large shape in the trees, nor could we hear a sound. We had to get out of the car to remove the tree, but we kept the doors open in case we had to make a quick escape. The tree was not uprooted, merely snapped off at its base by the weight of a huge body. The smell of the elephants hung heavy in the air. After this disappointment, we saw no more game for the rest of the trip. My host said, based on past experience, that a wide variety of animals were watching us from the safety of the nearby trees.

There was very little traffic on the road, and, at noon we stopped for lunch at "halfway house" where there were no other customers. We were practically in Bulawayo before we saw signs of life, and then it was all around us. The road widened and cars and people on bicycles appeared. We passed large houses with nice gardens. We reached the paved road. Suddenly we were in the city. The transition from ageless bush to the 20th century had been startlingly quick.

When the blond salesman dropped me off in the center of town, the last thing I wanted was to go back to my RAF camp with its routine, timetables, and boring predictability. So I got a much needed haircut and checked into a hotel. After a good dinner, I sat on the veranda with a cold beer and gazed up at a large moon overhead, I thought back over the miles I had covered and the people I had met and the things I had seen. I began plotting how I could see more of this magic continent.

Day 32

Before catching the bus back to camp, I bought a road map of the Union of South Africa and tried to roughly work out how many days' leave I would need to see all that I wanted to see. The bus rattled and jolted me back to camp, and as I eased my stiff bones off the wooden seat, I decided that it was clearly the most uncomfortable ride I had had during the whole trip. Fortunately for me, the serviceman at the gate was half asleep, so I hurried through a strangely deserted camp back to my bunk. Nothing had changed. It was Saturday, and those men not on duty were lounging around the pool. My things were just as I had left them a month before. I got out my map and started some serious calculations.

Chapter Eleven: Life at RAF Camp Heany

Camp Heany, or more correctly, Royal Air Force Flight Training School #4, Heany Junction, was a sprawling collection of hangars and wooden barracks set in the open bush about twenty miles north of Bulawayo. It was one of a number of bases set up during the Second World War, and when I was stationed there, it was in the process of closing down operations. The base and the planes were due to be handed over to the Rhodesian Air Force in a year or two.

It was a relaxed camp with almost no military bureaucracy and no fuss as long as the planes kept flying. We had a cinema with a different film every week and a bar that served beer and snacks. The officers' and married men's quarters were far off on the other side of camp, and there was a good size swimming pool where many of the men went after lunch. Only urgent mechanical work was done during the heat of the afternoon.

One of the pleasures of the pool was the Girl in Blue. At rare intervals, usually when the grass around the pool was packed with young, healthy, servicemen dozing in the sun and thinking about their girls back in England, a lone girl would appear from the changing rooms. She was about eighteen and wore a one-piece, light blue bathing suit and carried a white bathing cap. She was blond with only the lightest tan and had a beautiful figure. All conversation would fade away as she walked to the edge of the pool and took her time putting on her bathing cap. Acting as if the pool was entirely deserted, she looked at nobody and spoke to nobody. The men in the pool would all drift to the side, and she would dive in and swim a few laps, then float lazily for a while before climbing up to the diving board. She was a good swimmer and dived with very little splash, but she liked to stand for a while on the end of the board, knowing perfectly well that over a hundred young men, some of whom had not seen an attractive girl for many months, were staring at her with open mouths. She was obviously the daughter of one of the officers and should not have been there, so nobody said a word. Nobody whistled or made a wolf call or clapped when she dived. Nobody ever tried to talk to her. After about twenty minutes, she would walk back to the changing room and disappear.

The planes were very basic, light training planes, mostly two-seat Canadian Chipmunks (properly, the de Havilland Canada DHC-1) and some Harvards (North American Aviation T-6 Texans). They were all painted bright yellow in case they came down in the bush. One day a lightning bolt started a grass fire near the runway, but as it posed no danger, it was allowed to burn itself out. Next day, we could see the bare ground around the runway littered with the rusting remains of at least a dozen planes.

We had a number of deaths from flying accidents. Usually the remains were flown back to England, but one casualty was to be buried in Bulawayo. As the only person with any experience on a funeral guard of honor, I was delegated to find five other men of my height to make up a funeral squad and make sure they knew how to slow-march and shoot their rifles. Next, we had to ask the Rhodesian army for a dozen blank cartridges. The funeral went off quite well, and some months later, when some visiting royalty arrived, I again was told to find just the right men for the guard of honor. The ceremony was to be held at the tomb of Cecil Rhodes in the Matobo Hills. I made up the squad, but included myself as just an "assistant" so that, while the others were sweltering in the sun, I spent the ceremony wandering around the lovely setting, photographing the extraordinary rock formations and sitting in the cool shade of the gigantic boulders. I had already been to the Matobo Hills with my cousins and had seen the simple but impressive slab in the ancient granite rock that is the last resting place of Cecil Rhodes.

One day some of us commandeered a truck and went up into the hills for some rock climbing. It wasn't serious climbing. We wore rubber-soled tennis shoes and scrambled up without ropes. I had chosen a large, beautifully rounded hill of solid granite with not a single blade of vegetation on it, and while the others were paddling in a little pool left over from the rains, I started up. It was quite steep. I had almost reached the top when I looked up and saw a family of baboons above me. There were about a dozen of them sitting in a defensive group, the mothers clutching their babies and staring at me with their mouths open just enough for me to see their large canine teeth. Suddenly a very large male dashed a few feet in front of them. He stopped about twenty feet from me and opened his mouth wide, showing off his very large and very sharp looking teeth. It was clear that he was making up his mind whether to attack me or not and I was petrified. I had no weapon of any kind, not even a small stick, not even a rock to throw. All I could do was cling to the bare rock and wait. The baboon watched me carefully, all the while flashing his teeth, but he seemed to be more puzzled than angry, so I slid about six feet back down the rock and found a ledge where I could stand up. When I looked up again, all the baboons were gone. They had simply vanished without a sound. I never did get to the top of that hill. I slid all the way back to the ground and joined my friends splashing in the pool.

In the hills east of Bulawayo there was a large reservoir near which, many years before, some airmen had built a clubhouse and formed a sailing club. When I was there in 1952, the club had vanished and the clubhouse was abandoned. When somebody learned about it, one Saturday half a dozen of us "borrowed" a small truck, found the reservoir, and—with the help of a crate of beer—refounded the RAF Sailing Club of Southern Rhodesia. The sailing fleet we found consisted of one dinghy rotting in the mud and the remains of a small sailing boat sitting half full of algae-green water near a rickety little pier. We had big plans, including blazer badges and club ties, which we discussed in great detail over our beer while sitting in the shade of the old clubhouse. We never did sail anything, however, nor did we even swim in the water because of the fear of bilharzia, a parasitic disease. But the Sailing Club was a nice place to go whenever we could. Unfortunately, it wasn't long before questions were asked, and we soon found that our access to any form of wheeled transport had been cut off. I still have the blazer badge somewhere. It never got sown onto a blazer.

I got out of the camp as often as I could, bumming lifts all over the place. One place I could never get to, however, was Great Zimbabwe, the ancient stone ruins discovered by the Portuguese in the 16th century. Said to be the royal palace of the Kingdom of Zimbabwe from the 11th to the 14th centuries, it was explored by

Europeans primarily in the 19th century and has been argued about ever since. Great Zimbabwe is a complex of walls and buildings carefully constructed of stones without mortar. Among the artifacts discovered are birds carved out of soapstone, one of which can now be seen on the flag of Zimbabwe. It lies about 200 miles east of Bulawayo and is one of the places in Rhodesia that I particularly wanted to see, but I could never find anybody who was going there.

Trainee pilots arrived every month at Camp Heany. They were newly commissioned officers, but they were also young and very green, and the failure rate was high, which was a good thing because those who passed went on to fly the new jet planes that were appearing in the 1950s. A brand new batch of trainees had just arrived when we were visited by royalty and the Station Commanding Officer called for full dress uniforms which, for the officers, meant swords. Unfortunately, the RAF does not issue swords, and so the mad scramble to find enough swords in the city of Bulawayo was quite amusing. All the young officers eventually managed to borrow something resembling a sword, some of them valuable museum pieces, many of them souvenirs from Indian army veterans, and quite a few only cheap decorative imitations designed to hang on the wall. From a distance, they all looked good.

The CO was an interesting man. He was so upper class that I doubt that his eyes could even focus on any creature below the rank of squadron leader. I had very little contact with him, but I got the impression that he was a nice, harmless chap who knew very little about what he was supposed to do and had the good sense not to interfere with men who did know what they were doing. Nobody had ever heard of the CO actually flying a plane.

He was tall and good looking and wore his blonde wavy hair down to his collar, with his cap perched at just the right angle. He also had the regulation RAF moustache. The RAF moustache is never bushy or waxed. It is always brushed severely to each side as if pressed into shape by an oxygen mask.

What I admired most, however, was his uniform. Depending on the weather, we had the choice of wearing our blue uniforms with trousers or our tropical khaki uniforms with shorts. The CO's perfectly tailored uniform was neither. It was a very green shade of khaki with a nice finish to the cloth, which the sergeant complained was "obviously chosen by his wife." Instead of the regulation black shoes with gleaming toe caps, our CO wore a pair of tan suede chukka boots with crepe soles. Those suede boots were so comfortable that many of the men wore them during the working day and nobody said a word. I still have a pair.

Also smartly turned out were the men of the Rhodesian African Rifles (RAR), a very old regiment of black soldiers led by white officers that dated back to 1916 and had seen service in Burma, Suez, Malaya, and Nyasaland. Their camp was right next door to ours, and many of them worked at various jobs around the RAF base. One RAR was assigned to me as a messenger. His name was Joshua. As there was little for him to do, we talked quite a bit about Rhodesia and his regiment and his home life. He was mission-educated and had been married in the Catholic church. His wife was living in the camp, but a few months after we met, he announced that he had "bought" another wife when he went on leave to his village. He had paid a couple of goats and a new bicycle for her, and she took care of his village house and plot of land.

One day Joshua brought an old African man into the office. Although this man was a Matabele, Joshua, who was Mashona, treated him with respect. He wanted to show me the old man's earrings. They were carved and colored ivory and so large that they almost touched his shoulders. The old man spoke no English, but between us, Joshua and I learned that a boy has to have approval from his tribal elders to wear his first earrings, which are just slivers of ivory inserted directly into the ear lobes. As he matures, the elders allow him to increase the size of the earrings, and, if he is well respected for his wisdom or activities, he can wear large and highly decorated ear ornaments. These were so big that I asked the old man if he wore them all day. He laughed and said that they didn't hurt his ears, but they slapped his jaw when he turned, so he only wore them for special occasions. When he took them out of his ears, the ear lobes hung down like strips of rope and touched his shoulders. He simply flicked them up and over his ears to get them out of the way.

After the old man left, Joshua snorted his disgust and said, "Mashona don't do silly things like that. Those Matabele are not civilized. They are a Zulu tribe. They should all go back to Zululand."

Joshua's regiment, in Matabeleland (now a region of Zimbabwe), was composed mostly of Mashona men, whereas the regiment in Mashonaland (now another region of Zimbabwe) was composed mostly of Matabele men. There was no love lost between these two major tribes, and this prevented any fraternization between the soldiers and the local population. All the officers were white, but the sergeants and corporals were both black and white. Regimental spirit and loyalty to the regiment were cultivated, and the soldiers were told to think of themselves as members of their regiment first, with no regard to color or tribe. During the Zimbabwean war for independence, the RAR remained loyal and fought alongside the white troops with great bravery, resisting all attempts to change sides. They were even called in to try to quell the civil war that followed independence.

Black officers were introduced in 1979, and after independence the RAR became the Zimbabwe National Army. The soldiers loved a good parade and their turnout was always impeccable, with every button gleaming and every uniform pressed and starched to perfection. Their formation marching was a sight to delight even the most gloomy drill sergeant and they usually celebrated in the evening with drums loud enough for us to hear on our base.

Although the Mau Mau Rebellion (or Uprising) had already started in Kenya in 1952, Rhodesia was still quite peaceful and no talk about independence had started. The country was prosperous, there was work for everybody, food was cheap, and everybody seemed to be happy. One night, however, half a dozen of us were playing cards at a table in the middle of the barracks, which was a long, plain, wooden building with rows of beds and lockers. All the windows and the doors at the ends were open to let in a little night breeze. There was just one light over our heads. Suddenly we heard a buzzing noise, and the light bulb shattered with a loud noise. For an instant, we all sat there in surprise, then we threw ourselves flat on the floor. Somebody had shot at us, and we had no weapons. The nearest rifles were in the guardhouse on the other side of the camp, and the guards had only one small box of live ammunition.

We had no knives or clubs, either, and we had not seen a bayonet since graduating from boot camp many months before.

We lay there for about two minutes, listening, but there was absolute silence. Nobody was shouting, there were no sounds of running feet in the dark.

Then somebody said, "I didn't hear a shot. Did you?"

We all agreed that we had not heard the shot fired. But then we heard another sound. This was a scratching sound coming from the pile of our playing cards. As our eyes grew accustomed to the moonlight, we stood up. And that's when we saw the biggest, ugliest beetle that any of us had ever seen. It was about four inches long, black and shiny, and looked like a rhino with too many horns. We all roared with laughter and relief, and after the alien invader had been passed from hand to hand for careful inspection, somebody took it to a window and released it into the tropical night where, with a bit of luck, it might frighten the daylights out of another group of brave and fearless young airmen.

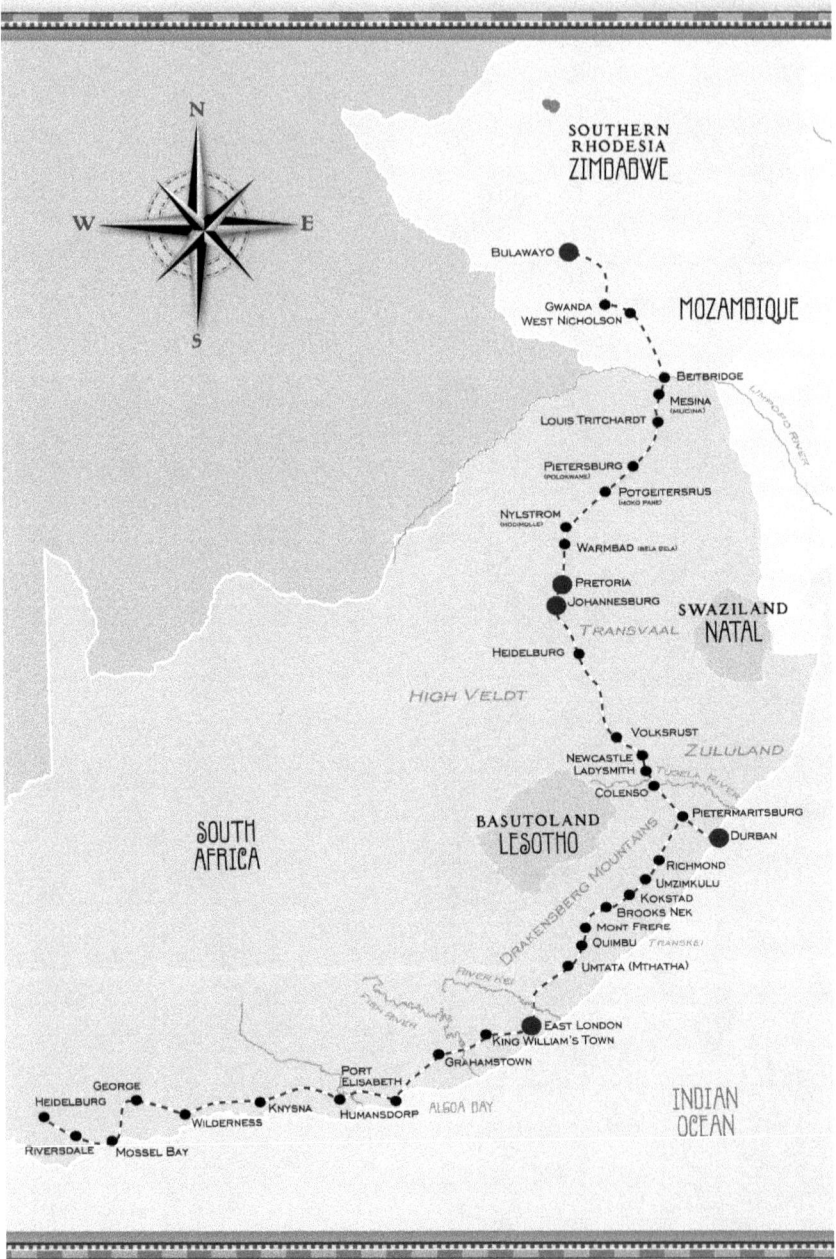

Map Two. Traveling South into the Union of South Africa

THE SECOND TRIP:

SOUTH INTO THE UNION OF SOUTH AFRICA

Chapter Twelve: Bulawayo to Johannesburg

Day 1

To give myself some extra time for my second trip, I made out a twenty-eight day pass, which was my limit, but added a forty-eight hour pass at the beginning. The sergeant signed them both without looking, and, a couple of days later, with my little bag in my hand, I thumbed a lift into Bulawayo.

There was a large trade fair and festival at the exhibition grounds. My hope was to catch a visitor returning to the Union of South Africa, so I strolled down the avenue under the jacaranda trees reading license plates. The first short lift got me out into the country. I walked up a hill from which I could look down the long, winding road until it vanished into some blue hills. The air was so crystal clear I could see the sun glinting on tin roofs nearly twenty miles away.

Soon I spied a little car speeding along the road towards me, its tail of dust drifting lazily behind it. It climbed the hill and stopped at my wave. The driver was a small man with a strong Yorkshire accent who didn't talk much except to make polite remarks as I explained what I was doing, but his driving style was remarkable. He sat facing me in the passenger seat, with his legs crossed and one arm draped over the back of the seat. The other armed rested on the steering wheel, and he would occasionally glance ahead to see where he was going. He drove fast, and at first I was quite nervous.

When I asked him if he knew the road well, he replied, "I drive this road about four times a week. Know every inch like the back of my hand. Have done for two years now, and never an accident." This reassured me a little.

We soon entered rougher country. The road twisted and turned as we skirted the Matobo Hills, then we were in open country again and sped through the little towns of Gwanda and West Nicholson. All along the way we saw signs of industry, sometimes a factory or a mine, sometimes a quarry or a mill, but where the railway ended at West Nicholson, all sign of industry ended abruptly. The road was being rebuilt and the detours were miserable, but my host did not seem to mind and continued to drive with his elbow as we went over roots and pot holes that would have torn the wheel from my grasp.

Strangely enough, there was at that time no direct rail link between Johannesburg and Bulawayo. The first rail line to the Rhodesias was built through Bechuanaland (now the Republic of Botswana) from Kimberley to Mafeking and then to Bulawayo, thus skirting the South African Republics later known as Transvaal and the Orange Free State. The line north of Pretoria had been extended to the border, and the Rhodesians had built a branch line south, but the two lines had never been linked and a train ride to Johannesburg meant a wide detour via Mafeking.

When I mentioned this "missing link" and wondered why, my host laughed and said, "Depends on who owns the railways and who'll make the profit." He paused, then added, "They don't build railways for convenience. They build them to make money. A direct line would mess things up badly." It was the longest speech he made the whole 150-mile drive.

For the next few hours we drove through hilly country covered in virgin bush with here and there a wide natural meadow. We passed a few kraals, but the only other signs of life were the half-wild cattle that roamed at will through the bush and wandered onto the road.

It was a strange ride, and I was glad to reach the border between Southern Rhodesia and South Africa at Beitbridge just as the sun set in all its golden glory. As luck would have it, the only hotel in town was packed with businessmen and tourists, but my host was well known, and so he soon got us a double room. After dinner, I started to check out the other guests to see if any were headed south, but my host wanted to talk.

"I don't like to talk when I'm driving," he explained. "Don't even have a radio. Got to concentrate on the driving." After all those long miles of silence, he talked, and talked until well past midnight.

Day 2

My host was gone when I awoke, and so were all the businessmen and tourists. After a leisurely breakfast, I strolled down to the border. Beitbridge is nearly two thousand feet lower than Bulawayo. The little town, which consisted of a large customs post, a hotel, a store, a garage, and a police post, plus some mud huts and houses hiding in the trees, slumbered in the heat. I produced my passport at the customs post, but the officer ignored it.

"Are you in the RAF?" he asked. When I said that I was, he said, "Good luck, man, and have a nice holiday."

I thanked him and stepped onto the bridge. Alfred Beit, after whom the bridge and town were named, was Cecil Rhodes' partner in the British South Africa Company. The two men shared the risks, but it was Rhodes who got the glory and whose name was everywhere. When they died, the huge Rhodes fortune went to international scholars, whereas Beit's fortune went into a foundation to serve the people of the land that bore his partner's name.

I walked across the large, handsome Beit Bridge to the monument to Alfred Beit in the middle. There I peered over the railing at the river far below. I have always loved Rudyard Kipling, and, as a small boy I had dreamed of "the great grey-green, greasy Limpopo River, all set about with fever-trees," (which is from Kipling's *Just So Stories*) but I was sadly disappointed. Below me was nothing but a shrunken mountain stream, although the polished rocks indicated that it was obviously a raging torrent in the rainy season.

When I reached the South African side and handed my passport and leave pass to the officer, I said, "So that's the famous Limpopo River, eh?"

He laughed. "Another disappointed Kipling fan. But don't you worry, man. You just go a couple of hundred miles downstream into Mozambique and you'll find your jungle river. Complete with elephants and pythons and mosquitoes and yellow fever and malaria. And lots of poisonous snakes." He handed me back my papers and said, "I've never been there myself. I don't think I particularly want to go."

While we were chatting, somebody called out. It was the driver of a small family car, and he offered me a lift. As he already had his wife and two children in the car, I tried to refuse it, but everybody insisted that there was enough room. So I squeezed in with the children, and we set off for Messina, about ten miles away, where we changed our Rhodesian money into South African currency.

My hosts were a pleasant, cheerful family returning from a vacation visiting relatives. They were Afrikaner and bilingual, but the parents spoke English by choice and made sure the children spoke English, too. Everybody showed a lively interest in my stories about England and those parts of Europe I had visited.

We traveled across flat, open country with great baobab trees standing here and there like lonely beer bottles, their massive trunk tapering sharply up to a bunch of distorted branches. These massive trees are often rotten and hollow, and when we passed one that had lost its branches, one of the children said, "It looks like a giant sentry box guarding the land."

As we approached the Zoutpansberg (now Soutpansberg) mountain range, the road began to climb. After a few twists and turns we were in Wylliesport, a magnificent narrow gorge, where we stopped for a picnic lunch in the cool shade.

After lunch, I took the children for a clamber over the rocks. The cliff walls rising sheer on either side were studded with a wide variety of rock plants and flowering cacti, all eking out a colorful existence in the rocky wilderness. Near a tiny stream we found a sturdy root, and the children traced it up the bare rock where it clung and twisted higher and higher until, about forty feet up, it fed a little grey plant with a flaming pink flower no bigger than a penny.

The road climbed higher and each turn as we rode along brought marvelous views across the veldt or down into sheltered valleys where little white houses stood out against the greens of the orchards. We stopped often to admire the view. At one point, the mother said, "How on earth did the pioneers get those clumsy ox wagons over the pass? It must be a thousand feet."

Her husband shook his head. "Just muscles and faith," he said, "and an awful lot of stubbornness."

At the top of the pass, where we ran into a wall of mist as thick as a London fog, we crept along with our headlights on. Then the fog vanished as quickly as it had appeared, and we dropped down onto the High Veldt, where the high plains spread out below us like a huge green and brown blanket quilted by roads and river beds.

On the outskirts of the little town of Louis Trichardt, we stopped at a pretty little cottage where the family went in to visit their grandparents. I wandered around the garden and was staring at a plant that looked exactly like a pineapple, except that it was three feet high, when the little girl invited me in.

My visit with the family was quite an experience. Grandfather was an elderly gentleman with a perfectly trimmed Jan Smuts beard and wearing an old-fashioned, tight black suit. His wife was a little lady dressed in Victorian black, complete with cameo brooch. Neither of them spoke a word of English. Through the grandchildren, they asked me formally polite questions, listened patiently to the translated answers, then carried on talking to the others in rapid Afrikaans. There was no way that I could join in the conversation, so I studied the room. The heavy curtains, the lace trimmed settee, and the potted plants on spindly tables told of a room that had not changed in fifty years, except for the old fashioned radio hidden away in the corner. A collection of china figurines stood on an upright piano, along with a dark framed portrait of a man with a huge moustache and a high stiff collar. I sat there, balancing a cup of tea on my knee, and listened to the conversation until it was time to go. After the grandfather wished me a polite but unsmiling farewell, we stepped out into the blinding sunshine.

When we were on our way again, the mother turned to me and exclaimed, "Well, I never thought I'd see that! I suppose you are to be congratulated. You are the first Englishman to set foot in that house since it was built, and Grandpapa built it himself."

Her husband explained. "They were both children during the Boer War and still have very unhappy memories. You see, they survived the British concentration camps."

During the Boer Wars (1880-1881 and 1899-1902), the British troops were dependent on their supply lines, as most armies are, but the Boers could stop off at any convenient farm for a square meal and a rest. Toward the end of the second war, the British generals realized that the only way to solve this problem was to systematically destroy the farms as they advanced. It was a drastic but effective method that had been used before and has been used since. Unfortunately, as in Sherman's March to the Sea during the American Civil War, the memories left by this scorched-earth policy festered for many generations after the war was over. Unlike previous conquerors, in southern Africa, however, the British felt some responsibility towards the women and children who were left standing in the vast and terribly lonely veldt. These tragic refugees were packed into whatever transport was available, often open railway cattle cars, and shipped to camps, called concentration camps, where they could be cared for and kept separated from their fighting men. It was wartime and everything was in short supply, and the camps were completely unplanned and poorly managed. There were nearly fifty camps containing over 100,000 people, most of them from isolated farms, where the families had never built up any resistance to disease. The result was a tragedy of horrifying proportions. Measles, typhoid, dysentery, pneumonia, scarlet fever, influenza, bronchitis, whooping cough, diphtheria, and malaria epidemics spread through the camps and the children died like flies. About 20,000 children died, and the Afrikaners have never forgotten what they call the Slaughter of the Innocents. To this day, English-speaking South Africans have difficulty defending what was basically a humanitarian gesture, but one that had such tragic results, so the people remain silent and most histories of the Boer Wars do not mention the epidemics.

About twenty miles further on, we turned off the main road, and I said farewell to this kind family. The veldt was now a flat, open plain, and the road was a quivering black ribbon across it. The only shade I could see was a sign post, so I was facing a long, hot wait. But suddenly, a large American car sped out of the heat haze. As it came alongside me, it put its nose to the ground and skidded to a long halt, then reversed.

The driver was glad to see me. "My radio is broken," he said, "and I'm in a hurry to get to Johannesburg. It's damn hot and this long, straight stretch of road is making me sleepy. It's so easy to fall asleep at the wheel. So talk!" Since talking is what I do best, we talked about cars, politics, soil erosion, and anything else that came into our heads, while he kept his foot hard down.

All the land that we passed was being farmed, and we occasionally passed a lonely farm house nestled in the shade of a low hill, adding its red and white to the browns and yellows of the great plains. We stopped for petrol and a hurried soft drink at Peitersburg (now Polokwane), which was a pretty town, clean and white with green trees and well tended gardens. But there was no time to waste, and we raced off and soon passed the town of Potgeitersrus, with its citrus orchards and then we went over some low hills to the town of Nylstroom (also known as Modimolle), where we stopped again. While we sipped our soft drink, my host gave me a brief history lesson.

"The first settlers here found a river flowing north," he said. "They thought it was the source of the Nile, so that's what they called their settlement. In Afrikaans, *Nylstroom* means Nile Source." For the rest of the trip we discussed towns' names as we sped across the extraordinarily level plains of Springbok Flats to Warmbad (now Bela Bela), where we were forced to slow down and crawl along the main street past a string of hotels catering to visitors to the thermal springs.

"Just think," my host said. "All these people have come miles just to sit in tubs of hot water, while I would give my false teeth just for a nice cold shower!"

It was late afternoon—after 300 miles of hard driving and even harder talking—when we arrived in Pretoria, now one of South Africa's three capital cities. (The other two are Cape Town, the legislative capital, and Bloemfontein, the judicial capital.) It looked like a lovely city with wide avenues lined with hundreds of jacaranda trees, comfortable-looking buildings, and an air of calmness despite the Saturday crowds. In the center of the city we ran into huge crowds coming from a rugby game. It must have been an important game because twice fans shouted the score at me from a passing car. All I could do was smile and say, "Dankie." The remaining forty miles to Johannesburg took nearly two hours, as the road was a solid mass of cars.

The proud citizens of Johannesburg claim that their city breeds the worst drivers in the world, New York included. But they also say that they have genuine sympathy for anybody from out of town who is unlucky enough to get trapped in their city.

"I'm from Jo'burg, but this car has Natal license plates," said my host. "Just watch this." And he proceeded to act the country bumpkin, passing every car he could, cutting in, changing lanes and sliding through red lights while I kept an eye open for the police. Curiously, nobody leaned on their horn and nobody waved an angry fist.

Outside Pretoria, we passed the Voortrekker Monument, a huge white block of granite on a hill top. A museum and a memorial to the pioneers, it was fashioned to represent the covered wagons of the settlers formed into a circle, or *laager*, for safety. The effect of the sculpture against the setting sun was dramatic, and the crowds of holiday-makers crawling over the hillside looked like colorful ants around a honey pot.

Later, while we were still some miles from Johannesburg, the sun set and we could see the blaze of lights that marked one of the biggest, and by far the richest, city in Africa. When we were well into the city, my host told me what tram to take to get to the city center and even went to the trouble of overtaking one and stopping in front of it until I was safely aboard. Then, with a cheerful wave, he roared off into the night. I had not the faintest idea where to go so I bought a ticket to the central station, where there are always hotels, and settled back for a leisurely ride. We clattered through miles of brightly lit streets crowded with people. After the wide open countryside, the buildings seemed to tower into the night sky and the roads seemed narrow and congested. I had expected a large city, but the expanse of Jo'burg quite surprised me, as the tram seemed to go miles before we reached the downtown area. A few blocks from the station, I found an attractive older hotel and, as I had made such good time from the border, I checked in for two days in order to see the fabled city.

After a cool shower and a hot dinner, I took a stroll around. My immediate impression of Johannesburg was of a lively city. There were bright lights everywhere, crowds going into neon-lit theatres, crowds coming out of bars and smart restaurants, crowds looking into the shops, and crowds of cars jamming the streets. There was vibrant life everywhere, but it had been a long day for me, and so I soon returned to the hotel, where the noise of the city lulled me to sleep in my room six floors up.

Day 3

It was ten o'clock when I awoke. The silence was uncanny, and I stood looking out of the window at the deserted streets below for some time until I remembered that it was Sunday. The weather had turned suddenly cool with a sharp breeze, but the sky was clear. It was an ideal sight-seeing day, so I spent most of it on my feet. Everywhere I strolled, there were new tall buildings, almost-finished tall buildings, and older buildings being torn down to be replaced by newer tall buildings. Some parts of the city were already canyons of concrete and glass. The shops contained everything and anything that money could buy, and the prices ranged from reasonable to absurd.

Lunchtime found me completely lost until I found a tram that would take me back to the hotel, where I experienced one of those very strange coincidences that happen once in a lifetime. During lunch, I caught the eye of a lady sitting with her husband across the room. She looked vaguely familiar, but as she did not seem to recognize me, I forgot the incident. Later, when we were all three standing and waiting for the elevator, the man turned, looked at me, and said, "John Fulford?"

Then I remembered who the couple were. He was my uncle. The only time we had ever met was at my cousin's home in Bulawayo, but that was some months past and then for only for an hour or two.

They were in Johannesburg on a short vacation. We went up to their suite, where I was made welcome, and they both insisted that I just had to stop by their place in East London and stay as long as I wanted. I was happy to take them up on their kind offer.

"You solved a problem for me," I said. "I was wondering whether to go straight down to Cape Town or to cut across to Durban and go down the coast. East London is about half way between Durban and Cape Town, I think."

They both agreed that it was a good plan and insisted that I should not miss Durban.

The rest of the day was spent sightseeing, planning my route, and gossiping about family with my relatives. They suggested places along my route that I had to visit, if I had the time. Interestingly, neither of them was at all worried about my hitchhiking in Africa. In fact, they were quite enthusiastic, and after a couple of drinks my uncle said, "You know, if I was a couple of years younger and not tied to a desk, I'd just love to do what you're doing. We've been here over twenty years, and there is so much of this beautiful country that I have never seen."

I promised to see them both again very soon, and he gave me his office address.

Chapter Thirteen: Johannesburg to Durban

Day 4

I decided to take a suburban train out of the city, but there was a variety of trains to choose from and I had no idea how far out the suburbs extended. I finally chose one that seemed to parallel the road to Durban, and then I chose a station that seemed far enough out. As the train clicked smoothly through the city, I could see white mountains towering above the gold mines. These "mountains" were actually huge dumps of pulverized rock that blows across the city when the wind is in the wrong direction and makes life miserable, but Johannesburg had grown around the gold mines and their tailings, and nobody knew how best to remove them. So there they stood like gleaming pyramids, a reminder to why the city was there.

We also passed a shanty town of little houses made of flattened tin cans, bricks, and sheets of corrugated iron. Most of them appeared to be clean, as they were painted in bright colors and the squalor was thus hidden under a bright façade. The Monday washing already fluttered in the breeze.

Abruptly, the city was gone, we were out in the country, and there was only open farmland stretching off into the distance. The change was so dramatic that I caught myself taking deeper breaths, like a swimmer surfacing from a pool. The station I had chosen turned out to be a whistle stop consisting of just a sign and a fence with a gate in it, but nearby, a factory chimney peered over some trees. The station was deserted, but the gatekeeper at the factory pointed me in the right direction and I strolled off down the road.

Leaving the shelter of the trees, I felt the full force of the wind that swept across the veldt. Despite the bright sunshine, it was cold. As I put on my jacket, I reminded myself that South Africa has a winter just like many countries I'd visited, and that the altitude of the high veldt was over 4,000 feet. After a while, I got a lift to a cross-road where I was told the traffic would be better. I was able to shelter near a grove of trees there. It was wild and open country, and the wind whistled through the phone wires overhead and cut through my light summer clothes. The few cars that passed completely ignored me until, eventually, a farm tractor came chugging down the road. The driver smiled and waved, so I climbed onto the tractor and leaned against the warm engine.

The farmer was a cheerful fellow, and we chatted about the problems of farming in that region. He was a fund of interesting facts about erosion, wind breaks, and grass fires and drought, so he talked and I listened and thawed my frozen bones for half an hour as we crawled slowly along the deserted road. When at last he turned off at his farm, I was left once again standing in the biting wind. Fortunately, not for long.

My next lift was from a middle-aged salesman for a tobacco company. He was a very nationalistic Afrikaner, a fact that he made clear from the moment I stepped into his car because he immediately started to discuss politics and apartheid. A well-traveled man who had been to England, he was appalled at the ignorance of most non-South Africans about conditions in his country.

"What really gets me hopping mad is the absolute nonsense printed about us," he said. "Obviously, by reporters who have never even been here, and fed to readers who couldn't find South Africa on a map."

My own hastily acquired knowledge of South Africa pleased him immensely, but I had not the background to be able to argue politics and apartheid, which was probably fortunate because it was obvious that he had only picked me up to have somebody to argue with. So I let him do the talking, and we got along fine.

The white South African is not an immigrant. He does not see himself as a transplanted European any more than the Australians in Australia and the Americans in America see themselves as transplanted Europeans. While some Americans describe their country as a new country only recently wrested from the original inhabitants, the South African sees his as an old country with deep roots and old traditions.

"Did you know that the Dutch settled the Cape Province 300 years ago?" my host asked me. When I told him that I knew that, he added, "But I bet you didn't know that there were no Bantu in the Cape region when the Dutch settled it. They never taught you that in school, did they?"

I agreed that it was news to me, and he explained that the Dutch had found only Hottentots and Bushmen, who are now extinct or who live in the wilds of the Kalahari Desert. The northward expansion of the white settlers was unimpeded for over one hundred years until it clashed with the southward drift of the Bantu tribes from the Congo. "So I suppose," he said with a laugh, "you could say that the white man was here first. Not that anybody would believe you."

His deep and angry pride in his native land extended to the language as well. "Afrikaans is not just a Dutch dialect," he said. "It's no closer to Dutch than Portuguese is to Castilian Spanish. It's our national language. But will the English learn it? Oh, no! You're going to meet hundreds of Afrikaners who speak English, but you won't meet many English-speaking South Africans who speak Afrikaans fluently. That's insulting."

I was learning a lot from my host, but, unfortunately, he had to stop in Heidelburg, so he dropped me on an open stretch of road where the traffic was good. It took some time, but eventually I stopped a very large station wagon with a pile of luggage on the roof. The driver was an American missionary of the "hot gospel" type, and I was hardly in the car before he asked me, "Are you saved?"

When I assured him that I was, he said, "I never stop for hitchhikers. Never!"

It was a very interesting ride. He was a large man, an American with a strong Southern accent, and I gathered that his missionary work consisted of lightning-fast trips out to some unfortunate African village, where he denounced drink and the devil for a couple of hours, then dashed off to another victim village or back to Johannesburg, leaving behind a pile of tracts that most of the natives could not read. He carried enough luggage for a six-month safari and had dragged his wife along, too. The poor woman didn't get a word in edgewise as her husband talked continuously, mostly complaining about hotel service.

His mission was obviously a well-financed campaign, but I couldn't help thinking that all the money—all those nickels and dimes so generously given by people back home in the United

States—could have been better spent on a small clinic or a school room rather than wasted on gasoline and hotels for this man. What he was doing did not compare favorably with the patient, time-tested methods of other missionaries that I had met.

The missionary turned off at a small town, where a long stretch of road was under reconstruction and the high wind blew the exposed earth into clouds of gritty powder that covered parked cars, trees, and even coated the houses in grey dust. It was a miserable place to stop, so I hurried through the haze to the top of a low hill. It was no better there. The road lay torn up and exposed for miles ahead, and the drivers who came bumping up the road were too busy groping through the dust to notice me. Soon I was as grey as the road, and the windward side of my face began to feel raw. To make matters worse, big black clouds rolled across the sky with awful suddenness. Soon it grew dark.

There was a small house near the road, so when the large, wet drops began falling, I retreated to the shelter of the front porch, where, through a curtain of rain, I watched my nationalist friend drive slowly by again. It was already afternoon, and I had not covered much ground, but my first priority was to keep dry under the little porch roof.

My predicament seemed to worry the lady of the house also, because after a few minutes, she opened the door and said, "Would you like to come in out of the rain and have a nice cup of tea?"

We sat by the stove, and she produced biscuits to go with the tea while I explained who I was and where I was going as lightning flashed, thunder rolled, and the rain drummed on the roof. Within half an hour it was over, and the sun came out as bright as ever, so, thanking the lady for her hospitality to a complete stranger, I stepped out into air that was fresh and completely purged of dust.

Soon I got a lift from a young insurance salesman who was keen and enthusiastic and tried to persuade me that I should take up selling insurance. It was a great life, he said, and the money was fantastic. He had only been selling for six weeks. I wondered to myself how he would feel after six years.

After a few miles, I found myself once again at a crossroad in the middle of a huge expanse of open country with a bare road and the nearest trees over a mile away. There were more black clouds on the horizon, and I could see the rain falling far in the distance, so I walked along until I found a large culvert that ran under the road. It looked like a miserable hole, but it was better than freezing in the rain. Fortunately, I did not have to use it. Just as the rain started to fall again, a large, black, chauffeur-driven car passed me, stopped, and reversed right up to me.

The driver was a small, wrinkled, African man, and the passenger was a very tall, very large salesman who was bored and wanted somebody to talk to. We talked about cars and taxes and anything that came to mind until we stopped for a drink about twenty miles from Volksrust. If I had known what lay ahead, I would have said goodbye right there and then. But I didn't know, and so we had a couple of beers.

Some farmers came into the bar, and we had a game of darts and some more beers. Then the talk turned to politics, and my host, who was strongly anti-nationalist, aired his views, and the farmers argued with him. The beer flowed, and the conversation got serious. It would have ended in a fight except that my host was such a huge man. When the beer changed to whiskey, however, I decided that we had had enough. I tried to persuade him to leave, but he was just getting warmed up. It was dark and cold outside, so I had to sit and listen, but after what seemed an eternity he cursed all Afrikaners and told me to get the car.

I woke the chauffeur, and he and I sat and waited another half an hour until the owner of the car staggered to the door and almost fell down the steps. The freezing night air seemed to put new life into him, and he decided that he wanted to drive. The chauffeur and I argued with him, but it was useless, so the chauffeur sat ready to grab the wheel and I cowered in the back seat. I had hardly closed the door, when the car shot forward into somebody's garden, then jerked and bounced onto the street. Swearing like a trooper, my drunken host switched the headlights full on and drove right onto the main road at full speed. As we shot across the late night traffic, I had a brief glimpse of a car skidding violently out of our way. A pair of headlights flashed and somebody shouted angrily, and then we were tearing down the main road. Two or three more cars swerved by us, their horns blasting, until we came to a steep hill with a very narrow bridge at the bottom.

"This is it," I muttered to myself and prepared to crouch on the floor but the chauffeur had a more practical idea. He switched the engine off and put the keys into his pocket. We rolled to a blessed stop, but then the drunk got out and, muttering to himself, began to push the car downhill. I reached over and pulled the handbrake. When the owner got back into the car, he saw the keys were missing. He guessed where they had gone and began to demand them from his servant, shouting and swearing and waving his arms, but never actually hitting the brave little man. Eventually the chauffeur got out of the car and began to walk away into the night. That seemed to do the trick. He was immediately called back. After one last tirade, accompanied with multiple threats of firing, he was allowed to drive us the rest of the way into Volksrust. We had hardly crossed the bridge when there was a load snore from the back seat.

In the town, I got a double room in the hotel, garaged the car, and saw to it that the black chauffeur had accommodation. While I was doing this, the chauffeur was trying to get the drunk up the stairs to the room. If I had not been so miserable, I would have laughed at the sight, but I was not in the mood for humor, so between us we dragged him into the room and dumped him onto a bed. He must have weighed 300 pounds. With quiet efficiency, the chauffeur removed his employer's suit and shoes. I asked him if this had ever happened before.

"Yes, Boss," he replied. "They took away his permit to drive. That is why the company pays me to drive him." He shook his head sadly and said, "But it has never been this bad before."

Day 5

I woke up next morning expecting to find the salesman nursing a horrible hangover. Instead, I was completely surprised to find him already up, shaved, dressed, and whistling like a schoolboy. He was entirely cheerful and did not mention the previous night until after breakfast, when he said, "I must have had one too many last night. I can't remember a thing after that darts game."

I looked at him in surprise and told him what had happened. He was horrified and hurried down to check on the car, returning in a couple of minutes to report that everything was fine. "It's a company car," he explained. "They look for the slightest scratch." Then, rather embarrassed, he apologized for the scary ride. Since he had work to do in that town, we parted company.

Volksrust was a small farming town, and so I was very soon out in the country. There was very little traffic, but I thumbed every vehicle that passed. When a very small car with suitcases on the roof and a child's face at the window came by, I kept my hand down and merely smiled at the child as the car passed. But it didn't pass. It stopped and the driver offered to give me a lift to Durban. The car was crowded, and I would normally have politely turned down the offer, but 250 miles in one lift was quite a temptation after the short jumps I had had since Johannesburg, so I squeezed into the back seat with two small children. They were another extremely nice, middle class family from Johannesburg, where the father was a college lecturer in history and geography. They were going to Durban on holiday, so we took our time and discussed the countryside as we traveled. I offered to do some of the driving, but the couple liked driving and shared it between them.

We soon left the Transvaal and the high veldt with its miles of open country and entered Natal (now KwaZulu-Natal), a region of rolling hills that gradually became steeper. "We will be crossing the Drakensberg Mountains before we drop down into Durban," said the father. "Some of the peaks are eleven or twelve thousand feet high, and they have enough snow up there for ski resorts." He shuddered. "Not that I am very interested in snow and ice."

His wife smiled. "Snow looks best on Christmas cards," she said.

The city of Newcastle looked exactly like its namesake in England—coal mines, heavy industry, and dust—so we did not stop but pressed on towards the coast and the Indian Ocean. Every now and then, one of the parents would point out something of importance to the children and me, which not only kept them from getting too bored on the long journey, but also gave them a little geography and history. At Newcastle, the children learned all about coal. Soon the road leveled out, and the temperature rose as we dropped from the interior plateau. By the time we reached Ladysmith, it was quite warm. We took a few turns around the town and found it a sleepy, pretty place with a quiet charm and relatively unspoiled by commercial tourism.

During the Boer Wars, however, Ladysmith had been far from sleepy. "When the Boer Republics invaded Natal," the father explained, "they attacked Ladysmith first. But they got a big surprise when it resisted so strongly and they had to besiege it. It was under siege for months. Conditions were pretty bad. They ran out of everything, but they held on. Of course the British sent troops to relieve the city, but they suffered some disastrous defeats before they even got here." He sighed. "The stupid British generals and their parade ground tactics lost a lot of good men to the hard-riding, fast-shooting Boers. It was months before the British realized they would have to use completely new methods of fighting."

Now his wife spoke up. "One of the things they did was to get rid of their pretty red uniforms. They gave the men khaki to match the countryside. Did you know that *khaki* is a word from India? It means 'muddy brown.' It is rather ugly, but it was a lot better than bright red."

History lesson over, we were soon in the hills again, and we stopped often to admire the view and let the children run loose. At the top of a pass called Colenso Heights, we could see the Tugela River winding slow and yellow in the valley, with little farms in the middle of acres of neatly planted orchards, green and cool against the blue hills. The scene was so peaceful that it was hard to imagine the slaughter these fields had seen during the Boer Wars.

"This is Colenso," said the father, "and somewhere down there the British army suffered its worst defeat in the whole Boer War. An idiot of a general called Buller marched his men across flat, open land towards the river, as if he was on some parade ground. But the Boers were well dug in on those hills overlooking the river, probably over there." He pointed across the Tugela. "To make matters worse, the Boers were using the latest German Mauser rifles. It was a bloody slaughter, and the British lost a thousand men as well as ten field guns. The battle was all over by noon."

Now and then we ran into rainstorms, but they only added color to the wild scenery. At one viewpoint, we stood in the rain to admire the Valley of a Thousand Hills, where the Umgeni River meets the Msunduzi (Duzi) River. It was exactly that: a huge valley filled with dozens of low, grey-green hills. Above us, leaning out over the valley, was a rocky outcrop, and there, perched on the edge, was a house. The lucky owner undoubtedly had one of the best views in Natal.

"That valley is a nature preserve," the father told us. "There are dozens of nature preserves, game preserves, and state and national parks throughout the Drakensbergs. And there are lots of resort hotels too."

From that point, the road dropped sharply to the coast of the Indian Ocean. There were more trees, and for most of the rest of the way the land was thickly populated, in sharp contrast to the emptiness of the high plains. We drove through villages and small towns all the way to Pietermaritsburg, the town founded by the Trekkers after the defeat of the Zulu chief, Dingane, successor to Shaka Zulu, in 1838. It turned out to be quite a large town with many churches, also quiet and conservative, with flowers and parks and little of the bustle of most large towns. I saw it as a sleepy hollow nestled in the cradle of the surrounding hills.

The rest of the way, as the children were getting sleepy and it was getting late, we drove on the Jan Smuts Highway. This was an excellent new road, and we quickly covered the fifty miles to Durban. On the outskirts of the city, the new highway turned back into a normal city road, edged with shops and houses, strung with phone lines and trolley wires, and crowded with cars and buses. My first impression of Durban was of a great rambling city with a very cosmopolitan population containing a high proportion of East Indians and many more black Africans than I had seen on the streets in Johannesburg. It looked like a prosperous city.

I said good bye to the family in the center of the city and found the YMCA. It was crowded, but I got a bed in a large dormitory with other young men of my age. Even after the sun went down, it was still warm. I looked forward to an evening of sightseeing, but a tropical storm roared in off the Indian Ocean, and it rained all night.

Day 6

Morning was clear and bright, with a stiff breeze off the ocean. I spent the day like a regular tourist, strolling and gawking and sitting. There was the long curve of beach backed by tall hotels and apartment blocks with tropical trees in their gardens, and there was the flower market with every color and type of flower, all dazzling and heavily perfumed. I strolled past fascinating shops and tourist traps and wandered the native market. At the docks, there were ships of every nation, and everywhere there were people. Sitting on a bench and licking an ice cream cone, I watched the crowds and remembered that, except for a few people in Johannesburg who were obviously tourists, I had not seen any East Indians in the Transvaal. But a large percentage of the population seemed to be Indian, and I saw Hindus, turbaned Sikhs, bearded Muslims, and everywhere were women in brilliant saris like butterflies in the sun. Many of the white South Africans were in cheerful holiday clothing, and the black South Africans were dressed more colorfully than in other parts of the Union, with the men in colored shirts instead of the usual dull khaki, and quite a few of the women in traditional dress with heavy skirts and pounds of copper, brass or silver bangles decorating both wrists and ankles. A few of the men wore huge, gleaming, white or brightly painted earrings, and some of the women carried pounds of Zulu beadwork around their necks.

There did not seem to be an Indian quarter in Durban, so I looked for the delicate, handmade, filigree gold and silver in the marketplace, but found only mass-produced jewelry. Many fantastic stories are told about the hidden wealth of the Indians. They are all supposed to have fortunes in gold hidden away and are waiting only for the opportunity to smuggle it off to India. According to one story, the easiest way is to hide it in the coffin along with a body being shipped back to India for cremation on the banks of the Ganges. In actual fact, while some South African Indians do get wealthy, many more do not.

The Indians in South Africa were imported from their homeland by the British to be laborers on the railways and the sugar plantations of Natal, since native African labor proved to be too much trouble. Many laborers remained in the sugar industry, but the majority quickly moved into the retail business and formed a middle class between the white and black Africans. Except in Transvaal and the Orange Free State, the Indians are generally accepted, although the whites are suspicious of their close-knit communities and the blacks complain that they overcharge. Nevertheless, they perform a useful function. Many of them are well educated, they work hard, and they usually stay out of politics...unless we exclude the most famous Indian of all time, Mahatma Gandhi, who was born in India but lived and worked in South Africa for over twenty years.

Day 7

I took a morning boat trip around the Durban harbor and was surprised to see a small fleet of whaling ships at anchor, their coal black sides streaked with blood-colored rust. Somehow, the icy seas and raging storms of the South Atlantic seemed a long way from this balmy city. At noon, I took a bus up into the suburbs that lay on the hills overlooking the city. This was where the expensive homes were, and the evening breeze was cool and fragrant. I envied the occupants their marvelous views. Some of the houses were exact copies of English suburban homes, and, here and there, tucked away behind high hedges, were expensive private schools, most of them sporting very British names.

No visit to Durban is complete without a visit to the snake farm, where every snake found in Africa is on view and many snakes are bred for medicinal purposes. It was quite fascinating to see the snakes that infest the regions through which I had traveled, where I had strolled through long grass and sat for hours on rocks and under trees. Yet I didn't recognize any of them. Outside the snake farm were the famous rickshaws, colorful two-wheeled vehicles pulled by men in full Zulu regalia, complete with pounds of bead work, leopard tailed kilts, whitewashed stockings, and huge headdresses of horns and porcupine quills. Everybody wanted a photo of them, but they cannily took off their headdress and turned their back until a tip had been paid. Then they posed for the cameras.

The actual ride was most uncomfortable. If he was in the mood, your "horse" might leap into the air, blow a whistle, and kick his feet wildly, tipping the chair so far back that it scraped a little safety wheel that prevented it going completely over. A sedate trot was little better, and the fare was always haggled over. I had gone barely a quarter of a mile when, with a straight face, the Zulu said, "One pound, sir." I laughed, and it dropped immediately to ten shillings. I snorted, and it dropped to five. I haggled him down to two shillings and a cigarette and felt quite proud of myself until an elderly gentleman who had been watching remarked, "The correct amount is usually one shilling."

In the crowded YMCA (which was for whites only), I sat next to a young man about my age who asked me where I was from and where I was going. When I told him, he immediately invited me to his home for the weekend. I accepted eagerly, and we arranged to meet next day at the station.

Chapter Fourteen: A Friendly Invitation

Day 8

After another day of sightseeing, I was at the station at five to meet my new friend, Bernard. We caught a local train, which soon left the city and took us into rolling country-side. As we went further, the hills grew greener and greener, but it was not until I saw a mill that I realized I was looking at sugar cane. I had seen it growing before, but only in flat, irrigated fields, and had never pictured it growing on hillsides. But there it was, miles of it, a rolling blanket of green and brown broken only by the Lilliputian lines of the cane railway.

It was dark when we arrived. Bernard's father drove us to their home, where I was warmly greeted by his mother and two teen-age sisters. After a light supper, I was shown to a bedroom and we all went to bed.

Day 9

In the morning, Bernard borrowed a car and drove around the district. There was no actual town, just a post office, a store, and a service station, where he signed for a tank of petrol. "The company owns everything," he explained as we picked up a few items at the store. "All we have to do is sign, and it's deducted from Dad's paycheck."

"Even your home?" I asked.

"Oh, sure. The company owns it, too. That comes with the job."

The houses were widely spaced along neat, tree-shaded avenues, and everything was spotless and peaceful. At the fruit and vegetable market, Indian and African women stood calling out the quality of their produce; their costumes competing with the colors of the wide variety of fruit.

"These are private vendors," Bernard said. "They just pay a small fee to the company. It saves the trouble of shipping in fresh fruit and veggies every few days."

Next we went over a hill to the sugar cane mill where his father was an engineer and gave us a quick tour. I had toured a sugar cane mill before, in the West Indies, and found it very similar though much more modern and efficient.

At the top of a hill, we stopped at a tall, stone, fire-watch tower and climbed the steps. In the clear air, every little detail stood out sharply all around us. The hills were brilliant green, and in the distance we could see the deep blue of the ocean. On one side, I saw a small mosque perched on a hill, its gilded dome shimmering in the sun, while on the other side the steeple of a church poked up from a cluster of trees. Bernard pointed to the north and said, "A few miles over there is the Tugela River and Shaka's grave. Beyond that is Zululand."

In one short sentence he had covered a hundred years of extraordinary history, including the rise of the bloodthirsty, military genius called Shaka, the arrival of the Boers from deep inland and the English from the sea, the clash of Zulu against Boer and Zulu against redcoats, and, finally, under the treacherous Dingane, the collapse of the Zulu empire. Like most English schoolboys, I had read numerous fascinating, and usually wildly inaccurate, accounts of the Zulus and the lands beyond the Tugela River. Now I stood where, only little more than a hundred years ago, the huge regiments had once marched, their spears red with blood. Around me now were only the gently whispering fields of sugar cane.

From there, we drove through the cane fields on a narrow trail that led to a heavy windbreak of trees and thick brush. We had to walk the last few yards and then, suddenly, we were out of the bush and standing on a long stretch of golden sand with the Indian Ocean tumbling great blue and white waves at our feet. Two or three large black rocks added contrast to the scene, and the blue sky overhead completed the picture. It was a perfect, unspoiled place with not a soul to be seen for miles in either direction. But we had only time for a glimpse before we had to dash back for lunch.

In the afternoon, we drove the girls twenty miles to a convent school, where one of them was to play hockey. A spacious old building set in well-tended grounds, except for the brilliant sun overhead, it could have been any expensive girl's school in England. The students wore the exact same uniforms of blue with the school badge, the deck chairs and tea cups and even the spectators were exact replicas of their English counterparts so many thousands of miles away. After the game, as I was introduced to various people, I found many of them using the term "back home" when they referred to England, although most South Africans use the term "overseas."

When I mentioned this to Bernard, he said, "Yes. I doubt if there is anybody in this crowd who has ever been to England." He looked around. "Everybody that I can see was born right here and their parents were born right here, too." He shrugged. "I suppose it's a form of loyalty. Or tradition. Or a way to irritate the Nationalists. Those Boers in Transvaal and Orange Free State get so irritated when English-speaking people in Durban or Cape Town act like newly arrived Englishmen." He smiled and added, "I bet there isn't anybody here who can speak any Afrikaans."

That evening, there was to be a movie in the company hall. This was the only manufactured entertainment in the small town, except for the radio. I dressed as formally as possible, considering my limited wardrobe, and had a very pleasant time. The movie was not important. There was a long break half way through, and this was the opportunity to meet socially and gossip and exchange news, plus have a few drinks. I was very nicely received by everybody, even more so when Bernard mentioned that I was in the RAF. He very tactfully did not mention that I was a mere clerk, not a glamorous fighter pilot.

Day 10

Early the next morning, Bernard drove me out to a small, white-washed chapel that he said was run by German Catholic missionaries. "I thought you might like to hear the music," he said. The congregation was mixed and unsegregated, and the service was in the traditional Latin. What surprised and pleased me was the way the ancient Gregorian plain chant had been translated into Zulu and put to Zulu music. It was magnificent. At first, the unusual tones and half notes startled me, but after just a few minutes, the beauty of it engrossed me completely. There was no organ, just the male and female voices harmonizing in that strange language and producing something lovely that would never be heard in the great stone cathedrals of Europe.

I spent the rest of the day picnicking on the beach with some of Bernard's family's neighbors and their children. It was very relaxing, although the surf was too high for the smallest children. About mid-afternoon, a lone fisherman appeared, working his way down the coast. This was Bernard's father, an avid surf fisherman who had been out since before dawn.

Back at the house, we all squeezed into the car and set off for Durban to visit friends who had a house in the hills overlooking the city. It was dark when we arrived, and the town and its port lay spread out before us in a mass of twinkling lights. It was a lively party of three generations, and our host knew every corner of South Africa and had an endless supply of hunting stories. Bernard's great grandparents had come out from England with the first settlers.

"The ships anchored off the coast, and they had to come ashore in boats," his mother said. "I remember my mother telling me how embarrassed she was when she had to be carried piggy-back to the beach by a semi-naked black. All she worried about was showing her ankles to the heathens."

The settlers had worked with an axe in one hand and a gun in the other to build a little town in the wilderness. At one time, the Zulu attacked so fiercely that they had to retreat to the boats and watch all their hard work go up in flames. "But they came right back and started all over again," our host said proudly. "When my farther chose this spot to build this very house, he did so because it was his favorite spot for hunting leopards and hyenas. As for snakes, the place was crawling with them."

This started the grandmother off, recounting hair raising tales about snakes. But, alas, it grew late and we had to be going. They dropped Bernard and me off at the YMCA. I was extremely sorry to say good bye to these kind people.

Chapter Fifteen: Durban to East London

Day 11

Waking early to get a good start, I decided that my best route was along the inland road from Pietermaritzburg south to East London. The road ran through the mountains, but there would be more traffic than on the winding coast road. I took a tram most of the way out of the city, but by ten o'clock I had still not got a lift and it was getting very hot. A sudden rainstorm forced me into a shelter, where I watched Indian buses racing up the road. Ancient, gaudily painted, and crammed to capacity, they tried desperately to pass each other, risking lives and vehicles for the doubtful honor of arriving a minute earlier, if they arrived at all.

Out into the rain I went again, thumbing, smiling, thumbing, and silently swearing, but it was midday before I got a lift. It was only a few miles, but it was better than walking. That ride left me on a fast stretch of road, and nobody going fast on a slippery wet surface wanted to slam on his brakes for a bedraggled hitchhiker. After an hour, a man in a small van did stop. He took me about twenty miles and assured me that "After lunch most drivers will be in a better mood. You'll see."

He was correct. I was picked up by an engineer on his way back to Johannesburg who dropped me off in Pietermaritzburg. The rain had stopped by then, and I walked along what I hoped was the main road, although the traffic was very light. It was much too light, in fact, and I began to wonder whether I was on the correct road. I had walked quite far out into the countryside, and it was beginning to get dark. Just as I was about to turn around and look for a hotel, a young couple gave me a ride to Richmond.

"I really don't think there is much traffic on this road," said the driver. His wife nodded her head in agreement and said, "You could wait hours for a car."

In the dark, Richmond looked very small and gloomy. Fortunately, I found the hotel and had dinner in an empty dining room, and then I went directly to bed. It had not been a good day.

Day 12

In the bright light of morning, Richmond did not look quite as bad as I had first thought. Although there were some nice houses, there was not much activity. And there was almost no traffic. The morning was cool, so I strolled quite far out into the country, where I was surprised to see how bare the hills were. The land was being cultivated, but there were almost no trees and hardly any signs of life. At rare intervals, a lonely farm wagon trundled along a track in the distance, or a solitary woman, her bundle balanced on her head, trudged to market along the empty road.

After a long wait, I got a lift for a few miles, then another long wait and another short lift, and so it went all day—a farmer or a delivery truck for a few miles followed by a long walk. By three o'clock, I had covered about thirty miles. What was only an hour's bicycle ride had taken me seven hours. At one point I found myself in the middle of nowhere. There was not a thing to be seen in any direction except the bare, rolling hills. The road lay brown and empty with no signs, no rusting advertisements, no scattered bits of trash. Nothing but the lonely phone poles to remind me that I was not on Mars.

I also saw more rain clouds were gathering. As I stood there, staring at the sky, a car suddenly appeared. It was going very fast. I thumbed as it approached, and the driver gave the wheel a sudden twist and aimed his car straight at me. By sheer luck, I was well clear of the road. As I jumped back, I was splattered with gravel, and then I just stood there, horrified and angry, as the car roared off over the horizon.

After that nerve-wracking experience, I gave up and started walking down the road. After a while, I came to a farm gate. It wasn't much, but it was a sign of civilization and it meant company. Almost immediately, in fact, I had more company than I cared for, as a large herd of cattle rounded a hill and headed straight for my gate. I quickly scrambled up on the gate and perched on the top, feeling rather foolish, but they were big, wild looking beasts and they flowed right to the gate, which swung wide under their pressure. It was then that I noticed that the herdsmen were half a dozen little boys in bare feet, the oldest not more than six years old. He was controlling the herd with a handful of small rocks which he flung at stragglers.

It was from my awkward vantage point on the top of the gate that I spotted a car coming down the road. The cattle did just the right thing and completely blocked the road. The car had to stop. This gave me the opportunity to ask the young couple in the car for a ride. They were ready to help me out, and when I mentioned the deadly attempt to kill me by the last car, they said that only a few days earlier, a pair of teenagers had hitched a lift from a clergyman and shot him in the head.

"Just bad luck that you should come by right after that nasty bit of work," said the driver. "It will be many a month before anybody around here gives a lift to a hitchhiker."

When his wife heard that I had been on the road all day, she found their left-over sandwiches and gave them to me. It was not until I had started eating that I realized just how hungry I was.

They took me as far as Umzimkulu, a small town on the Umzimkulu River that forms the border between Natal (now Kwazulu-Natal) and Pondoland (in the Eastern Cape Province). There were a post office, a hotel, a service station, and a few stores, but not much else. I was beginning to think that I had hit a dry spell, but there was still a little daylight left, so I stood hopefully in the bitter wind, stamping my feet in the rapidly increasing cold and wishing, for the hundredth time, that I had packed a sweater.

I was so busy trying to keep warm that I almost missed the car when it appeared, but it stopped at my wave. The driver, a young salesman for a clothing company, was immaculately dressed and very serious. Although he had been on the road for just a few years, he was making good money.

"I hope you won't mind a couple of stops and detours before we get to Kokstad," he said.

"With the luck I have had today," I replied, "I don't mind if you make a dozen detours."

As we drove through the wild and empty country, he talked

about business and the changes in the clothing industry. "There was a time when the Bantu bought just what was cheap," he said "Every penny counted. But not anymore. Now that they have money, they want the very best. They see it in a magazine, and that's what they want."

I looked at the empty landscape and asked, "Where do they get the money?"

He smiled at my ignorance and said, "The mines, of course! A couple of years in the mines, and they come home with their pockets full and they spend it. Boy, do they spend it!"

I gathered that the women do the farming while the men are away. The two-year limit on mining was strictly enforced; otherwise, the land would be completely depopulated.

"Of course," my host said, "a lot of employers turn a blind eye, and then the whole family moves to the cities and you get slums and squatters. Personally, I prefer them to come home and spend their money here. Much better for business."

In the dark, Kokstad looked quite attractive, with a long, broad main street and a wide variety of shops and houses. The town is about 4,000 feet above sea level, and the night had turned bitterly cold, so we shared a bottle of wine at the hotel to warm us up. Later, we played billiards in the bar and chatted with other salesmen. Before long, the subject switched to motorbike racing, and the hotel owner, a big hearty man, showed off his photos of the local racing team. Everybody except me appeared to be a racing enthusiast. Now the party began. When the bar closed, the party simply moved into the lounge, where it got decidedly wilder. It was about one in the morning when I left them, still merry, still thirsty, and crept thankfully into bed. But the night had only just begun. About two o'clock, I woke to find the whole gang in my room. They were removing my bedclothes, piece by piece, and dropping them out of the window, while singing an unintelligible song, mostly in Afrikaans. I gave a yell and dashed out in my bare feet to retrieve my bed clothes from the rain-soaked rose bushes and flung them back on my bed where my salesman friend slowly poured a jug of water all over them. Then, laughing like hyenas, they staggered off down the corridor.

It was hopeless to remake the bed. My bare feet were blue with cold, and I was shivering violently. But I had been given a double room, so I locked the door and slipped into the other bed, hoping that I had had the last laugh.

Day 13

I had no hangover the next morning. Although the rest of the drunks were already wolfing down their breakfasts, I noted that the young man who had given me the lift and led the revelers was absent. We all gloated that he obviously must have a huge hangover and went to his room to torment him. But his door was firmly locked, so we went outside and looked in through his window. We could see a grey face that turned even greyer on seeing us. When he said something impolite and groaned, we left him to his misery.

It was raining again. Between the showers, I could see that Kokstad lay on the outer slopes of the Drakensberg Mountains, which loomed bleak and grey. It was also freezing cold. Hoping that a good walk would warm me up, I walked out of town to the shelter of some trees. A bit later, I stopped a salesman, who greeted me with the comment, "Glad I saw you. I just might need somebody to push." He was quite serious and in a little while I found out why.

The road climbed steeply to a mountain pass called Brooks Nek. "We usually call it Broken Neck," the salesman said, not smiling.

The highways department had chosen that time to completely rebuild the road, so there were machines everywhere and the road's surface had been reduced to about nine inches of soupy mud. The only way to avoid getting stuck was to race through at top speed, which we did for a mile or two until we rounded a bend and were abruptly stopped by a line of stationary vehicles winding up the mountain.

After a while, a workman made his way through the mud toward us. "There's an Indian bus stuck at the summit," he said. "It's been there all night, and the dozer we sent to pull it down has got stuck, too. Best thing to do," he advised, "is go back to Kokstad." Then he slithered on to the next car.

A group of drivers gathered to discuss the situation, and everybody decided to sit and wait a while longer. One driver, a Catholic priest in a little French car, could not wait. He said something unholy about the roads department, jumped into his car, and slipped and skidded his way past all the other cars to the top. There he stopped, and with some extraordinary maneuvers managed to turn his car and start back down.

My host watched this. "If he can't get through," he said, "how did the bulldozer get through?" He looked around, "There must be another way."

He pulled out of line and went back down the hill until we came to where they were building the new road. It was very raw, little more than a line of white surveyor's sticks.

"God! That looks rough!" he exclaimed, "but it's got to go somewhere."

Bouncing like a dinghy in rough seas, we set off across open country. As we topped a rise, we could see all the other cars following us like lemmings heading for the edge of the cliff, the priest well in the lead. Weaving in and out among the rocks, we made good time until we came to a great boulder that was being drilled for blasting. Here the way was blocked by heaps of jagged rubble. One of the workmen pointed up a grassy slope and suggested we go around. Not bothering to investigate further, my friend put the car in low gear and up we went, our wheels spinning until they reached rock, at which point we shot over the crest...

...and before us lay one of the most hair raising sights I have ever seen—a great, mist-filled, mountain valley with steeply sloping sides that dropped nearly a thousand feet. The grass we were on sloped steeply to the edge of a precipice that was barely twenty feet away. My friend hit the brakes immediately, but they were useless. We slid towards the bottomless drop. Suddenly, at just the right moment, he hit the gas again and swung the wheel hard. The tires spun, then gripped, and, in a shower of mud and grass, we were able to drive along the edge of the precipice, around some rocks, and back onto the road.

"That was rather tricky," said my host. "I just hope it's in better condition when I come back."

Looking back up the hill, I could see the other cars shooting over the ridge and swinging frantically away from the edge of the cliff. I hoped they were all good drivers. A few minutes later, the priest splashed by us in his little car. The rain soon turned to sleet, and we could barely see the road winding down the valley in front of us and hugging the cliff face above us.

"See that bit of road just there?" my host said at one point. "I got stuck in the snow there a couple of years ago. Three or four of us all got stuck together. One was a big delivery van with boxes in it, so we all squeezed into it and somebody lit a little fire with bits of wood. The snow was so bad, it covered all the cars to the roofs, Boy! That was scary!" He shivered at the recollection. "By the time the snow plows found us next day, we had burned almost everything in that van that would burn."

If I had not learned it already, this story was a clear sign that South Africa is not all sunshine and blue skies.

After we left the pass we entered a native reserve. "This is the Transkei," said my host. "These are protected tribal lands. You and I can't buy any land here, or even lease it." He explained further. "There's a handful of Indian stores here, but the only non-tribal people you'll see will be in the towns, and there are not many towns."

As I had worked my way slowly south, I had seen very few of the typical, round native houses, but from Kokstad almost to East London, the countryside was liberally sprinkled with villages. Sometimes the huts were arranged in a perfect circle, others were in neat straight lines, and there were rarely more than a dozen in any village. Unlike the rather crudely built huts of the Rhodesian natives, these were a pleasure to see. The thatch was trimmed as neatly as in an English cottage, the mud walls were decorated with simple tribal patterns, usually done in white around the door, and many of the huts also had bands of white around the eaves and the base of the walls. Some were fenced or had a cattle pen of twisted sticks, but most just sat on the bare hillside, their simplicity and neatness matching the stark surroundings.

When I commented on these huts, my host agreed that they were picturesque. "Yes," he said, "it's pretty all right. Pretty horrible. Take a look at the land."

I looked again. Erosion is one of the great problems of Africa. In rural districts, it ranks with the price of fertilizer as a primary topic of conversation, and billboards along the roads remind all and sundry to stop erosion. Even suburban housewives know enough to prevent the slightest gully from forming in a flower bed. The African continent is old and the soil is thin. Once it is washed into the sea, it can never be replaced. Gangs of laborers are constantly at work, building little soil-catching dikes of rock in the roadside ditches and in stream beds. In this land, the farmer dams a stream not just to catch water, but also to prevent erosion.

In the reservations, the erosion was terrible. Everywhere I looked, there were great, jagged, open sores on the face of the hills and gullies, which are called *dongas*, as deep and as wide as a house, exposing the stained yellow bedrock. There were narrow slits as deep as a man is tall that crumbled as we watched, and in many places, so much of the bedrock was exposed that the land was dead.

When I asked what had caused this terrible thing, my host snorted in anger. "Look at the stupid bastards," he said, pointing at fields plowed vertically up steep slopes and at tracks made by generations of people going straight up the slope to a village. Here and there women dragged bundles on sleds straight up the hills through the soft, wet earth, and there were goats everywhere. "The women take even the smallest twigs for firewood," he said, "and what's too small to burn, the damn goats will eat. This is one battle Mother Nature can't win." He sighed and after a while continued. "The government sends in teams of experts who show these people how to prevent erosion. But do they listen? My father says that when he was a boy, there were trees on these hills. Look at them now! It's their land, and that's the way they've always lived, and they're not going to change just because the white man tells them to."

In the next fifty miles, we passed through one small town, then we reached Mount Frere, another town, where my host stopped. It was actually just a village, so I walked to the last building and sat on the veranda, where I could look down the road. While I was waiting, a young African man of about eighteen came across the fields. He was well over six feet tall and wore a red ochre-dyed blanket draped over one shoulder, Roman style, plus copper anklets. His face was powdered with red ochre, with extra highlights on the cheeks and forehead, and the whole effect was very striking. He carried a long spear handle with no blade and was very handsome. He knew it, too. He walked slowly along with just the right smile on his face. Around him flocked a bevy of giggling females, all young girls, who hung onto his every word and went into fits of laughter whenever he smiled at one of them. Whether he was a son of a chief or just the village glamour boy, he was having a wonderful time.

As the group passed, heading for the Indian store, I noticed that the girls all had bare feet but carried pounds of copper bracelets on each ankle. I remembered what somebody had told me. "A lot of that copper comes from up a phone pole. If the line suddenly goes dead it probably means some young buck is busy collecting a few yards of copper to impress his girl friend."

The owner of the store where I was taking shelter came out and locked the door. Then he turned to me. "You need a lift? I'm going south, but not very far."

I eagerly said that, yes, I needed a lift, and we got into his car.

"The Bantu around here are Griquas and Pondos," he told me. The Pondos were an important tribe before the Zulus invaded in the 1820s. "When you get south of the Umtata River," he said, "you'll be in Tembu country. Then south of the Kei River, it's Xhosa territory. Lots of other tribes, too, but everybody just calls it the Transkei." He seemed to be very knowledgeable about the various tribes and I said so. "Oh, yes," he agreed. "Very interesting people. This is the heaviest concentration of Bantu in all the Union. Actually, it's horribly overpopulated." When I mentioned that I had seen a lot of women but not many men, he explained, "That's because they're all off earning good money in the mines or working in factories. They can be away for two or three years, then they come back just long enough to spend all their money, then they're off again."

The storekeeper took me as far as Qumbu, another small village twenty miles further on. It was still cold, but the sun had begun to appear intermittently, creating a bright mist. I walked to the last building, an Indian store, where I had lunch and waited on the veranda for my next ride.

Now and then along the way, I had seen Africans on horseback, but we had always passed too quickly for me to see them clearly. Now, out of the mist appeared a couple of riders who rode up and stopped directly in front of the store. The horses were short and wild looking, with sturdy legs, long manes, and shaggy coats. They had bridles, but no saddles. The man was wearing store clothes and a Stetson cowboy hat, but the woman wore traditional costume with a bright blanket draped over her shoulders and a heavy skirt, with so many pounds of copper coils on her ankles that I was sure she had trouble walking. There was almost as much weight around her neck, in the form of beads and other jewelry, much of it bright plastic. Her hair had been painstakingly braided into dozens of little tassels, and on her head she wore a curious, flat, black cape that resembled a cobra's hood. Like the born horsewoman she probably was, she sat on a sheepskin for a saddle, looking more like a Balkan peasant than an African native, ignoring me and the occasional spattering of rain. When her husband came out of the store, they were off without a sound, back into the misty hills of Basutoland.

About half an hour later, a car drew up at the store and an elderly salesman climbed out. He had a black driver who also carried his sample cases. While he was inside, his driver came out again, and I told him that I was looking for a lift. When the salesman came out, the driver spoke to him and I saw him appraising me out of the corner of his eye. He must have been satisfied because he called out, "I'm heading towards Umtata. Would you care for a lift?" (I still can't think why I didn't just ask him for a lift myself.)

This salesman was of the old school, politely formal, immaculately dressed, and careful to avoid talking about politics or religion. When I had explained who I was, he asked, "Have you learned any Afrikaans yet?" When I rattled off the few words that I had learned, he said, "In the selling business, it helps if you can speak the language of your customers, so I learned Afrikaans many years ago. I have picked up quite a few useful phrases in half a dozen native languages. Some of them are damn difficult for a white man to pronounce." Here he smiled and added, "Oh, and I have picked up quite a bit of Hindi, too. Very useful when talking to Indian storekeepers."

As we chatted, I learned that my host seemed to know almost every hotel in the Union, but his great pleasure was tracking down good restaurants. For about forty miles, he talked about excellent meals he had eaten over the years. When we came out from under the cloud bank, he sat back, quietly enjoying the sunshine. When we reached Umtata in its wide valley, he dropped me at a hotel that was popular with traveling salesmen and wished me good luck.

Umtata, capital of the Transkei region, was a big town and quite attractive, but there was still an hour or two of daylight left, so I thought I would try my luck once more. I had no luck, however, and, as the sun set behind the mountains, I returned to the hotel, which was full of salesman. After supper, I drifted around, letting it be known that I was looking for a lift south, but nobody seemed to be interested.

Day 14

It turned bitterly cold again during the night, and nobody bothered to turn on the central heating in the hotel, so I filled up on a hearty breakfast and was on the road quite early. But all the traffic seemed to be going the other way. A cold wind was blowing down from the mountains, so I took shelter from it in front of a high garden hedge. I was standing there and shivering when a young doctor offered me a lift to a hospital a few miles up the road. He had been accepted as part of the crew on a *Kon-Tiki*-style raft trip from the east coast of Africa to Australia and was eager to talk to somebody about it. He was so enthusiastic that I was disappointed to read some weeks later that the project had been abandoned.

The road outside the hospital was high, wide, and lonely, with only one or two trees that offered no protection from the cold wind. Within minutes, I was shivering again and wondered what to do. If I walked to stay warm, I would be far from shelter when the inevitable rain came, but if I took shelter in the hospital lobby, I would miss what little traffic there was. I decided that the worst thing I could do was get soaked, so I walked to where some engineers had been laying a cable and met a watchman with a small fire.

Leaving my bag at the side of the road, I jumped across the open ditch and squeezed into the little canvas watchman's hut, where I could keep an eye on the road. The watchman was a cheerful old black man with a shock of snow-white hair. He put more wood on the fire for my benefit and accepted a cigarette, and we discussed the weather until a car appeared on the horizon and I leaped back across the ditch. The car roared by, and I returned to the hut and for over an hour I carried on with this routine until I felt like a cross country racer in training. The old man sympathized with me. We spent another hour warming ourselves while I scraped the mud off my shoes, and the wind rattled the canvas.

Finally, I could stand it no longer. After thanking the watchman for his company, I made my way back to town. At a restaurant, over a cup of hot coffee, I worked out new tactics. Standing on the open road had proved useless, so now I made my way along from gas station to gas station, looking at license plates and talking to drivers who looked as if they were heading south. At the biggest and busiest service station, I hung around for a while until I heard a voice asking, "Would you like a cup of tea?"

The manageress of the station had been watching me. She was curious about a young white man hitchhiking in Africa. "So," she said, "where are you from and where are you headed?" She passed me a mug filled with hot tea and slid a sugar bowl and a milk jug across her desk.

When I explained what I was doing and mentioned that I was in the RAF in Rhodesia, her eyes lit up. "Oh, my favorite uncle was in the RAF! He had to go to England to join up and he never came back." She sniffed and added, "He married an English girl."

And then she called to one of the black mechanics and ordered him to find out the destination of every car going south. "We'll get you a lift," she assured me. "Never fear. They're doing a lot of road repairs, and this horrible weather doesn't help. Umtata is normally much busier than this. I'm so sorry you couldn't see it in the summer. Have some more tea."

We sat for about an hour discussing the places I had been, and she promised me that the weather would be much better around Cape Town.

"I'm beginning to think this storm has been following me all the way from Durban," I told her, "and now I'm beginning to worry about running out of time. Nearly half my leave is up. I just hope I'll reach Cape Town before I have to head back to camp."

Just then the attendant came in and announced that his customer was going to East London, 150 miles south.

Both the manageress and I pounced on the startled driver, who put up quite a resistance at first. It transpired, however, that he was not worried about me as a stranger; what he was worried about was that I would not be comfortable with all the luggage he had squashed into the car. I merely smiled and told him that I had hitched lifts on Italian bullock carts, French motorbikes, and had even shared a trailer with a prize German heifer, not to mention cars full of children, so a little luggage would not bother me at all. In a few minutes, we were off and out into the rain-swept countryside again.

My new host, born and raised in the area, did not apologize for the terrible weather. "I know it must look pretty miserable to you," he said. "The rain and mist make these hills look rather depressing. But we need the rain. In the spring, these hills will all be green and the sky will be an unbelievable blue and hundreds of wild flowers will cover the ground. Tourists come from all over just to see the flowers. In the summer, thousands of vacationers come through here, all heading for their summer cottages on the coast." He shook his head, "Most people don't realize how many tiny little harbors there are all up and down the coast. Some of them are almost impossible to get to."

I sat back and tried to imagine the picture his enthusiastic words painted, but it was not easy.

After an hour or two, we turned off on a side road and drove up to a house where we were to pick up a lady. Her son, a young man about my age, was an invalid confined to his bed, but this had not shut him off from the world. He was an amateur radio enthusiast, and his bedroom was a maze of radio equipment. I squeezed in through the tangle and introduced myself. When I mentioned my camp in Rhodesia, he became quite excited.

"Camp Heany! The RAF base near Bulawayo. I have three contacts there." And he rattled off some names that I vaguely recognized.

"They're radio mechanics," I said. "The ground crew billets are closer to the airfield, and I'm afraid we never really meet. I'm just a clerk in the squadron offices."

This did not dampen his enthusiasm, and we discussed military life while his mother packed. He showed me a filing cabinet filled with the names and the call numbers of thousands of people all over the world that he had conversed with over the years.

"I can't go out and see the world the way you're doing," he said, "so I have brought the world into my bedroom." He laughed and looked out the window. "Considering the weather, I think my method has advantages."

His mother was soon packed, and I squeezed into the back seat with her luggage. The miles flew by. In one small town, where we stopped for tea, the restaurant walls were covered with sketches and paintings of native costumes and African scenes, all for sale at quite reasonable prices. Here in the Transkei, the tribes have probably the most colorful costumes and most artistically decorated houses in the whole of southern Africa, but thanks to the foul weather, I had seen very little of the beauty. I would love to have bought some of the drawings and paintings, but I had no way of carrying them. Later, I saw similar art work offered at fabulous prices in London and other cities.

It seemed to be downhill all the way to East London, so we made good time. There were more farms, then, after we crossed the big bridge over the River Kei, the rocky valleys vanished and trees appeared, among them a tree called the Kaffir boom, a mass of scarlet blossoms that could be seen for miles. It was a wonderful sight. Like so many African trees, the blooms appear before the leaves and shout their colorful message to the world.

At East London, I said good bye on the rain-lashed ocean front and dashed for the nearest hotel, where after a hearty dinner in a nearly empty dining room, I stood and watched through thick glass windows as giant waves of the Indian Ocean pounded against the sea wall. A raging storm, I told myself, looks best from inside a large, modern hotel where silent waiters bring coffee in china cups, and central heating banishes all memory of the biting wind.

Chapter Sixteen: Visiting My Uncle and Aunt

Day 15

Next morning I woke to brilliant sunshine. The clouds were gone, the sky was blue, and the rain was just a memory. It was a bracing day. After a hearty breakfast, I set off to tour the city and find my uncle, Charles Couchman, whom I had phoned the previous night to let him know that I had arrived. He had given me his office address. East London was a large town with a friendly, residential atmosphere, and I suspected that during the tourist season, it would be full of tourists and vacationers. In the winter, however, it was quiet and relaxed, perfect for casual touring.

I had never asked my uncle what his job was. I knew that he was some kind of executive in a large American or British company, but I didn't know at what level. I was rather surprised therefore when the receptionist at the big modern office building asked me if I had an appointment. I told her that I did, and she spoke into an intercom. A few minutes later, I was handed over to a young lady who escorted me to a plush suite of offices, where I was given a cold eye by yet another secretary. She obviously did not much like what she saw. When she asked my name and business, I told her that the gentleman that I sought was my uncle. That brought an immediate change in her attitude. She pushed buttons on her intercom and announced me, and when a cheerful voice told her to send me right in, she led me through an office of smartly dressed clerks, all of whom stared at my casual hitchhiking clothes and battered bag. Finally, she ushered me into a giant office where, across acres of carpet and yards of polished desk, sat my uncle. Only then did it dawn on me that my cheerful, friendly, and completely unassuming uncle was one of the most important businessmen in South Africa.

He stopped work immediately. "John! I'm so glad you got here. I'll just ask them to bring my car around and we'll go out to the house right now. Nothing important is going to happen on a Friday." He spoke into the intercom, then added, "Your aunt will be so pleased to see you."

Within a few minutes, we pulled in to a beautiful converted farmhouse set in a large expanse of garden about eight miles out of town. My Aunt Rhoda was preparing lunch. I was welcomed as if I were an old family friend instead of a relative from the other side of the globe, and after I had settled into the guest house, we lunched and talked of South Africa and England and things in general.

"I saw the look on your face when you came into my office." Uncle Charles said with a smile. "Didn't know I was a big wheel, did you?" Then he explained. "We got married during the Great Depression. I was a salesman, and things were pretty tough. One day I was offered a selling job in South Africa. I grabbed it right away. Neither of us knew a thing about the country, and Rhoda thought I'd be selling baby powder to Zulus with spears. Well, to cut a long story short, we both fell in love with the country, and neither of us has ever been back to England. Plenty of nice places here to take our holidays." Modestly, he didn't mention the hard work and long hours that had got him to where he was.

As we talked, I noticed that neither of them ever used the phrase "back home." Their pride in their adopted country was obvious.

"This country is not only beautiful," said Uncle Charles. "It is a modern, industrialized country with a lot to offer the world, and I don't mean just gold and diamonds."

When we discussed politics, he could see both sides. "The Afrikaners have a long history and their own unique culture, but— let's face it—English is an international language. It's the language of trade and commerce. The harder they struggle to retain their way of life, the more enemies they make. They hear everybody speaking English and nobody is learning Afrikaans, so they have developed a dangerous, defensive attitude." He sighed and added, "That's not good for the future. We can't keep things the way they were a hundred years ago. Everything changes. We just have to adapt."

My uncle was experimenting with a windmill operated generator and had a small garage filled with car batteries. It was a neat and apparently functional system. "You know that South Africa has no oil wells and very little hydro power," he explained. "Just coal. One day we will have to produce electricity from wind power. And we have plenty of that!" He laughed, "Maybe one day wind-generated electricity will be useful."

We spent a quiet afternoon sitting on their patio watching the weaver birds, which had covered a huge tree with their perfectly woven hanging nests. It was the male birds that did all the work. The females were off somewhere else. "Probably shopping." my uncle suggested. The poor male bird would slave from dawn to dusk to create a masterpiece, then the female would take a quick look, find instant fault, and refuse to accept it. The unhappy male would then tear it down and start all over again. "It often takes two or three nests before her ladyship is satisfied," said Aunt Rhoda.

Day 16

It was a grandchild's birthday, so after breakfast we drove to my cousin's house to celebrate the event. There was a good crowd there, and I blended quite well into the mixture of family and friends. Since it was a glorious spring day, we lunched casually on the patio. My cousin owned a two-story house. Upon seeing it, I realized that this was the first two story-house I had been in since I'd left England. It seemed strange to climb stairs in a private house. After lunch, as we drove back home for a "siesta," I realized that this, too, was something I had adjusted to. I recalled what I'd heard somebody in Rhodesia say. "In these parts, without a proper siesta, a woman loses her looks and a man loses his mind."

In the cool of the late afternoon, we all three admired the view across the valley to the green slopes of a low range of hills where, my uncle assured me, there were deer that came out at night and raided his garden, then we strolled around the huge garden admiring the turkeys and the geese and the vegetables and the various fruit trees. I asked if they did their own gardening.

"Oh, we used to," said my aunt, "But it has become just too much for us. There is a very good gardener who comes in every few days. He sometimes brings his son. Very reliable. We've had him for years."

I had not seen any black servants around the house. In fact I had seen very few black people anywhere in the neighborhood. "So where do the blacks live?" I asked.

"They have their own part of town," my uncle answered. "We have a maid who comes in during the week. She takes the bus, and the gardener usually rides his bike."

My aunt added, "I suppose we should have a live-in girl and a full-time gardener, but the rules and regulations about employing blacks are such a nuisance that most people I know just hire daily help and pay them in cash every week."

Dinner that night was home-grown turkey and South African champagne. The other guests were my cousin and his wife, who had found a baby-sitter. After weeks of making small talk with complete strangers, interspersed with long periods of talking to myself, it was delightful and refreshing to be talking with relatives. The conversation switched rapidly from one topic to another. When I happened to mention television, there was mild interest but no real enthusiasm and I learned that there were no television stations in the Union. (Remember, this was 1952.) The government would not allow them "just yet," and there was no serious demand, anyway. Everybody was quite happy with radio and newspapers, and there was always the cinema.

Day 17

I spent most of my second morning with my aunt and uncle in a deck chair on the lawn with a pair of binoculars, watching the weaver birds again. Their nests, which were pear shaped with the hole at the bottom, were suspended a foot below the branch. That made it impossible for snakes to reach them. The males were busy diving to the ground in search of straw or dry grass, then dashing back to the nest, where they wove and sewed each strand rapidly in and out, using just their beaks and one claw, while holding on to the nest with the other claw. They were building roomy nests, and the whole tree was decorated with them, making it look like a strange Christmas tree. When a male was finished, he would flutter about in a fit of anxiety while his mate examined his work, hopping in and out and giving it a careful inspection. Quite often, the nest was not up to standard, and twice I saw an unfortunate male snip through the strand holding the nest and watch sadly as it crashed to the ground, where it was immediately torn to shreds by other males seeking building material.

After lunch, my relatives and I went for a drive around town. "I had a monstrous big American car up to last week," said my uncle, "but the damn thing was such a problem to park that I traded it in for this thing." He sighed dramatically, "She was a really lovely car. Lots of chrome and push-buttons."

East London is a major city and sea port, but in the summer it is also a holiday town catering to the family trade. It was quiet that Sunday, and there was little to see, so we drove out of town through the green hills and well-farmed countryside, where cattle grazed in the stubble and plows had already opened the damp soil. Along the coast, we drove past dozens of tiny cabins among the sand dunes. These were holiday retreats, all locked up for winter. Some were miniature houses, but most were rough, comfortable looking, and gaily painted. Despite the brilliant sunshine, it was far too cold to consider swimming, so we walked a bit on the beach where the great white breakers rolled up the yellow sand and nibbled at the dunes, warning the world that it was not time for the small boats and rubber rafts of summer. Nearer town, we passed the docks where ships of all nations rode quietly in the channel, surrounded by cranes and dark, quiet warehouses. I told my aunt and uncle about the convoy of cars and trucks from Port Elizabeth to Nyasaland that I had joined in the depths of Mozambique.

That evening, we checked the calendar and the map. It was time for me to move on as quickly as possible. Leaving this pleasant home was not an easy decision, as my relatives all insisted that I stay at least a week and have a real holiday, but Cape Town looked so close on the map, and there was a lot more that I wished to see before my leave was up. Although nobody mentioned it, we knew that there was very little likelihood that we would ever meet again.

Chapter Seventeen: East London to Humansdorp

Day 18

Morning was clear, fresh and warm. After many long farewells, I walked away from my relatives' house and waited for my first lift. It came quickly. The driver was an old farmer with his daughter. They were going to Grahamstown. When I got into the car, they were speaking Afrikaans, but out of politeness to me they switched to English, and we discussed farming in that region. Except for the maize, the crops and the livestock appeared to be similar to those in southern England, and the old farmer had exactly the same complaints about the lack of reliable skilled farm workers, the high price of fertilizer, and the low prices paid for his harvest that one would hear in England.

As we drove, we could see a great column of smoke on the horizon. This was a grass fire, and as we came closer, we could see the red and yellow flames racing through the winter-dry grass faster than a man could run. The fire was heading for the road, and the old farmer decided to out-race it.

"Roll up the windows!" he shouted. "We don't have time to sit around and wait for it to go away." And he put his foot down hard.

Burning grass does not seem dangerous, but it was already less than fifteen feet from the edge of the road, and we could feel the extraordinary blast of heat. Despite the closed windows, we began coughing in the heavy smoke. We were through in seconds and when we could breathe again, my host said, "I never burn off my fields. It leads to erosion. Anyway, it's against the law now. But there are some who still swear by it." He shrugged his shoulders. "They say it brings on the new grass, but I'm not convinced."

We were still discussing the value of burning off fields when we reached King Williams's Town, which looked rather like an old English market town with a large square in the center.

The daughter turned to me and said, "This is a very old city. It was founded long before the Great Trek. It was what you would call a 'frontier town,' and there were many wars with the native tribes. This whole region between the Fish River and the Kei River was once the frontier for settlers coming up from the Cape and the Bantu tribes coming down from the north." She smiled and looked around. "It's hard to imagine what it was like then, it is so peaceful now."

For years, the white settlers had plowed their fields with a loaded gun handy while the tribes of Kaffirland, the Xhosas, the Tembu, the Pondo, and others struggled to push them back. It was a war of cattle raids and punitive expeditions, interspersed with years of relative peace. Much of the trouble was caused by Chaka and his Zulu regiments in Natal. As the Zulu empire expanded, the neighboring tribes were forced off their lands. Trapped between the Drakensberg Mountains and the sea, the displaced tribes were forced onto the lands of their neighbors, and these waves of migration eventually crashed against the guns and block houses of the white settlers in the Cape. The pressure was not released until the Great Trek, when the Boers migrated into the interior of the continent, west of the mountains, and entered Natal from the west.

But this was just as British settlers were entering from the sea. The Zulus were forced to concentrate their forces at home to face this newer, more deadly enemy.

After a cup of coffee, we set off again for Grahamstown and rode across lovely open country, green and well farmed. The land rolled gently and offered wide views to distant hills with now and then a more rugged tree-clad hill. We crossed numerous rivers and somewhere crossed the Fish River, though it was not marked and nobody mentioned it. As we traveled, the daughter pointed out things of interest and the father commented on the crops and the farming. There were very few native huts, and I saw no full-size villages, just old but efficient looking farms spaced widely across the rolling countryside. We arrived in Grahamstown about midday, and I said goodbye to the farmer and his daughter.

Grahamstown turned out to be an extremely charming old town nestled in the shade of some hills. There were plenty of cool shade trees, and in the center of town was a very English-looking cathedral with a spire that must have been over a hundred feet tall. I strolled around for a while. It was so quiet and peaceful, it could have been Sunday. It was impossible to believe that in the early 19th century, this fledgling town had fought for its existence against 10,000 besieging tribesmen.

When I had looked around Grahamstown I strolled to the foot of a hill, where there was a grove of tall trees to shield me from the sun and wind. I sat under a tree, listening to the birds and watching some men chopping firewood. It was very peaceful, but, unfortunately, there was very little traffic and in the first hour only two cars passed. The hours ticked away and the men finished chopping firewood and took away their loot in wheelbarrows, and I was beginning to think that my luck had run out, when suddenly, a shiny new car purred up the road toward me. It was sleek and powerful, but was going quite slowly.

The strange car stopped for me, and I got in and explained who I was and what I was doing.

"Well, I'm going to Port Elizabeth," the driver, another salesman, said. "That should help you on your way. But this is a brand new car and I'm 'running in' the motor. I won't be going very fast for a couple of hundred miles."

All the windows of this car were tinted green, which made me feel like I was riding in a fish bowl, but I did not comment. My host had no stops to make before Port Elizabeth. As they say, *Beggars can't be choosers*, so I was quite satisfied to crawl along at a little more than forty miles an hour. The scenery was beautiful, with the first green touches of spring and from the rolling hills we could sometimes catch a glimpse of the Indian Ocean, blue and sparkling in the distance.

Now and then I also caught a glimpse of a rail line winding through the hills. I had seen tracks before, but these looked different somehow. "Is that a narrow gauge rail line?" I asked.

"Oh, yes," said my host. "There's a network of narrow gauge lines along this coast. Some are really narrow, and many of them are quite old. Not many of them are connected to the main line, but they're very useful and they don't cost much to run. There are lots of isolated places along the coast that depend on those little tracks." After a while, he continued, "With the government building roads everywhere, I suppose one day those narrow gauge lines will be obsolete and disappear. Pity, really, I've always liked them."

One of the drawbacks of being a foreigner, I have learned in my life, is that you have to be ready to take the blame for everything foolish that your government happens to have done, whether you voted for it or not. My new host was an English-speaking nationalist who could trace his ancestry back to Scottish settlers. The political turmoil in southern Africa had convinced him that the nationalists had the right approach. As the long miles crept past, he took me to task for every blunder that the British government had made in Africa over the past two decades. He was a well-educated and extremely well-read man and was probably a good example of the many proud South Africans who had been forced into an extreme position by the ceaseless, loud, and terribly uninformed condemnations heaped on them by overseas critics.

"It always seems to me that those politicians who have never been here are inevitably the most critical," he said. "And as for the writers…well, we have a saying about them. 'To Africa, Africa. Have a quick look. Home again, home again. Write a big book.'" He turned to face me. "You wouldn't believe some of the absolute rubbish that I've read."

I must have been a good listener, because my host talked continuously with a quiet, suppressed anger that I knew was not aimed at me but, rather, at all the overseas critics of his country.

"Most foreigners must think that our blacks are nothing but slaves," he said at one point. "Starving on miserable wages, dressed in rags, living in squalor. You've traveled a lot now. Does it look like that to you?"

I had to admit that I had not seen anything like squalor.

And then...he was just explaining in great detail that the blacks were never subject to physical abuse but were treated just like any other human being, when we rounded a corner and came across a chain gang.

It was the first time in my life that I had seen men chained together. They were convicts, about a dozen black men, and they were cleaning out a roadside ditch that was badly overgrown. They wore plain khaki prison clothes with sturdy shoes. They were not being overworked; in fact, most of them were leaning on their shovels and could easily have been mistaken for casual laborers, except for the long steel chain that ran from ankle to ankle, and the guard, who sat half asleep on the bank, his rifle lying in the grass next to him.

The sight stopped my host in mid-sentence. "Well. They're doing something useful and it's better than sitting in a cell all day, I suppose."

I thought this was a rather lame explanation, but I said nothing.

As we rounded Algoa Bay, I saw the blue and white water flashing in the sun. The quiet, rural scenery changed dramatically. Towns sprang up, the railway appeared, there were factories and freight yards and all the paraphernalia of a modern industrial city, including a thin layer of smog. There was also much more traffic on the road, so my host decided that he could increase his speed for the last few miles. Soon we were in Port Elizabeth. We stopped at a bus stop, and he told me which bus to catch to reach the city center, then with a polite good bye he was off. It had been an interesting ride, and I had learned a lot.

There were some fine public buildings and an air of prosperity in Port Elizabeth. I found a clean but inexpensive hotel, and after supper I strolled along the crowded streets where the bars and the theaters were full and many of the shops were still open. I walked along the sea front and up the steep, winding streets of the old town that dated from the time when there was no other seaport between Algoa Bay and Delagoa Bay (now Maputo Bay) in Mozambique. Port Elizabeth was obviously a major city, but it was a harsh contrast with the idyllic rolling countryside that I had been traveling through, and I saw no reason to stay more than one night.

I went to bed convinced that such a city would produce plenty of traffic bound for Cape Town.

Day 19

After an early breakfast, I took a bus out to the edge of the city, where I saw two or three miles of residential area with dozens of houses and bungalows, all freshly painted and very new. When the bus came to the end of the line, I found myself once again in the open countryside.

There was indeed a good flow of traffic, so I saw no reason to walk any further. As car after car sped by, however, my high hopes began to fade. I thumbed cars, vans, and trucks without raising even a smile until, two hours later, a car finally stopped. There were two men in the car, and it was only when they began speaking to me after I was in the car that I realized that it was an unmarked police car. What, I wondered, was the official view of hitchhiking? I need not have worried.

Turning to his companion, the driver said, "Bet you a beer," and the other man said, "I'll take your bet." Then he turned to me. "The sergeant says you're in the RAF and you're stationed in Rhodesia."

I must have looked as surprised as I felt, because he started laughing. "You're absolutely correct," I said. "How did you guess?"

"He's pretty clever, for a sergeant."

There was a grunt from the driver. "That's why I'm a sergeant, and you're not."

For about ten miles, the two policemen tried to explain how my haircut, suntan, clothes, and general appearance had all been clues, but I still found it uncanny. I was still quite puzzled when they stopped at a crossroads, where they assured me the traffic was good. They let me out in the shade of some trees, and then, with a cheerful wave, vanished in a cloud of dust down a side road.

The shade was welcome, as the sun was now huge and glaring in a white hot sky. But there was very little traffic. Two or three cars raced by, but there was no sense in walking away from my shade trees. Fortunately, I had found an old *Reader's Digest* somewhere and pulled it out of the little shapeless canvas bag I had been carrying everywhere. Even reading, however, the time still dragged on.

I was half asleep when a car stopped right in front of me. The elderly farmer who was driving a well-used car offered me a lift of about ten miles, and I scrambled in. The road climbed up Van Staden's Pass, then continued out into open country. That was where my host had to turn off. It was very open country indeed, and ahead of me the road lay long, hot and dusty, with not a single tree within a mile of the road.

I had not thought that I would need a hat in the springtime, and there was a slight ocean breeze, so for the first hour or so I was not too uncomfortable. But when the breeze dropped, I felt the full force of that huge, hot sun. Sitting on the dry grass with a knotted handkerchief on my head, I felt like a pork chop under a solar cooker. Remembering the cold and sleet of the past few weeks, I wondered which was worse.

As I sat there, staring at a cow that was staring at me, I remembered a small hotel that we had passed about two miles back. It was set back from the road, but anything was better than just sitting in the sun, so I started down the road. As I walked, my little bag seemed to grow heavier and the road became hotter. I had covered only a mile when I stopped for a rest. Just then a bus going in the opposite direction, toward Port Elizabeth, passed me. That's when I decided that if I got no further before nightfall, I would go back to East London and spend the rest of my leave with my relatives. All day and just twenty miles was a very uncomfortable way to waste my precious time. Soon I could see the whitewashed walls of the hotel gleaming in the distance, but I was too tired and despondent to walk any further, so I just sat down on the grass and broiled and wondered at the complete lack of traffic.

It was late afternoon before a car stopped. The driver, a young man who hit his brakes and gas pedal with equal enthusiasm, offered me a lift to Humansdorp, about thirty-five miles inland. We had hardly introduced ourselves when he decided to stop at a hotel to wash down the dust. It was a charming little place, tucked away under a cliff and with a stream running through the grounds and flowers around the door. The cool stone floor and the ice cold beer put new energy into both of us.

We were soon in Humansdorp. It was only a small town, but I stood hopefully in the shade of a tree and prayed that somebody would decide to go to Cape Town that afternoon. After an hour, I bought a lemonade and nibbled some cake and walked a few yards up the road for exercise. No cars. Nothing stopped for me.

As the sun began to set, another bus bound for Port Elizabeth appeared. I almost flagged it down, but decided instead to wait for just one more car. When the next car passed me without even slowing down, I told myself, *Just one more, then I'm going back*. And so it went, "just one more car" after another that didn't slow down, until it was almost dark. Back at the hotel, I had a good meal and went to bed with a splitting headache from too much sun. I had covered about fifty-five miles in ten hours. It wasn't worth the effort.

Chapter Eighteen: Humansdorp to Strand

Day 20

At dinner the night before, I had spoken briefly with a salesman who had a large car. He was from East London and was obviously going south, so after breakfast, I lay in wait for him. But my luck had not changed.

"Sorry," he said, "but every inch of space is taken up with my sample cases." He shrugged his shoulders, "Just don't have the room."

When he drove off I picked up my bag and set off slowly and reluctantly, walking down the road. It was a useless gesture, and I was risking sunstroke but it was better than just standing there.

My luck suddenly turned for the better. Within ten minutes I was picked up by two weather-beaten farmers in an ancient car. They were Afrikaners who spoke very little English, but I didn't miss the first question. The smaller of the two peered closely at me and said, "You got a gun?"

When I assured them that I did not have a gun, they were both clearly relieved. The taller of the two could only say "Goot. Goot." but the other man explained that I would find it hard to get lifts in rural areas because of the fear of hold-ups.

"Have there been many robberies around here?" I asked.

"No." he replied "We have not had any hold-ups around here. But you have to be careful."

Perhaps that explained why my hitchhiking had been so unproductive during the past few days. After only three miles, however, they turned off the main road and let me out. I stood under a row of poplars and thumbed the few cars that appeared, but no one stopped. As the hours passed, the shadow of the trees moved to the other side of the road, so I left my bag on one side and sat on a handy rock on the other. It was reasonably comfortable until a hot, dry wind sprang up and drowned out the sound of approaching cars. Soon the wind became a small gale, tearing the winter-dry leaves off the trees and snapping small twigs from the wildly waving branches, even though at ground level, I felt almost nothing. I was so busy staring up into the trees and studying the strange phenomenon that a car suddenly appeared and sped by before I could flag it.

I was still sitting on the rock when the speeding car stopped and reversed back towards me. It took me two seconds to leap across the road, grab my bag, and race to the car. At first glance, it looked as if there might not be room for me; but the driver, a very tall young man, climbed out and, with the aid of his black assistant, moved suitcases and boxes of samples until we had room for me in front and space for his assistant in the back seat. Then we were off.

The car was a French Citroën with Johannesburg license plates. It was an older model of the type used by the French police, black, low-slung, and powerful. It was so low-slung that with three adults and all the luggage, it seemed to be much too close to the ground. But this did not worry the driver, who put his foot down hard and kept it there.

"My name's Chris," he said, "I sell leather goods. Belts, purses, stuff like that." After I introduced myself, he said, "My radio is broken and I haven't had anybody to talk to since Jo'burg. I'm going crazy from boredom." He nodded towards his assistant. "That's Benjamin. He's a farm boy, and this is his first trip off the farm. Only speaks a bit of English and Afrikaans so I don't get much conversation out of him."

Chris offered me a lift to the next town, but when he heard about my recent bad luck, he had a better suggestion. "If you don't mind waiting while I do business, I plan to be in Cape Town in a couple of days. Could be a bit boring for you, but I would welcome the company."

Naturally, I jumped at the offer.

"This stretch of road from Cape Town to Port Elizabeth is called the Garden Route," Chris explained, and I could easily see why. The road led through a succession of deep, cool woods, wide dry meadows, narrow winding gorges with foaming streams, and sharply climbing hills that opened up vistas of sandy beaches and blue sea. Now and then we came across a cottage tucked into the shade of some trees or a house perched on a cliff overlooking the sea, but for the first hundred miles the scenery was lonely, wild, and beautiful, and our business stops in the little villages served only to heighten the beauty of the countryside.

Out on the wide plains, it was scorching hot in the little car, even with the windows down. "They call this part the Little Karoo," Chris said, "and there is another area further inland that they call the Great Karoo, but damned if I know what a Karoo is." After a hot, flat stretch, the car would plunge into some deep valley where the pine trees grew tall and cool, and we would feel the temperature drop. Chris always slowed down to admire a rushing stream and breathe the pine-scented air. Two or three times, we came across an area of barren rocks where great cactus plants were in bloom and seemed to flame with pink and mauve blossoms atop tall stems.

As he drove, Chris explained that he was on commission only, and at the moment nobody was ordering. This was because the shopkeepers were waiting to see what the summer's fashions would be. But he was philosophical about it. "Just part of being a salesman," he said.

We also talked about cars and military service and the scenery. Cars were his main interest, and he admitted, rather sheepishly, that he had invested a small fortune in the Citroën. "Much more than I can afford," he said, "but isn't she a beauty?"

He was from Johannesburg and took immense pride in the bad name that Jo'burg drivers had acquired. "Sometimes," he boasted, "I get tickets from small town policemen just because I have Jo'burg license plates." Two or three times, we had bad skids on sharp corners, and once we ended up almost in the ditch, prompting Benjamin, who normally sat quietly in the back seat, to say, "Boss. I think that time we all die!" That was exactly what I had thought, too.

But Chris only laughed and said, "Don't worry! It's impossible to roll a real Citroën with front wheel drive."

It was wonderful to have a lift to Cape Town but if my host insisted on demonstrating the marvelous performance of his car, I just hoped that we would get there alive.

Benjamin, a small man, had never seen a big city and never been far from the family farm near Krugersdorp, where he had two wives. He was not quite sure how old he was (although he seemed to me to be about thirty) nor how old his numerous children were.

They had run into snow in the Drakensbergs near Kokstad a few days after I had been there, and Chris described how the snow had clogged his windshield wipers so badly that Benjamin had to lean out and clear them. At first, Benjamin did not want to touch the strange white stuff and had swatted at the snowflakes as if they were insects. Eventually, he took a handful of snow and studied it for a while, watching it melt through his fingers. "Like ice cream, Boss," he observed. His boss had agreed that that was a good description, but Benjamin was still worried. Finally, he admitted that he was going to have a hard time explaining snow back on the farm. He was convinced that his wives would call him a liar.

At Knysna, Chris stopped to visit a friend. With its attractive cluster of buildings clinging to the rocks at the mouth of a large bay and surrounded by sharp hills, the town looked rather like a quaint Cornish seaport town. Numerous cottages were scattered around the almost land-locked bay, and dozens of chalets were dispersed widely over the hills. Boats of all size were tied up along the shore. It was obviously a favorite place for artists, and the walls of almost every restaurant and café were covered with samples of the local talent. Much of it was very good.

The friend's cottage was perched on the rocks where the bay opened to the sea. It was a fascinating little place, but the friend was not home and nobody knew where he was, so we had to go on. For the next thirty miles, the road ran along flat land around shallow bays and over numerous little rivers. The scenery was well sprinkled with little cottages and holiday chalets, most of them locked up for the winter.

As the sun set, we reached a seaside town with the curious name of Wilderness, where we decided to spend the night. It was one of the loveliest places I have ever seen. The road ran close to the shore, and the town was squeezed between the steep cliffs and the ocean. There was little more than a beautifully laid out hotel, some shops, and a few rows of attractive houses. The rest was hills and wide beach, with palm trees and well tended lawns, and it seemed more like a private estate than a town. It was quiet enough there that even the most hyper-tense businessman could relax.

Since it had been such a hot day, we decided to take a swim in the ocean before dinner. We took Benjamin along to watch our clothes. He had not seen the ocean before this trip, though he had gotten some glimpses of it from a distance. As we drove onto the beach in the fading light and he studied the vast expanse of water and the little waves that washed up on the sand, he said, "Boss. You not swim in that water."

Chris laughed and assured him that everybody swam in the sea.

Benjamin shook his head, "Not safe," he repeated, and he walked back to the car.

We were almost out of light and I was eager to dive into the cool, clear water, so we changed quickly and, using the car head-lights, we ran into the water. It was freezing! I went in up to my knees and stopped. Chris went in only up to his ankles and stopped. We stood there daring each other to get wet but, within a minute, we were blue with cold and, feeling a little foolish, we ran back to the car where Benjamin sat. There was the shadow of a smile on his face, but he said nothing.

After a good dinner, we went for a stroll, then Chris met a fellow salesman in a bar. We tried some German beer, and I was introduced to a popular drink, South African brandy and ginger ale. It went down well.

Day 21

After a very early breakfast, we drove under a perfect sky through beautiful scenery, across rushing rivers, and through cool forests to George, the next town, which was a medium-size town and quite busy. Chris set to work visiting his customers, with Benjamin carrying the sample cases, while I sat in the car and watched the people or strolled up and down the street. After Chris and Benjamin had visited half a dozen customers, we moved on to Mossel Bay, the place where in 1488, the first European, the Portuguese Bartolomeu Diaz, landed in South Africa nine years before Vasco da Gama. What I saw was a pretty little town at the end of a high ridge of land with a superb view of the sea. It was obviously a popular holiday town. From there, the road turned inland and we raced from town to town visiting a score of customers. There were Riversdale and Heidelburg and Swellendam, sitting amidst its orange groves. Next were Rivier Zonder End and some smaller towns, then Caledon.

It was at Caledon that I saw my first protea flower. After Chris had visited his customers, he found me outside a small flower shop admiring a large, brilliantly colored flower that looked very much like an artichoke.

"That's a protea," he said. "They only grow around here." He reached into his pocket and found a very old silver sixpence. "See? It's on some of our coins. I think it's the national flower."

Sure enough, the strange flower was indeed on the coin. "The botanists say that this is the only place in the world where the soil and the weather are just right for proteas to grow wild," Chris said. "It's a bit early in the season, but there may be one or two flowering. In the middle of the season, the hillsides are just covered with them. It's a wonderful sight."

We drove slowly up and down a few side roads looking for more blooming proteas and in a sunny hollow, protected from the wind, we found a large shrub with two or three blossoms holding their wide bright faces to the sun. I looked around and saw that the hillside was covered in the plants.

"You'll just have to come back in a month," Chris said, and we sped back to the main road.

Many of the South African towns we visited were founded in the 18th or early 19th centuries, and as we drew closer to Cape Town, they became older and more solid looking with their century-old buildings and lots of ancient shade trees. Almost all the towns in the Cape region could have been towns in Western Europe. This was quite a contrast to the new or almost-new buildings I'd seen in Rhodesia.

The open countryside was intensely farmed, and there were very few hills to be seen except for a blue range in the background we approached as we worked our way south. The bright morning had not lasted. The weather became as changeable as an English spring, as showers and bright sunshine followed each other with uncanny regularity.

It seemed that whenever we came to a town, it rained. The open country would be bathed in sunshine, but as we approached a town, there would be a neat, dark cloud above it waiting for us, and so the sample cases had to be dragged out into the rain. As we left each town, the cloud seemed to sneak ahead to wait gleefully for us at the next town. At one point, where the land was bare and open for miles, it was quite hot. Chris and I had been discussing why the rain fell in one area but not in another.

"I think we learned in school that it's something to do with the ground temperature," he said. "The rain falls where it's coolest."

Just then, we came over the crest of a low hill and saw a huge tree plantation ahead of us. Thousands of trees had been planted in neatly regimented rows with fire breaks at regular intervals. Over this artificial forest, but nowhere else, a rain cloud was emptying its contents in long streamers. The sun, reflected in the rain, made it look as if the cloud was anchored to the trees. As we entered the forest, there was an immediate drop in temperature, and Chris slowed down so that we could enjoy it.

"Well!" he said proudly. "Mother Nature just proved me right. The trees keep the ground cool, so the rain falls there. The rain keeps the forest cool, so that attracts more rain." He laughed. "I knew that one day I would find some use for all that expensive schooling."

Late in the afternoon, he shoved his order book into the glove compartment and called it a day. He had been working hard and it had been a good day, but we had eaten very little since breakfast. We headed for the next large town and a good hotel. The road twisted through a region of apple orchards and small farms, and we soon reached the blue hills that had been overshadowing us all day.

As the road climbed, long and steep, through heath and forest, this gave Chris the opportunity to really prove the power of his Citroën. There were also one or two sharp bends to whet his appetite. Suddenly we shot through a gap in the high cliffs and found ourselves looking out into space. Before us was a sharp right-angle turn and nothing between us and a fearful drop except a low stone wall. As we arrived at the turn, a bus appeared from the opposite direction. There was a horrible screeching of brakes. I glimpsed the front of the bus, just inches from my head, then we spun away and slithered towards the low stone wall. When the Citroën stopped just inches from the wall, we could clearly hear the bus driver swearing loudly and fluently in Afrikaans. To this day, I still remember thinking what an expressive language it was when the occasion demanded.

After the bus drove off, Chris, Benjamin, and I got out and, rather shakily, admired the view. "I think this is called Sir Lowry's Pass," Chris said. "But I don't know who he was. I seem to remember that it's nearly 2,000 feet high, or at least well over a thousand."

The pass gave us a superb view across the plains, almost to Cape Town itself, and we could just make out the grey blur of Table Mountain, almost forty miles away. Below us, the road snaked down the steep mountainside in dramatic bends to the plains below. To the east, the Indian Ocean lay dull and grey under a rain cloud, but we were in bright evening sunshine with darkness already creeping across the land below.

By the time we reached the bottom of the pass—at a much

reduced speed—it was quite dark, so we stopped in the first town we came to. This was the seaside resort of Strand at the northern end of False Bay. There were plenty of hotels to choose from and we soon found an inexpensive hotel. Gazing back up at the pass, I thought it looked as if the road we had just descended had been scraped on the cliff face with a knife. We could clearly see the lights of descending cars.

Here in Strand, there was a long promenade with plenty of shade trees and seats, and what looked like a fine beach, but the water was angry black in the dark, and waves crashed against the sea wall.

After we had cleaned up at the hotel, Chris discovered that he had a friend in this town, too, so he phoned and we were invited for supper. The friend turned out to be a very pretty girl. I found myself making polite conversation with her parents for most of the evening, but it was more interesting than I had expected. Chris was an English-speaking Afrikaans, whereas our hosts were strongly anti-Afrikaans.

As the father explained, "You cannot get a civil service job of any kind unless you are bilingual. You have to be fluent in Afrikaans as well as English, which means thousands of well-qualified people are excluded from jobs because they are not considered fluent enough." He laughed bitterly and added, "It's just a trick to find work for all those Boers who come in off the farms with practically no education."

When I asked about non-government jobs, he said, "Oh, yes, there are plenty of jobs, but they need education or training. We can't have a white man digging ditches or doing any kind of unskilled work. That's for the blacks. The white man has to be the supervisor. He can't do a black man's job, even if he wanted to."

After a fine dinner, the conversation turned to education and I asked about education for black South Africans. Our host sighed and said, "Oh, I know what they say. That we don't let our blacks have an education, that we keep them ignorant and don't provide schools for them. But the truth is quite different. We provide a better education for blacks than any other African country. The schools for blacks are free, and we have built thousands. No, they are not as good as the schools for the white children, but what do you expect? There is just so much tax money to spread around, and the blacks don't pay hardly any taxes." He paused and then continued, "Did you know the blacks have their own university at Fort Hare? Did you know there is a medical college reserved just for blacks and Indians? Where do you think the black doctors and nurses and lawyers and teachers come from? And who do you think pays for it?"

He looked at his wife and daughter and said, "None of us went to university, but we don't mind paying taxes so that blacks can go to university. God knows, we'll never have enough black doctors and teachers, but the fact remains that white people expect their tax money to go to white schools first. That's life."

It had been an interesting evening. I had learned a lot. But Chris had gotten absolutely nowhere with the pretty daughter, so I bought him a drink in the hotel before we went to bed.

Chapter Nineteen: Strand to Cape Town

Day 22

During breakfast, Chris said, "I think we'll go directly to Cape Town from here. I have lots of good customers there, and they'll give me bigger orders than I'm getting in these little towns."

As we drove off, the morning mists solidified and took the shape of Table Mountain. That great, rectangular shape stood, squat and massive, at the end of a range of mountains that formed a grey background to the lovely countryside, which was green and damp in the morning light. In a very short while, we were in the outer suburbs of Cape Town and completely lost.

The inland side of Cape Town consisted of a twenty-mile-long string of intermeshed towns with sign posts that were either vague or non-existent, and so it was only by sheer luck that we found ourselves on the main highway that curves around the mountain and into the city. It was an excellent road that took us through well-kept parkland, past the famous hospital where, years later, in 1967, the first heart transplant was performed, past the beautiful memorial to Cecil Rhodes who had once been prime minister, then past the zoo and a stretch of forest where, Chris claimed, there were wild deer. Soon we turned a corner and found ourselves in Cape Town.

Just like visitors in any other major city in this modern world, our first task was to find a parking space. We eventually parked near the town hall in the older part of the city, and Chris went off to do his work, with Benjamin carrying the sample cases. I set out to do some touring. In my usual, unorganized style, I wandered up and down, admiring the public buildings and looking into the shops. The streets were busy but not crowded, the pedestrians were a mixture of city workers and suburban shoppers, and the pace seemed to be a trifle more leisurely than in other big cities I had known. Many of the streets were quite steep and, at the top of one particularly steep road, there was a charming little park with a pool of goldfish and some benches, where I sat and gazed up at Table Mountain. The tablecloth of white cloud was neatly draped over the edge of the plateau, and, as I watched, a whimsical draft of air lifted it a few feet to reveal a small, white, concrete speck perched on the very edge. This was the cable car house. I wondered if I would have time to take the trip up to the top of the mountain.

Strolling downhill again, I found myself standing at the foot of the Jan van Riebeeck Statue. Originally, the statue was at the water's edge, but there has been extensive reclamation and landfill as the city has grown, and now Van Riebeeck stands in the heart of the city, far from the docks and the ships. To the South Africans, the landing of Van Riebeeck in1652 is as important as the Pilgrim Fathers to the Americans, and the details of the settlement by Van Riebeeck are engraved on every schoolboy's memory. (The early history of the two countries is astonishingly similar in many ways.)

I was making my way over to the star shaped, 18th-century citadel when I remembered the time and hurried back to the square in front of the governor's residence, where we had planned to meet. Chris was patiently circling the square, and we immediately drove out to Bellville and Goodwood where he had more customers. The whole area was completely urbanized, and the level farmland had long vanished under a sea of houses and shops. When we returned to the city, we realized that we had not yet found a hotel.

As luck would have it, there was an international rugby match that weekend. Rugby is the most popular game in South Africa, so the hotels were filling rapidly. We could easily have found a room for ourselves, but finding one for Benjamin proved to be a problem. Many salesmen took helpers along to carry the heavy sample cases and, quite often, to do some of the driving. Small-town hotels always appreciated the steady business that salesmen brought and almost always provided accommodation for their black servants. In the bigger cities, however, most hotels were unaccommodating. We tried five or six with no success. There were no hotels for blacks in the city, and no garage would allow Benjamin to sleep in the car. We were soon at a loss for a solution to this problem until Chris remembered yet another old friend.

This friend was an ex-policeman and, although he had no servants' quarters in his tidy little house, he had an idea. We all squashed into the car and drove around to the local police station. The sergeant in charge agreed that there was no place for a black man to sleep in the white part of the city, and we could not go cruising around the black part at night. It took a little time for the sergeant to realize what we had in mind, and then he was immediately against the idea. But we worked on him and, eventually, he admitted that he had unused bunks in empty cells. Our next step, of course, was to persuade Benjamin that it was perfectly safe in the police station. It took longer to persuade him than it had the sergeant, but in the end, he reluctantly got his own blanket from the car and entered the cell. It was spotlessly clean, freshly painted, and as comfortable as a prison cell can be. But Benjamin was not happy. We left the door wide open as we white men trooped out of his temporary bedroom. He was staring at the solid walls and, quite obviously, wondering how he would explain this to his wives,

With that problem safely solved, Chris and I found a room for ourselves, piled all the sample cases and suit cases on the beds, and went in search of yet more friends that Chris remembered that he had. They were nurses at the large, beautiful hospital that we had passed earlier. But the girls had just come off duty and were too tired to go out, so we went to their place and had a late tea and argued the relative merits of Johannesburg and Cape Town. This is always a good subject to warm up a party, and very soon, with the aid of something stronger than tea and joined by a few more friends who dropped by, the hustling city of steel and concrete on the lonely high veldt was doing noisy battle with the lovely garden city on the coast.

What fascinated me most was the ease with which people switched from English to Afrikaans and back again, often in mid-sentence. As more people joined the party, it became impossible to tell anyone's native tongue, as a sentence that started in one language would often end up in the other. A word or a phrase in either language would tumble off the lips wherever it fit smoothly into the sentence. I spent much of the evening sitting in a chair, clutching a cold beer, and listening to the flow of words and trying to guess the meanings of many of the words and phrases.

Chris seemed to be doing quite well with a particularly pretty girl, but his romance came to an abrupt halt when, on the stroke of midnight, the girl who owned the apartment declared the party at an end. We drove a couple of the girls back to the nurses' residence, then made our own way back to the dark and silent hotel.

Day 23

Although it was a Saturday, Chris still had a full day of work ahead, so we agreed to meet at the main railway station that evening. I wanted to put in another day of sightseeing before I returned to camp in Rhodesia. Perhaps it was the sparkling sunshine or the champagne air, but the city looked much more inviting than the tourist posters I had stared at back in grey, damp London, so many miles away.

Table Mountain dominates the city of Cape Town. Whichever way I turned, the great shadow loomed over the roof tops or blocked the end of a steep road. On the hillsides were dozens of little houses, some only reached by a steep flight of steps, all of them graced by a magnificent view of Table Bay. The architectural styles in the city ranged widely from Dutch gables to the Spanish stucco of Southern California. Most houses were whitewashed, but I also saw many painted in soft pastels, and there were flowers everywhere. Below me was the harbor with its swarm of toy-like ships and the hazy outline of Robben Island, and between the mountain and bay was the eruption of tall office buildings of downtown Cape Town. It struck me as humorous that a great mass of humanity lay squeezed between the mountain and the water while behind the mountain lay the vast expanse of a giant continent. But then, I thought of New

York, crowded onto an island at the edge of another giant continent.

Later, walking along the seafront, I found that a brisk wind had sprung up and the waves were quite high, though not high enough to drive away the determined surf fishermen. When grey clouds appeared, I took a bus back to the city center and got off at the post office, which was a huge marble palace fit for a sultan. I felt that my miserable little postcards were hardly doing it justice, but it was a good place to wait out the rain storm. Browsing through a city directory, I came across the address of the Union Jack Club, a British serviceman's club. It was close by and seemed like a better place to spend an hour or two than the public post office.

I met half a dozen friends from Heany Camp in the club bar. To say that they were surprised to see me would be an understatement.

"We thought you were only going as far as Durban," one said.

"Didn't think you'd get that far, actually," said another.

"No," said a third. "Remember that radio message that Ted got from the ham radio operator who lives somewhere south of Durban? He mentioned that you'd dropped in and were on your way to East London. But that was some time back."

I did a rough calculation and said, "Yes, I did visit a ham radio operator, but that was about ten days ago. Nice of him to pass the word along. More important, how the heck did you lot get here?"

They laughed. "We did it the easy way. Took the train." They then described three days of utter boredom as the train slowly wended its way across the eastern edge of the Kalahari Desert through Bechuanaland. Even as I thought of the heat and the cold and the problems I had experienced, I was still glad that I had hitchhiked.

"Now we spend three more days getting back," said the guy.

"Yeah," said another. "That's over half of our ten days' leave spent sitting in a train."

When it stopped raining, we went to a bio-café. At that time, many South Africans called the cinema the "bioscope," so the "bio-café" was a strange combination of café and movie theater. We paid for coffee and a hamburger at the box office, then found seats inside. In front of each seat was a narrow shelf, and a waitress brought our order when we were seated. We sat for half an hour, having our snack and watching cartoons and newsreels and wondering how the waitress found her customers in the dark of the theater. It was quite fascinating, but later, when I commented on it to Chris, he said, "You mean you don't have them in England?"

Back at the railway station, as I waited for Chris I watched the crowds lining up at the ticket windows. The waitresses in the cafés, the bus drivers, and most of the blue-collar workers I had seen were white, and now it struck me that I had not seen many non-whites in the city. But here at the train station there were all kinds of people, and each race seemed to have its own ticket window. There were ticket windows for whites, ticket windows for blacks, and a separate ticket window for Asians. The line of people at the black window in-cluded many Cape coloured, who are descendants of early pioneers who found their wives, sometimes more than one, from among the original inhabitants or the imported Asian labor. For generations, these people of mixed blood had formed a middle class between the Bantu and the Europeans, but now they were grouped with the blacks. I was astonished to see quite a few fair-haired and blue-eyed people in the coloured line. The Asians also included the Cape

Malays, a Moslem community of about 60,000 who were descendants of indentured workers brought over from Malaysia and have remained in Cape Town as a small, close knit community, avoiding politics and publicity and prospering modestly in a land where race is everything.

When Chris arrived, I pointed out a blonde, blue-eyed girl in the Cape coloured ticket line and asked him what the difference was between her and any legally white citizen.

"She's as white as you or me," he began. "But what if you married her?" he asked. "You'd live in the white part of the city, you'd send your children to a white school. Right?" I agreed. "But then," now he turned serious, "the third or fourth baby comes along and it is quite clearly black. What then?"

I remained silent, so he continued, "You have to move. Your children are tossed out of the white school, you lose your job, and your wife loses all her friends. Where would you live? What would you do for a living? Could you live in one of the black townships?"

I had no answers, and we left the station with Chris insisting that the rules had to be there. No exceptions could be made, he added; otherwise the whole structure would come tumbling down and the nation that his ancestors had worked so hard to create would vanish overnight. There was no middle road.

We arrived back at the hotel to find Benjamin sitting on the curb with his bundle. It seems that he had been forced to leave his quarters at the police station by the sudden arrival of tenants more deserving of the accommodation. I didn't think that he was reluctant to leave his jail cell. As we approached, we saw he was deep in conversation with a black mechanic from a nearby garage. Between them, they had worked out a plan whereby, for a small sum, the mechanic would take Benjamin to the black township and find him room and board until we were ready to leave Cape Town. It sounded good to us, so we paid the mechanic and they went off into the night.

Chris was finished for the weekend, so we cleaned up and set out for a night on the town. I fully intended to head back to Heany Camp first thing in the morning, so we went to a rather expensive restaurant and then bought good tickets to the theatre. Both the food and the show were very good, but the night was still young. Fortunately, my friend seemed to know every bar and nightclub in town, and his list of friends was inexhaustible. I found it fascinating how he could step through a door thousands of miles from his home and immediately see someone he knew. We ended the night in a sleazy but crowded bar near the docks. It was full of servicemen and cigarette smoke, along with lots of women trying to separate the men from their money. I had been sitting there for some time before I realized that more than a few of the girls were boys and many of the men were women. I also saw a small crowd of Royal Navy sailors who were clearly looking for a fight. One drunken specimen was standing on a table and, in a horrible Liverpool accent, insulting everything South African. Chris wanted to do something about this guy, but I restrained him and then we watched as the number of South African military uniforms increased. Eventually, when the sailors found themselves thoroughly outnumbered, they dragged the drunk off the table. It was clear that there was not going to be a fight, so we left. After a few wrong turns, we found our way back to the hotel, where we had to ring the bell for half an hour to wake the night porter.

Day 24

As it was early afternoon before we woke, I decided to put off my return to camp by one more day. Chris and I were both in surprisingly good moods, so we decided to visit the nurses again after lunch. A couple of them had Sunday off. We drove out of the city, down lanes shaded by tall poplars and cypresses, and wandered between fields of grape vines and past picturesque old Dutch farm houses. Everywhere, the tiny green buds of spring were bursting out into the soft sunshine.

We stopped at Groot Constantia, a beautiful Cape Dutch farmhouse built in 1691 and restored by Cecil Rhodes. It was now the official home of the prime minister and was open to the public. We strolled through the cool, lofty rooms and the great kitchens and admired the work of the early pioneers; their handmade tools, their handicrafts, and the carefully made furniture. There were not many other visitors that day, and afterwards we sat in the shade and had tea. Behind us stood the old house with its beautiful, whitewashed gables and neat garden, and in front of us the farmland, tinted blue by the grape vines, vanished into the pale grey mist, while all around us loomed the surrounding circle of mountains. Even Chris had to admit that it was more lovely and relaxing than anything Jo'burg had to offer.

We finally dragged ourselves away. We had to stop for gas at the pretty little town of Wynberg, where the white proprietor filled the tank and his black assistant cleaned the windows and checked the tires. We exchanged a few pleasant words and then were off. There was nothing unusual about this stop, but a few weeks after I had returned to camp, my mother wrote and told me that she had traced a relative who lived outside Cape Town. She did not have his name, she wrote, but he owned a garage in Wynberg.

We took the long way, along the coast, back to Cape Town. It was a spectacular drive, and we stopped so many times to admire the view that it was sunset before we reached the hotel, so we had supper with the girls and decided to go up Signal Hill. Somebody decided we should take beer with us, but the hotel could not sell beer to take out on a Sunday, so we ordered it in our room then carried it out to the car, two bottles at a time, tucked up our jacket sleeves. The desk clerk knew what we were doing, and we knew that he knew, but the ritual had to be gone through with solemn faces.

It was a steep road to the top of the hill, and the overloaded Citroën complained a little, but it was worth it. Cape Town lay spread out before us like a spilled sack of bright diamonds. Far out to sea we could make out the lights of ships rounding the Cape of Good Hope on their long run from Europe to Asia, while below us, the lights curved around Table Bay and up the slopes of Table Mountain, where they thinned to lonely pin-pricks of light. By the light of the moon, we could see the blanket of cloud draped, thick and fleecy, over the sharp edge of the mountain. We stood there in the dark and drank a toast to Cape Town. When it began to get cold, we drove down into the lights and became part of the city.

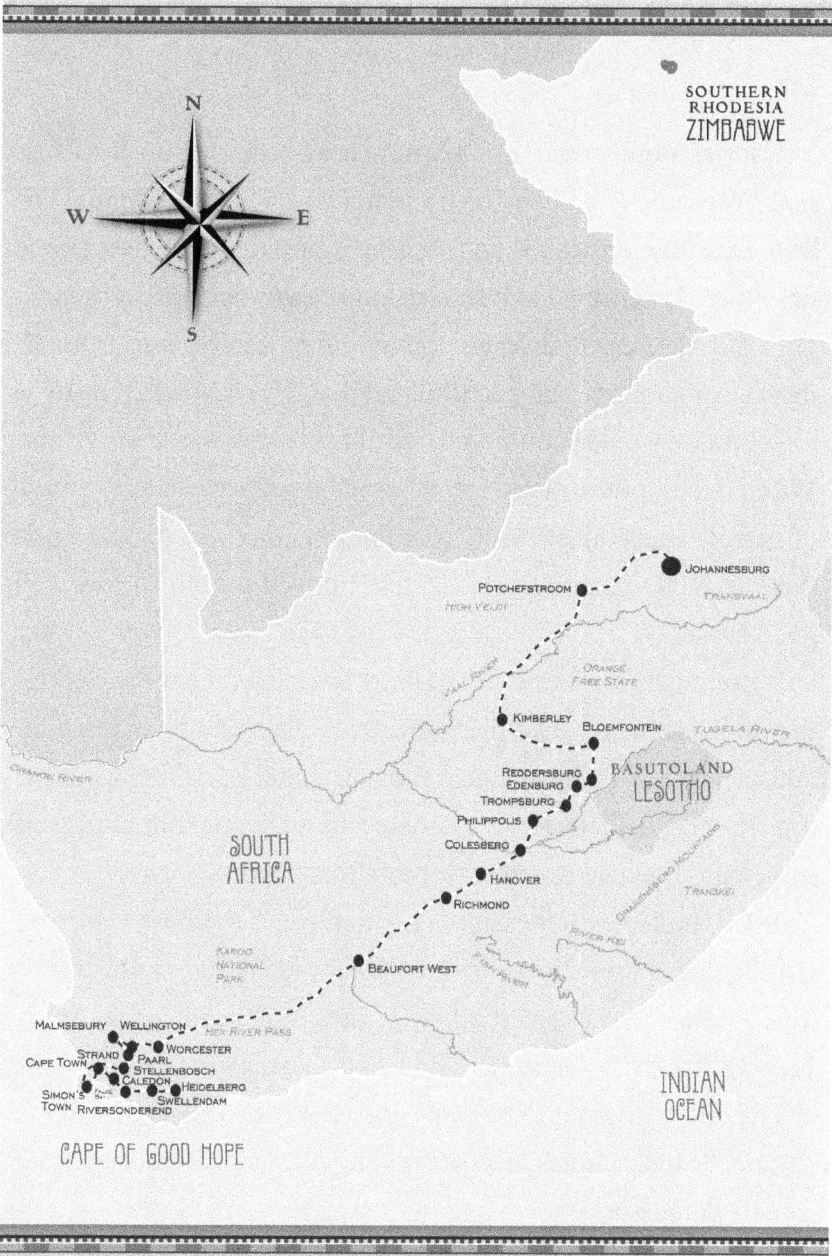

Map Three: Traveling North, Back to RAF Camp Heany

Day 25

Now it was Monday and time for me to head back to camp, But Chris said, "You can't visit Cape Town and not go up Table Mountain! I've been here so many times and, believe it or not, I have never gone up, either." He grinned at me. "One more day won't hurt."

The cable car that serves the mountain can be seen from almost any point in the city, so thinking that if we headed in the right direction we would soon find it, we didn't bother to ask directions. Within ten minutes, of course, we were hopelessly lost in the maze of narrow streets filled with charming little houses. All the roads there seemed to climb so steeply that I hoped the old Citroën had good brakes.

Eventually we found the parking lot and, while we waited for the cable car, we studied the rather slim cable that ended in a giant spring and the huge wheel that, presumably, hauled us to the top. To me, it all looked very simple and quite safe. But Chris was inspecting the machinery with more than normal interest. As we boarded the cable car, he casually remarked, "You know, I've never been in one of these things before. Never even been in an airplane." There were about a dozen other tourists in the car, and he made his way quickly to the center and stood there staring grimly at the ceiling and trying not to be conspicuous. When we were almost at the top, he took a quick look at the view and swiftly returned to the middle of the car.

At the top of Table Mountain, over 3,000 feet above the blue sea, there were a small curio shop and a restaurant, but otherwise it was clear of any commercial clutter. It was flat, as I had expected, but not level. The surface was covered in rocks and boulders, which made walking tricky. Everything was also slippery wet thanks to the little streams that ran between the rocks. There did not appear to be an ounce of soil anywhere, yet small bushes, ferns and tufts of grass were growing here and there. It was cool, and when the fog drifted down it got quite cold, but the fog seemed to be constantly breaking up and reforming so that we alternated between bright sunshine and the damp gloom.

It was a strange new world, and we roamed about for hours, peering over the surprisingly steep edge of the mountain, discovering strange plants, scrambling over weather-worn rocks, and investigating crevices. Once we sat on a jutting rock and yodeled to a party of climbers far below. It seemed like a hard way to get to the top, but they were not the only hikers. We soon discovered that most of the people we talked to had climbed up. In one party coming up, we could clearly see several small children, so we waited for them and, as they were resting, one of the tots told me that this was the "easy route." He was not old enough yet to go up the proper climbers' trail.

From almost any point on the mountain, we got wonderful views of the city and the bay, while behind us, there were equally spectacular views of the distant mountains of southern Africa, blue and grey against the sky and broken by wide green valleys. Soon, alas, it was time to go, and so we headed back to the cable car. On the way down, we passed close to more climbers, resting on their ropes or walking the narrow cliff-face paths. Instead of planting himself in the center of the car again, Chris joined me at the window. "This contraption seems to be safer than I thought," he told me. But I noticed that he still did not look directly down at the thousand foot drop.

That evening, Chris remembered yet another friend worth visiting, and so we drove out to a quiet tree-lined suburb to visit an uncle. We were welcomed enthusiastically, and as his aunt set the table for supper other relatives appeared as if by magic. It was a cheerful group. I was made to feel quite at home, but the recent international rugby match was the main topic of dinner conversation, and I knew almost nothing about the game, the teams, or the players. South Africans are enthusiastic sportsmen; I am convinced, in fact, that if the price of gold or diamonds dropped overnight, nobody would mind as long as South Africa could beat Australia in cricket, New Zealand in rugby, and England in soccer. During a lull in the conversation, I asked about American football and baseball but the idea of playing rugby while sheathed in pounds of padding and a plastic helmet was greeted with polite scorn, while baseball was looked on as a childish form of cricket, not really worth taking seriously. When I suggested that baseball was slowly becoming an international game, everybody assured me that it would never replace cricket, not anywhere in the world.

I learned that the color bar affected even sports, and segregation tended to limit international competition. At the time, it was said, the Indian and West Indian cricket teams would probably never play in South Africa, and, if the New Zealand rugby team included a Maori player (considered non-white), it would not be invited to South Africa. South African tennis players could compete anywhere overseas, but non-white players could not compete in South Africa. With the huge number of non-white players in international sports, even in the 1950s, South Africa could never host any important international meet, and, of course, no white South African could ever face a black opponent in the boxing ring.

When I asked the family why a black sportsman of international caliber could not be considered an exception, Chris's uncle asked, "Yes, he could…but where would he stay?" When I hesitated, he continued, "I bet there isn't a hotel in the city that would, or could, put up a black man."

Everybody agreed, and somebody added, "And you couldn't put him up as a guest in a private house, either. It's illegal." When I suggested that arrangements could surely be made, somebody else asked, "But where would he practice? I can't think of anyplace that would allow a black man to use their locker room or swimming pool."

And with that, the subject was dropped.

Day 26

I woke bright and early, fully determined to get on the road and hitch back to camp just as quickly as I could. Now I had less than a week to get from Cape Town to Bulawayo, a distance of well over a thousand miles. I had spent far too long in Cape Town, and the specter of fourteen days in the guard house hovered over me. At breakfast, when I told Chris my plans, he said, "You're right. I have an idea. It's time I visited customers in the Orange Free State. There are just one or two customers left to see here, so if you help me with the damn parking, we can be on our way in a couple of hours."

That decided, we turned our thoughts to Benjamin. Neither of us had the faintest idea where he was, but when we stepped out of the hotel we found him leaning against the wall and looking very embarrassed. It took us some time to get the story out of him, but he eventually confessed that he had hardly reached the black township before he had been quickly and painlessly relieved of all his money by smooth-talking city slickers. For one wild evening, he had been surrounded by a host of friends, eager to show a country boy the delights of the big city…and then, alas, he found himself broke and alone. He was vague about where he had slept and what he had eaten, but somehow he had found his way back to the hotel in time to leave the wicked city. It was such a classic tale that Chris and I both laughed, and even Benjamin, after he had finished two large sandwiches, eventually saw the humor of it.

That morning, I drove slowly around the busy streets while the other two hauled the sample cases in and out of stores. With me cruising the block, instead of wasting time looking for parking space, they managed to get their work done by early afternoon. We said goodbye to Cape Town and headed for Stellenbosch.

This famous university town, which lies about thirty miles northwest across the Cape flats behind Table Mountain, proved to be such a lovely place, set in a cradle of low tree-covered hills, that, despite the early hour, we decided to stop there for the night. While Chris and Benjamin drove around to their customers, I strolled along tree-lined streets past old, mellow buildings. Spring was in the air, and after the excitement of Cape Town, I was enjoying the wonderful atmosphere of peace and relaxation. At sunset, we dined at the hotel. As usual, Chris remembered some friends from his university days, but I was not in the mood for another party, so when he drove off, I went for another leisurely stroll in the cool of the evening.

The second oldest town in the province after Cape Town, Stellenbosch was founded in the 17th century, when the settlers at the Cape could be counted in the hundreds. Bushmen and Hottentots still plagued the European settlers, and the Bantu were still far to the unknown north. Simon van der Stel, the town's founder and first governor of the Cape Colony, was the son of the Dutch governor of Mauritius and his Indian wife. He worked hard to build up a strong agricultural base for the colony and it was he who invited French Huguenots to settle in the Cape, although he scattered them widely among the Dutch to force them to assimilate. There were not many Huguenots, perhaps two or three hundred, but they were skilled and educated and proved to be of immense value. Today's flourishing wine industry can be traced directly to those early French immigrants.

The buildings of Stellenbosch University stood solid and silent in the yellow lamplight, and I wandered for a while under ancient oak trees, then headed past a cinema and back to the hotel. The brilliant red and white neon of the marquee clashed with the evening, so I hurried on down sleeping streets and silent churches to the hotel, where I sat in a rocking chair on the veranda, sipping a drink and listening to the insects in the gardens.

Chapter Twenty: Malmsbury to Kimberley

Day 27

In the morning, we drove to Paarl. Famous for its wines, the town was founded by Huguenots and sits in a valley with vineyards and orchards climbing the steep hills around it. Paarl was a big town, and Chris picked up plenty of orders. Next we drove on to Malmesbury, about forty miles to the west, through well farmed land, much of it looking like the south of France with its acres of neatly pruned vines and ancient farm houses. Malmesbury also provided some very good orders for Chris. It was a cheerfully prosperous town in the heart of a farming district where everybody seemed to have money. There were new cars everywhere, the shops were full, the restaurants crowded, the women well dressed, and the farmers openly boasted of their good fortune.

For us, however, it was quite a different matter. We had stopped to fill the car with gasoline and were poking around in our wallets for the money to pay the man, when we realized that we were both almost broke.

"I have a bad feeling," said Chris, "that I spent too much in Cape Town."

"I have exactly the same feeling," said I.

As we both stared into the barren depths of our almost empty wallets, Chris said, "If we go straight back, without making too many stops, we might just make it." Then he thought for a minute.

"I could wire my father for some money, but then we would have to sit around here for a day or two."

I shook my head. "I have almost run out of time. My leave pass expires in a few days. Then it's the guardhouse for me if I'm not back. I vote we head north just as fast as your Citroën will go."

With that, we drove straight to Wellington for a couple of quick business calls. From Wellington, the road climbs over the Bains Kloof Pass, the loveliest eighteen miles of mountain pass that I had seen during the whole trip. Just outside the town, the road began to climb into wild and rugged mountainside, where we could see the road twisting away before us across the bare face of the hills, and the town below became a cluster of tiny buildings. Higher and higher we climbed, until clouds drifted across the road and we had to use the headlights. There were no birds or insects up there, and all was silent except for the sound of the car engine. We drove without speaking for about five miles through this strange land, then suddenly we were through the fog and into another world. The bare hillside was now rock-strewn and savage. Above us, the snow gleamed in the sun. Far below us, a stream rushed, foaming and wild. The road twisted like a wild thing and great boulders were balanced precariously over our heads. In the shadows, we felt the icy blast from the snow fields, but in the sun we squinted from the glare. The road was so narrow and the drop-off was so unnerving that even Chris slowed down to a crawl.

The transition from mountains to plains was quite sudden. The sun had more warmth in it now, and after crossing a wide river swollen by melted snow, we were back in farming country again. The road to Worcester lay in the center of a wide valley where the road never rose or fell more than a few feet. The black, plowed fields and bare orchards lay on perfectly flat land surrounded by mountains whose sides were roughly painted with snow. An icy wind blew dead leaves across the road.

The Cape was now behind us. It had been a wonderful visit, and Chris had to agree that Cape Town was very attractive. "Oh, it's a very nice place to *visit*," he said. Then, like a true, loyal citizen, he added, "But Jo'burg has so much more to offer. Yes, go to Cape Town or Durban for a nice holiday, but if you want to get rich and get ahead, Johannesburg is the only place." He looked over his shoulder. "What do you think, Benjamin? Jo'burg or Cape Town?"

Benjamin smiled and said diplomatically, "Boss, I think we all will be glad to be home."

At the far side of Worcester, a road sign informed us that we were 850 miles from Johannesburg. Chris did some rough calculations and said, "If we don't eat, sleep, or drink, and I drive carefully, we just may reach Jo'burg, or pretty close, before we have to get out and push." He laughed. "Hey, man. We've had pretty good luck so far. Let's see what the gods have in store." And we set off again.

For fifty miles we drove down the middle of a winding valley where the mountain walls sometimes crept to within yards of the road and sometimes stepped back to reveal well-tended farms, orchards, and vineyards that were spaced out evenly down the valley. We could still see patches of snow tucked away in the gullies, but the icy wind had given way to a warm breeze. Once or twice we sped through a small farming community, but the bulk of the settlement was strung out along the highway and the railway line.

At the head of the valley, we climbed the Hex River Pass. The road was not too wildly twisty here, but the old railway line was contorted into a fantasy of hairpin bends. At one point we stopped to watch a train slowly descending. There were passengers leaning out of the windows, and, as the engineer carefully navigated one particularly sharp bend, some children in the first carriages waved to their fellow passengers in the rear carriages that were going in the opposite direction. The mountain was almost sheer at that point, and we marveled at the skill of the engineers who, back in the 1880s, had, with blood, sweat, pickaxe, and dynamite, taken the line up onto the high plateau.

At the top of the pass, 3,000 feet above sea level, we entered what looked like a desert. Before us lay miles and miles of perfectly flat open country almost devoid of trees and the ground was thinly covered with little clumps of tough grey-green grass.

"This is the Great Karoo," said Chris. "The pioneers wrote it off as a useless desert. But they were wrong." He waved his hand from east to west. "Just look at it now."

On both sides of the road we could see flocks of great, fat, healthy sheep, their wool so long and thick that their heads and feet seemed to poke out of a dense grey bundle.

"It's the grass," Chris said. "That tough looking stuff seems to be just right. It's the only kind that will grow here. Some farmers claim that they shear their animals three times a year. I think that's an exaggeration. Twice, maybe. But it's a fact that if a sheep gets too heavy and falls into a drainage ditch, he has a tough time getting on his feet again." Then he pointed to the large black birds sitting on the fence posts. "Those crows just sit there waiting for that to happen. They peck out their eyes."

The land was divided into huge pastures by tall wire fences to keep out the jackals that are sometimes a menace to the lambs. The only signs of human life we saw for hours were one or two farm houses set far back from the road.

A great silence seemed to reign over the Great Karoo. It was lonely, but not dreary, and, just as our eyes had grown tired of the emptiness, we came across masses of white daisies shining like fresh snow along the edge of the road, with here and there a clump of yellow flowers around the telephone poles, brilliant in their loneliness.

All through the late afternoon we traveled, and mile after mile sped under the wheels. We passed a few cars going south and overtook a few local vehicles going north, but mostly we had the road to ourselves. After about a hundred miles, the sun sank reluctantly, going down like a penny in the poor box. In a few minutes it was dark.

"This is a good road," Chris said. "Maybe we can drive through the night. What do you think?"

I was not sure that it was a good idea, but we had no alternative. "Okay," I said, "but as soon as either of us gets sleepy, we find a hotel. Where there is a road, there's sure to be a hotel."

The moonless night closed tightly around the headlights and the monotonous flash of the phone poles was all that we saw for hours. To keep each other awake we talked about anything and everything. In desperation, we even tried to get an argument going, but the smooth purr of the Citroën lulled us until, suddenly, in the distance appeared a white light. It was too bright to be a farmhouse. As we watched, it rushed towards us, then, with a roar and many flashes of light, it passed. It was an express train, and through the windows we caught glimpses of dining tables and made up sleeping compartments.

It was too much for us. When we reached the next town, Beaufort West, we made straight for the hotel, where, within minutes we had Benjamin and the car settled for the night. Then we dashed into the dining room. It was very late, but a bull-like roar from Chris brought swift action, and soon we were wolfing down our first meal since breakfast. If the bartender thought he was going to have trouble with us that night, he was quite mistaken. All we wanted were hot baths and comfortable beds.

Day 28

A quick breakfast, and we had the car out of the garage before Benjamin had rubbed the sleep from his eyes. Beaufort West was a busy crossroads town, and, despite the early hour, the wide, dusty streets were already filled with farm trucks and station wagons. While the town looked like an important railway stop and service center for the sheep ranchers, Chris decided that it did not look like a likely market for his fancy leather products.

After a brief stop to check the car and fill the gas tank, we were once more out on the wide, flat plains. Within a few miles, some hump-backed hills appeared on the horizon, bald and red in the morning sun. They were a welcome sight that gave us a feeling of movement as the miles slowly passed. When we reached them, we saw that the soil itself was bright red. I suggested that the redness might be iron ore, and then we argued about setting up a steel industry in a region that had neither coal nor water. We argued about it all the way to the Three Sisters, where the road forked.

To our left, the road to Johannesburg went by way of Kimberley. This was a slightly longer route, so we chose the right fork, which went via Bloemfontein and would probably have a better surface. I had dearly wanted to visit Kimberley and see the diamond mines, but it would have taken more time and more gasoline, and we could not afford either. Fifty miles further north, we passed through Richmond, a small town that seemed to mark the end of the Great Karoo, then we were back on the high veldt, where, through the sharp, clear air, we could make out the mountains to the east. To the west, the land stretched endlessly.

Next, Hanover and Colesburg flashed by, and then we arrived at the Orange River. We stopped in the middle of the bridge and looked down at the river, which was shrunken to a trickle, although the tumbled rocks were evidence of its power during the flood season.

"That's a historic river," Chris said. "It starts up in the Drakensbergs and joins with the Vaal, just west of Kimberley. Then it goes out into the Kalahari Desert. It's the only major river south of the Congo that empties into the South Atlantic." He laughed, and added, "But some years it doesn't get that far. Just vanishes in the desert. I often think that somewhere under the Kalahari there must be an awful lot of water."

Across the bridge, we were in the Orange Free State, the center of Afrikaner nationalism, where all the towns seemed to have names that ended in *burg* ("city") or *fontein* ("fountain"), although, surprisingly, my map also showed a town named Westminster.

There were more vehicles on the road now, and more farms on the horizon, but it was still very open and almost treeless. We saw sheep and cattle and lonely farms set well back from the road in shelter belts of carefully planted trees. Now and then we also saw a burst of color as we passed some wildflowers. We also passed gates in the jackal fence (miles from any farm) and an occasional African sheepherder on a horse jogging slowly down the endless road. Erosion had carved the hills here, and some were fluted as delicately as a great cathedral, others were worn to needle-sharp pinnacles, and still others were flat-topped mesas with their multicolored strata gleaming in the sun.

When we stopped outside Philippolis for a quick snack, I noticed a tame springbok wandering around the garden. It struck me that this pretty little gazelle was the only game that I had seen in the Union, so I asked the manager of the hotel what hunting was like.

He was a short, weather-beaten man with a strong accent, and as he tossed some table scraps to the springbok, he said, "This little bugger can hop over a jackal fence as if it wasn't there. When I was a boy, we had to chase the damn things out of the garden, but now I have to drive all day and camp all night, just to put a bit of fresh meat on the table." He shook his head and looked at the animal quietly nibbling the scraps. "And they're not as big as they used to be, either. Too many week-end hunters."

Through Trompsburg, Edenburg, and Reddersburg we sped, and then we reached Bloemfontein. It was only four o'clock in the afternoon when we arrived, having covered more than 350 miles in good time, and we were singing the praises of the Citroën.

Bloemfontein, the capital of the Orange Free State, was a big, bustling city with a mixture of new, modern office buildings and solidly Victorian public buildings. I thought it was an attractive, well-kept city, and while Chris did some business before the shops all closed, I sat in the car and watched the stream of cars and the swarms of people squeezing on to the buses and hurrying in and out of the buildings. After so many long miles of emptiness, it was like looking at a busy anthill in the middle of a wide meadow.

The sun was setting as we left Bloemfontein. The great orange disc hung for a few minutes just above the crest of the road, then it slipped quickly below the horizon, dragging the purple shadows after it. In those few glorious minutes of sunset, while the light was in our eyes, we took the wrong road.

But we didn't discover our mistake until, half an hour later, the concrete suddenly ended in a bump and we found ourselves on a gravel road. I grabbed the map. "It looks like we're on the road to Kimberley," I said.

Chris looked too. Then he said, "Well, it will get us to Jo'burg, but it's going to add a few miles. Maybe a hundred."

Did the car have enough gas? We sat and debated whether or not to turn back, and then Chris laughed, and said, "I have a couple of good friends in Kimberley. I should be able to borrow a bit of money from somebody. Let's go on."

The region had seen no rain for many months, and the dust rose in huge yellow clouds. It spun from under the wheels and whirled in through the windows, but it was too hot to close them, so we three sat and slowly grew our own coats of fine dust.

Whenever another car approached, there was a mad scramble to wind up all the windows before it passed so we wouldn't receive additional dust. We crept along through the murk until we were out of the dust cloud, and at last we were back in bush country, where the thorn trees stood grey in the moonlight, the grass was dry and yellowed, and the night insects were gone or silent. Everything was waiting for the rain.

And then, about half way to Kimberley, the road suddenly seemed to get worse than usual. We got out to have a look at the tires. One was almost flat, so Benjamin was awakened from his uncomfortable nest in the back seat, and we changed the tire. While we were doing so, a car, enveloped in a cloud of dust, came down the road at high speed. We were parked on the road, and it was clear that the oncoming driver would not see our tail lights in time, so Chris, Benjamin, and I ran towards the approaching car, waving our arms wildly. Fortunately, the driver was awake and slammed on his brakes and screeched to a stop.

"Good God, man," he said as he got out of his car "The sight of you three, all covered in dust, coming out of the dark, waving your arms like crazy men, would make anybody stop. Nearly gave me a heart attack!" He reached for his water bag, which was hanging from his front bumper. "Here, have a drink. You all look like you need it."

After that, at reduced speed, favoring the spare tire, watching for pot holes, and with our fingers crossed, we limped into Kimberley. Although the hotels were crowded, we found rooms. After seeing Benjamin settled, we headed for much-needed baths and supper. I could have gone straight to bed after supper, but Chris phoned a friend he had not seen in a long time and then we drove slowly around the dark streets until we found the friend's house.

He was an old army friend of Chris, who said he now regretted having left the service and was considering re-enlisting. We sat on the friend's front porch, drinking beer and talking about service life and relaxing in the cool dark. Our host was an expert on South African military history as far back as the Dutch pikemen who landed with Van Riebeeck in the 17th century. I learned a lot during that conversation.

"This modern word 'commando' is not modern at all," the historian told us. "The settlers could not afford a standing army. They simply grabbed their muskets and formed a militia whenever there was danger. The Americans called them Minutemen. When the Boers fought the English, it was the same, but instead of forming regiments, they worked as small, highly mobile groups called *Kommandos*. They were highly effective. The commandos were democratic, and they voted their officers in, or out." Hearing this last bit of information, we toasted commando democracy.

I also learned that nearly every white male in the Union had done some military service and that practically every school included rifle practice as part of its curriculum. Most women, too, could handle a rifle or shotgun in an emergency. It was just part of the culture.

"We're not gun-crazy, like the Yanks," the historian said with a laugh. "There is no cowboy gun-slinger mythology here, and since the blacks are not allowed to have guns, there is little gun crime." He paused and added, "But I'd bet you all the money in your pocket, that there is a weapon of some type in every house on this street."

This mention of money gave Chris an opportunity to explain our predicament. Our host immediately went into the house and returned with a small bundle of notes. "That should get you safely home," he said, "and you can pay me back next time I'm in the big city."

With enough to pay the hotel bill, fix the tire, and buy gasoline, we felt like celebrating.

Day 29

In the daylight, I could see that Kimberley was a sprawling city of low level buildings and the hot, dusty, casual look of an overgrown mining town, which it was. After Chris and Benjamin went off to work, I spent the morning in a garage getting the tire repaired and put back on the car. Although we had no time for an extended visit or a tour of the diamond company showrooms, I refused to go any further until I had at least seen the Big Hole. Chris admitted that he had never seen it, either, so he agreed.

It was well worth the time.

We drove some distance out of the city, parked, and walked up a slope to some small buildings. We soon found ourselves standing at a wooden railing at the very edge of an immense crater that was partly filled by a lake of jet black water. The lip of the crater curved away to form an almost perfect circle over a mile in circumference, and the city of Kimberley seemed to perch precariously on the other side.

The sides of the great hole, which is also known as the

Kimberley Mine, dropped straight down for well over a thousand feet to the surface of the dark water below. We stood in silent amazement at the vastness of it until Chris eventually broke the silence.

"God," he said, "you mean to say this was all dug by hand? By men?"

Victoria Falls had astonished me by its strength and thunder. It was a live and violent thing. The Big Hole at Kimberley awed me by its size and silence and its brooding sense of history.

When diamonds were first discovered, in 1871, thousands of men poured in from all over the world to scratch the magic stones from the dry earth. They soon turned the little hill into a hole, and working with spades, buckets, and ropes, they clawed their way hundreds of feet down until the danger of falling rock became too great. But the blue clay still held a fortune in diamonds, so they started digging a shaft alongside the hole. The mining continued until the hole reached an astonishing depth of 4,000 feet. When the hole was abandoned to rising waters in 1914, it had yielded over three tons of diamonds valued at fifteen million carats.

The Big Hole killed innumerable nameless men, and made the fortunes of a few. The flamboyant late 19th–century entrepreneur Barney Barnato was one, Alfred Beit (whose bridge I had crossed a month ago) was another, and Cecil Rhodes was yet another. Rhodes began by buying out small mining claims until he had enough in 1888 to establish the De Beers Consolidated Mines Limited, which was named after the farmer who had owned the land on which an 83-carat diamond was found. From there, and with astonishing daring, he took control of the entire diamond mining industry. The Genius of Kimberley next used his fortune to get into South African politics with his British South Africa Company and the conquest of Rhodesia, and thence into international politics. A hundred years after the first diamond was discovered, the region still produces diamonds from other mines and De Beers still controls much of the diamond industry.

While we were standing at the rail, I had the quite natural urge to throw a stone into the lake below. But perhaps the De Beers Mining Company, which owns the Big Hole had anticipated my wish, and the wish, no doubt, of every other visitor. The ground was bare. The entire area had been swept clean and every stone of any size had been carefully removed. But then, a black man came up the slope pushing a wheel barrow full of stones. With a wide smile, he offered to sell us some.

"Now that," said Chris, "is what I call enterprising."

We bought a rock.

The hole was so deep that after Chris threw the rock over the lip, we had to wait a long time before there came a long rumbling boom from out of the depths, the echo of the splash, but when we looked down we could see not even a ripple.

Behind us was a notice board and an illustration that showed an even more astonishing fact. We were looking at only one third of the hole! Two thirds of it was under water. In the small, but excellent museum nearby, we saw photos of the swarms of men struggling in the dirt at the bottom of a huge pit under a dense spider web of ropes and pulleys. There were thousands of worn and filthy men, all struggling to find that tiny bit of ancient crystallized carbon, first cousin to common coal, the *diamond.*

In the museum were also souvenirs of the Boer War, when, aided by a four-inch gun made in the De Beers foundry, Kimberley had withstood a five-month siege. The Boer War display irritated Chris.

"You realize, of course, that Kimberley was part of the Orange Free State," he said. "It was stolen by the English." I must have looked surprised, because he took me to a wall map in the museum and said, "The Orange Free State lies between the Orange River and the Vaal River. For years, nobody cared a damn about this chunk of useless bush. But when diamonds were discovered, the English produced some unknown tribal chief to claim the land. It was a farce and everybody knew it, but it made no difference. The Cape annexed it."

Sure enough, the Orange and the Vaal rivers met well to the west of the city and the Cape-Orange border was just to the east of the city. The little triangle of land between the rivers is, or was, clearly a part of the Orange Republic.

Chapter Twenty-One: Kimberley to Johannesburg

Day 29 (continued)

From the Mine Museum, our way lay straight to Johannesburg. Chris put his foot down. Parts of the road were still rough gravel, but now that she was back up on the high plateau, the Citroën behaved beautifully and the miles flashed by. We crossed the Vaal River, which was sadly shrunken so we did not stop, although 200 miles later, we did stop at Potchefstroom to wash down the dust. Potchefstroom was a pretty little town in a prosperous-looking farming area where spring planting had already begun.

"This is the oldest town in the Transvaal," Chris informed me. "It was founded by the <u>Voortrekker</u> leader, Andries Potgeiter, some time in the 1830s."

The bar we chose to stop at had only one other customer, the salesman for a brewery who insisted that we have free beers. We had not eaten since breakfast, but we could not very well ignore such a kind offer, so we had a couple as we wolfed down some hot meat pies. The bar began to fill up quickly, and it looked as if there was going to be quite a party, so we reluctantly slipped out and headed, once again, for Johannesburg.

We were in the suburbs of the Golden City in record time, having covered about 300 miles in slightly over five hours. As we passed one of the gold mines, Chris gestured towards it and yelled, "Gold, man, Gold!" His pride in his city had not been reduced by his visit to Cape Town. In fact, it seemed to have increased. It was dark by the time we reached the city center and I thought we would go to his parents' house where, he had assured me, I would be welcome. But he had other ideas.

For what seemed like hours, he drove up and down the streets of Johannesburg, showing me buildings that had not been there a few months before. He also stopped frequently so that I could admire new apartment blocks or office buildings and he even dragged me into lobbies so that I could admire the interiors and into patios and gardens to prove that all was not just steel and concrete.

"Just think," he said, more than once, "less than a hundred years ago, this was just useless scrub. Now we have a gorgeous city with every modern convenience, from race tracks to a philharmonic orchestra." He stamped his foot on the ground. "And the gold seam stretches for seventy miles!"

His enthusiasm was extraordinary, and I was getting a wonderful guided tour, but it was also getting late, so I hinted that I should be looking for a hotel.

"Hotel?" he said. "I told you. You'll come home with me. We have a guest room. Mother will be pleased to see you." That sounded very good to me, and I had a momentary vision of a home cooked meal that vanished abruptly when he added, "But there's no rush. I have some friends who live close by...."

These friends proved to be a newly married couple living in a penthouse apartment. Both of them worked and were making good money and their standard of living was obviously very high. They were glad to see Chris and made me welcome and quickly produced snacks and tasty tidbits. A few phone calls soon produced more friends of Chris. Many of the new arrivals brought food and wine, so it was a lively crowd which eventually overflowed onto the apartment's wide balcony with its spectacular view of the city.

The talk was about apartments and cars, theaters and night-clubs, but not a word about politics or international problems. It was midnight before we knew it. Leaving the party just as it was getting noisy, we dashed off to Chris' home.

I could recognize nothing in the dark until we stopped in a large, three-car garage and Chris told me to follow him and not make a sound. Benjamin, who had been fast asleep in the back seat all this time, slipped away into the dark. As silently as pos-sible, Chris and I groped our way along a wide veranda and down a passage and, without putting on the lights, found our rooms. After a hurried wash, I tumbled into a soft bed and was soon fast asleep.

Day 30

I woke to the thought that I had less than two days to hitchhike the nearly 600 miles back to camp. Quite obviously, this would be impossible; so I decided to stop worrying, do my best, and hope that some fast talking at the other end would keep me out of serious trouble. Besides, I had come to see South Africa and meet people and I intended to do just that. It had been a stroke of incredible luck to meet up with Chris and see so many places in his company. All his many friends had been interesting people, but they were mostly white, middle-class, white-collar Anglo-Saxons with quite similar backgrounds. It was time, I thought, to get back on the road and meet other South African people.

After I showered and dressed, a rather subdued Chris led me down more cool passages and into an immense room that seemed to contain little more than a huge stone fireplace and an even larger curved settee that could have seated a dozen people. There were no pictures on the walls and no decorations except a tall vase of ornamental branches in the far corner. Everything was white. The fireplace, the settee, the thick carpet, even the vase was white. One entire wall was huge glass windows that offered a spectacular view over a gently sloping valley of wildly untouched grass and bushes and dark thorn trees.

I finally noticed a figure sitting in the far corner of the settee. This was Chris's mother, a young-looking middle-aged woman, slim and dressed in expensive cashmere and slacks. She greeted me politely but showed no interest in me or our travels, though she did invite me to join them for an early lunch. It was a rather strained affair, however, and, after a few minutes, I gave up trying to make small talk because it was obvious that there was serious friction between mother and son and they were only being polite because a guest was present. As soon as the meal was over, Chris hustled me back to the car.

Benjamin had taken all the cases, including mine, out of the Citroën and had vacuumed and washed it.

"Well," I said, "I suppose it's time to get back on the road. With a bit of luck, I could reach Pretoria by sunset."

But Chris was horrified. "You can't see Jo'burg in one evening," he said, "It took you nearly a week to see Cape Town." And with that, he hustled me into the car.

By daylight, I learned that his house was far out in a very affluent suburb. Through the trees, I glimpsed swimming pools, tennis courts, horse stables, and other very large houses in expensively manicured grounds. Over everything hung an air of peace and luxurious quiet.

A few minutes on an excellent road brought us back into the crowds and noise of the big city, and there, in the busiest part of town, the engine stopped. After all the rough treatment the Citroën had received in the past few weeks, I was not surprised. We pushed it to the side of the road and began to trace the problem. It took us two hours to find a clogged fuel pump, and we accumulated quite a collection of small children who insisted on playing with the various bits and pieces that we removed. By the time we had cleaned up and were ready to go again, much of the day had been wasted and there was little we could do except take a hurried tour of the more interesting parts of the city.

We were surprisingly close to the heart of the city when we stopped at one of the gold mines. We could just see the tops of the machinery and buildings hidden by the high steel fence, but it was easy to hear the dull roar of conveyor belts and wheels, and the air smelled of oil and dust. We were politely told at the office that all tours had to be booked one week in advance. Disappointed, we drove on to where we could see the mine's huge white dump. This was a small mountain of poisoned white sand, its sides completely bare of even the hardiest little weed. There was a faint blur along its flattened top where a slight breeze was disturbing the powder.

"If you could think of a use for all that stuff," Chris said, "you'd be a rich man and the city would give you a gold medal."

I suggested some ideas but they had all been tried, and discarded.

Near one of the mines was a soccer stadium, around which the streets were packed with black mine workers dressed in their best clothes. As we inched through the crowd, we saw that there were also quite a few women and some white people, too.

"Oh damn!" Chris exclaimed. "You know what we just missed? Tribal dancing! Every month, the mines organize tribal dancing. They say it's quite a sight."

Sure enough, as we watched, groups of men in various colorful tribal costumes came out the gate, their faces shining with sweat. They were soon swallowed up in a crowd of laughing, celebrating friends.

"Man, it's a shame we missed that," Chris said, "but I've just remembered something else I heard about that should be interesting."

He drove for a few minutes until we came to a busy street lined with little cafes and shops selling cheap tourist souvenirs. Then we found a parking space and walked to an arcade where the main building advertised *All The Gold You Can Carry! Absolutely Free!* We bought tickets and walked down a dark passage that led to a large, almost bare room, in the center of which, on the concrete floor, stood a steel box with a rope fastened to its lid. The rope led up to a pulley, and the other end was held by a huge white security guard standing in the corner. The other corners of the room also held security guards just as big and well muscled.

"Wouldn't like to meet them on the rugby field," Chris whispered.

When there was a good crowd, the door was closed and a sharply dressed little man gave his talk, rattling it off as if he had given it a thousand times. Then the guard pulled the rope and the box lifted to reveal an ingot of pure gold gleaming under the bright spotlight, and lying flat on the floor. The ingot was a little over a foot long and a little under a foot high, and its sides tapered just slightly, so that it would leave the mold easily when it cooled. While everybody stared at the gold, the little man assured us that it was absolutely pure gold and that we could just pick it up and walk away with it. We would not be stopped, he added; in fact the four huge guards would escort us to the nearest bank.

"So what's the catch?" Chris asked.

The little man grabbed him by the arm, led him to the ingot, and said, "Pick it up, sir. Just pick it up and it's yours."

Chris was tall and broad shouldered, clearly a strong young man. He reached down and grasped the gold with two hands and tried to lift it. His fingers slipped up and off the metal. He rubbed his hands on his trousers and tried again, and failed again, so he rubbed his fingertips on the bare concrete floor and made a third attempt. Again he failed. Now the little man called to the next customer to try his hand at walking off with an ingot of gold. When he also failed, the little man slipped a shovel under the ingot and lifted it enough for us to see that it was not glued or bolted to the ground. When it was my turn, I took a good firm grip with my fingers, squeezed as hard as I could and, using my knees, tried to lift it straight up. My fingers slipped smoothly over the gold and I was left clutching stale air. When everybody in the audience, even the women, had had a try, we filed out.

"Clever! Bloody clever!" Chris said. "There's just enough slope on the metal so you can't get a grip. The bottom has been smoothed so flat, you can't get your fingers under it, and the ingot is bigger than a regular one, so it's much too heavy to lift with only your finger tips." He laughed and added, "Every tourist who tries just adds more polish to the gold and makes it even more slippery." With that, he found a public telephone, dialed yet another friend, and invited himself to tea.

These new friends were another nice couple, though not as young and not as rich as last night's couple. As we drank tea and nibbled biscuits, the trouble between Chris and his mother came tumbling out.

"She just doesn't like the idea that her son is a traveling salesman." he said, rather sadly. "She wants me to get married and settle down at a nice job in a bank or something."

Our hosts sympathized and agreed that Chris was not the type to sit in an office. I gathered that he had been given the best education that money could buy and had excelled in a number of sports and had done his military service. He was a very likeable young man, a natural salesman who had made countless friends all across the land. He liked the freedom and the constant traveling.

There was not much else to say on that topic, so our host switched the subject to Rhodesia. To most South Africans, Rhodesia was rather like Canada is to citizens of the United States. It lies to the north and is large but thinly populated. It is culturally similar and is economically close, but it is still a foreign country.

To Chris's horror, his friends said they were toying with the idea of leaving Johannesburg for Rhodesia to maybe homestead a little farm or start a business in some little town. The ancient urge to pioneer and to challenge the wilderness had struck both of them.

"We are still young and healthy," the wife said. "It would be a fantastic experience," the husband added.

"You're a couple of raving idiots," Chris said. I did not offer an opinion.

As if by magic, other people began to arrive and soon there was quite a party going on. They were all apartment dwellers and none of them had black servants of any kind. What struck me was the extraordinary gulf between their lives and the lives of the black citizens of the huge city. Almost all of these people could go weeks without more than the minimum contact with a black person. Neither in school nor at work, nor in transportation, or entertainment or home life did they have more than the briefest contact with anybody who was not white. Some had parents who had homes in the suburbs. They had servants, but nearly everybody agreed that, with all the rules and regulations, servants were not worth the trouble.

There was no television in South Africa at that time, so somebody turned on the radio to a popular comedy show. It featured a man with an outlandish Afrikaans accent and a bumbling rural policeman. Many in the room were of Dutch descent, including Chris, but they roared with laughter along with the others and it was clear that the butt of the jokes was not the blacks or the Indians, but the Afrikaner country bumpkin. My impression was that the old antagonism between the Dutch and the English was rapidly vanishing and being replaced by the more universal city dweller-country

dweller conflict. When somebody switched the radio to an Afrikaans station, we listened to lively, foot-tapping, accordion music.
It was fun for a while, but I soon felt that, like most country music,
a little went a long way. As any good guest should, I offered to help
with the dishes and, to my surprise, I ended the evening with an
apron around my waist. At midnight, we slipped out and drove to
Chris's home.

Chapter Twenty-Two: Johannesburg to Bulawayo

Day 31

We both slept late and, just before noon, I met Chris's father. He was a solidly built man, an engineer at one of the gold mines, who spoke very little and asked no questions. He shared his wife's opinion of traveling salesmen, and so when Chris soon vanished, I spent a reasonably pleasant hour helping his father repair a water pump.

There was an air of Sunday formality about lunch. As we sedately discussed the building boom and property values, I learned that the architect who had designed the house had insisted on wooden shingles for the roof, but because of its location, the insurance companies had flatly refused to insure it for fire. When I suggested fireproof shingles, or tiles, the lady of the house coldly rejected the idea. It was a sad meal for me because I had to leave right away. So we drank a glass of wine and Chris's parents wished me luck.

Chris and I had been good friends for three weeks by now. After lunch, he drove me out to the main Pretoria road, and then he sat in the parked car to watch. When nobody stopped in the first twenty minutes, he came across the road, swearing at his fellow countrymen, and began to help me wave down cars. His method was not quite what I would have used, and I watched in horror as cars swerved inches away from his wildly waving arms. One or two drivers slowed just long enough to swear at him. In the end, I persuaded him to get back into his car and let me do it my way. Within minutes, I got a lift from a couple of students on their way to Pretoria and, with a wave to Chris, was on my way again.

The trip to Pretoria seemed to take only minutes. The students dropped me near a bus stop, where I could get a bus out of town. I got off the bus near the top of a small hill where some trees offered shade and the traffic was good. Behind me, I could see the city with its long, tree-shaded boulevards spread out in the hollow of the hills; ahead of me, the road vanished in the heat haze. There was certainly a great deal of traffic, but it was all Sunday traffic and the cars were either full or just going a short distance. In the late afternoon, all Pretoria seemed to be on the road, but nobody stopped.

The sun went down and a refreshing breeze sprang up, but still nobody stopped for me. When it was dark, I walked back to the bus stop, got on another bus, and got off at the first hotel I came to. It was very old and quite gloomy. The chairs in the lobby held silent old men wearing sharply pointed moustaches and uncomfortable suits and a few thin women in black with bad tempers. After a solemn dinner, I strolled around town for a bit and mingled with the family groups, all dressed in their Sunday best and walking up and down the boulevards after evening service.

The most important church in South Africa at the time was the Dutch Reformed Church. This is a powerful and conservative force, especially in the Orange Free State and the Transvaal, and the Calvinist DRC made sure that Sunday remained a day of worship and *only* of worship. Almost everything was shut on Sunday, and public services were reduced to the minimum. Although the church has never frowned on Sunday sports, I still found Sunday in Pretoria deader than an English Sunday and went to bed early.

Day 32

When I went to pay the hotel bill, I received a wonderful surprise. I had taken out my last remaining ten pound note, a brand new note, all crisp and fresh looking, and was holding it in my hand wondering just how I was going to make it last, when I found that I was actually holding two brand-new notes stuck together. Feeling like an angel had showered me in gold coins, I smiled at everybody all the way to the bus stop. My bad luck had changed to good, and I was hardly off the bus when I got a short lift of about five miles. The next car to stop held a pair of elderly ladies who only wanted to check that they were on the right road. They were going all the way to Bulawayo, but insisted that they had no room for a passenger. Almost immediately after they had gone, I got a lift to Warmbad. On the way, we passed the little old ladies chugging along at a sedate pace. It was hot and dusty, and by the time I had walked to the far end of Warmbad, the little old ladies had passed me again. Sitting in the shade, on a stone wall, I watched the middle aged and more than slightly overweight visitors to the public baths after which the city was named. They all seemed to look exactly like the visitors to hot springs and sulphur baths that I had seen in Germany. The next car to stop was driven by a very fat man who smoked powerful cigars with the windows closed. He was a Rhodesian businessman, but he was stopping for a day or two at Pietersburg. I was not too unhappy when he dropped me off.

I stood in the open air, gulping down the sweet breeze, then headed for the shade of some trees. Before I got there, two motorcycle policemen drove up and hid under the trees, waiting for speeders. Not knowing the local regulations regarding hitchhiking, I played it safe and sat in the shade for half an hour and watched them at work. They caught eight speeders, then, smiling happily, roared off down the road. When I got back to the roadside, I found that another hitchhiker had arrived on the scene. He was a few yards down the road from me, so I stood and watched him. He soon stopped a small van. The vehicle had been moving fast, so it pulled up right in front of me and I jumped quickly into the back while the other hitchhiker was getting into the front seat. The driver took it for granted that we were together, and the whole one hundred miles to Louis Trichardt, I crouched in the back. It was hot and uncomfortable, but I could peer out of the small window. I gave a wave to the little old ladies as I overtook them once again.

By the time we reached Louis Trichardt, the oppressive heat had conjured up black rain clouds, and I had hardly scrambled out of the van and eased my cramped joints when it began to rain. Many of the cars I now saw had Rhodesian license plates, so I worked my way through the town, thumbing everything that moved, but with no success. As the sun set, the clouds dropped lower and the tiny raindrops turned into huge drops the size of silver dollars. I hurried to the hotel,

After dinner, I sat on the veranda, savoring the smell of rain after a hot and dusty day and watching the water pour off the tin roofs and glinting on the dark leaves. Next to me sat a salesman cleaning a small hand gun.

"I'm in jewelry," he said. "Have been for years, and, you know, I have never had to use this gun. Not once. But she's a beautiful little thing and I feel better having her in my pocket."

He was in a talkative mood and told me about the early days in his business. "When I first started, I was in cloth and my territory was Zululand. Most of the roads were actually river beds. One day, I got caught in a flash flood. In a couple of minutes the water was up to the seats of my car. I spent a long, cold, night sitting on the back of the seat with my head pressed up against the roof and my legs in the water, praying that it wasn't going to get any higher. Next morning, I got out and walked about five miles to the nearest village where I borrowed a couple of bullocks to pull the car out. The whole village helped. They thought it was a lot of fun and refused to take money. Said it wasn't any use to them. What they did want were my cloth samples. Every scrap of cloth vanished in five minutes, and it took me the rest of the day to get that car running again. Then I had to go all the way back to Durban to get more samples."

Over a couple of beers he described the southwest around Walvis Bay as the worst desert in the world. "The great Namib Desert is the hottest, driest, and loneliest place in the world," he said, "but it has diamonds! Now getting in there and getting out of there is another question. They don't call it The Skeleton Coast for nothing."

Despite all that I had read to the contrary, he insisted that a man could walk along the beach and pick up diamonds with his bare hands and end the day with his pockets full. It was a tale that

I had heard many times in my travels, so I changed the subject to the wide variety of flowers and flowering trees I had seen. He was genuinely sorry that I had not arrived at the height of the season, but he was immensely pleased that I had managed to find a couple of protea growing wild and blooming.

That night I slept to the sound of rain drumming on the roof and hoped that it would not last too long.

Day 33

The rain let up a little the next morning, but dark clouds still threatened. I got a lift from a businessman returning to Messina who didn't talk much, preferring to concentrate on his driving as we crawled slowly through the damp fog over the Zoutpansberg range, where the lovely scenery was hidden and the rocks dripped grey. Out on the plain again, we picked up a young man whose car had broken down during the night. We were the only car he had seen since midnight, and he was in need of a good cup of hot coffee, so we stopped at the first garage we came to, and the businessman persuaded the owner to brew a pot of coffee while he was finding the needed spare part. Then, with perfectly casual charity, the businessman offered to take the young man back to his car and help him fix it.

Messina was a mining town where the shops and houses were overshadowed by the tangle of buildings and machinery and the great dump. In the grey light, the baobab trees looked even more fantastic than the ones I'd seen a month ago, but soon the clouds parted, the sun came out, and I was forced to shelter from the steaming sun under one of those giants.

After an hour, I got a lift to the border from the customs officer. When he heard where I was from and where I had been he said, "Well, they'll be glad to see you back." I asked who would be glad, and he said, "The RAF. They probably keep it very quiet, but every now and then one of you chaps goes down to Durban on holiday, likes the place, meets a pretty girl, and decides to stay. Can't say that I blame them. It's a thousand times nicer than some ugly city in England, and you can't beat the weather."

I was surprised and said, "But what about the police and the immigration people?"

He laughed. "There's no extradition and we can always use another white man if he has some useful skill. The authorities turn a blind eye, and the men soon blend in and vanish."

After he dropped me outside his office, I walked across the bridge to the Rhodesian side with no problems. But there I was stuck. In the next three hours, only four cars passed me. I spent most of that time watching a man making bricks with a wooden mold. He squatted by a small stream and packed mud into the molds, then carefully tapped the bricks out of the molds and carefully set them in the sun, where they were soon hard enough to stack onto a pile. Here, I realized, under the African sun, bricks were being made using a method that was old when Babylon was young, a method I have since seen used in many different lands far from the banks of the Limpopo.

Late in the afternoon, a jeep driven by a pair of cattle ranchers in bush hats and high leather boots stopped for me. I was so glad to get a lift that I didn't ask them how far they were going. About five miles up the road, we stopped for another hitchhiker, then, after barely twenty miles, the ranchers turned off into the bush. They were gone with a wave, and we were left standing in the wilderness on a very empty road.

The other hitchhiker told me that he had been driving to Messina during the night and had fallen asleep at the wheel. It had only been for a moment, but it was long enough to hit a phone pole and slide into the ditch, where he had remained all night until a car arrived and towed him to a garage. "My car is out of commission for at least a week," he said, "and I have to get back to Bulawayo, so I hitched a lift to the border. This last five miles I did on the back of a bullock cart!"

I pointed out that the next bit of civilization was at least seventy miles away and that, even if the road was smooth, it would take twenty-four hours to walk it. So we both sat down in the shade at the side of the road and waited.

After an hour we looked at the map again. "Our best bet," I said, "is to head on back to Beitbridge and try again tomorrow morning."

"But that's going back at least twenty miles," he protested. We looked at the map again, and he said, "There's a place called Musunga just up the road. It doesn't seem to be very big, but it's better than nothing."

So we picked up our bags and began to walk. The bush was quite thick and there was nothing to be seen except a few frightened cattle that took one look at us and vanished into the undergrowth. It grew dark, and we kept our eyes open in vain for the glimmer of firelight from a native kraal in the bush. A cool wind sprang up and clouds drifted across the moon, and still no vehicle came, so we walked faster to keep warm and prayed that it would not rain. Whenever we stopped for a rest, we peered into the forest looking for a large tree to shelter under in case it did decide to rain, but there was nothing that offered real protection.

About eight o'clock, we came to a large culvert that ran under the road. It was over three feet high and perfectly dry, at least for the moment. It looked as if this would have to be our shelter for the night so, while he inspected it for snakes, I groped around in the dark for dry twigs to start a fire.

"Well, it's not the Ritz," I said as I searched my pockets for matches, "but it's better than nothing."

He was not happy with the arrangement, so just to cheer him up, I told him of some of the strange places I had slept in while hitchhiking around Europe. "One night, in Austria, I sneaked into a barn and slept in a pile of hay. I woke next morning to find that I had spent the night with the breed bull! He was the biggest, blackest beast I had ever seen." Somehow, this story did not cheer him up.

Just as I finished, we heard the sound of a car and saw headlights coming north. Determined not to let it pass, we stood across the road and forced the startled driver to stop. He was extremely suspicious and kept the windows up and the engine racing while we introduced ourselves. Even after he allowed us into his car, the poor man was quite nervous and my hitchhiking friend made matters worse by asking if he had a gun. By his hesitation, I guessed that he did not, but he claimed that he did, so I promptly complimented him on his wisdom and changed the subject,

Our new host had also been driving all night and was afraid of falling asleep. His radio was not working, so he had spent the last few hours singing all the songs and hymns that he could remember. His repertoire left much to be desired, but we were only too happy to sing along. We sped through night singing a terrible mixture of sacred and profane songs in even more terrible harmony.

We were somewhere in the middle of "Alouette" for at least the third time when we rounded a corner and the headlights swept across a large herd of springbok crossing the road. They were small, light brown creatures with smoothly gleaming coats and curved horns. They panicked as the car approached. For the next few moments, the air was full of gracefully flying animals, leaping over the road in great soaring curves. Silently, and quite effortlessly, they sprang from one shoulder of the road, sailing like ballet dancers to the other shoulder, where they landed on four feet, then, with no apparent effort, rose again in another *grand jeté* and vanished into the bush. We sat there, astonished by the grace and beauty that had appeared out of the night. Then our host said, "And to think some people hunt them for fun."

Masunga turned out to be a cluster of thatched huts in a clearing and nothing else. But a couple more hours brought us to a hotel sitting by itself in the wilderness. There was no other building nearby, just a gas pump and a hotel where our maps said no hotel ought to be. It was not a mirage so, with a prayer to whatever saint watches over careless hitchhikers, we all checked in and headed for the dining room. Later, with a square meal under our belts, we sat on the veranda, listening to the crickets and watching the moon sliding in and out of the clouds. Our host explained that he was heading for Bulawayo and we were quite welcome to a ride, but he was selling the car and would take any reasonable offer he got between the hotel and Bulawayo. We agreed to take the chance and went happily to bed. It was a pleasure to lie between clean white sheets and think about the insects and other, much larger, creatures that must creep into culverts at night.

A few weeks later, I read about a woodcutter who was attacked one evening by a leopard. The brute leaped at the man, but he stepped aside and brained it with the axe he was carrying. It measured out as the largest leopard ever seen in that district, which was very close to where we had almost spent the night in a culvert.

Day 34

At six o'clock, I was off with my companions on the last lap of my African odyssey. The mist was still floating across the road in broad streamers and the bush was wet with dew, but the air was clean and fresh, and it was very quiet. We had a quick coffee and toast at West Nicholson, then pressed on to Gwanda, where our host met a man who showed keen interest in the car. So we said goodbye to him and took to the road again. In a short while, the traffic from Beitbridge began to pass us, and we were soon picked up by a man who was only too pleased to give us a lift. He was a cheerful, red-faced, clothing store owner who laughed uproariously when we described our adventure in the culvert the night before. He was a city man and his parents had been city people who came from some big English city whose name he couldn't remember. All he knew about the bush was the rough on the golf course.

"Hunting! Safaris! Great for those who like that sort of thing," he rumbled. "I wouldn't be seen dead where there isn't electricity and hot running water in nice chrome taps." Eager to be back in civilization, he drove as fast as the frequent detours would allow.

In a surprisingly short time, we were in the suburbs of Bulawayo. Our host dropped me off near my cousins' house, where a pot of tea was soon brewing. They had heard from my uncle and were anxious about me. They were also fascinated to hear about all the places I had been, but I was, alas, pressed for time. Rather than take the bus into the city, I hitched a ride in a builder's truck on the theory that I might as well finish my ride in style.

A haircut and shampoo later, I was ready to face the military police. The bus back to camp, with its wooden seats, was still the worst vehicle I had ridden in so far. Then I was at the gate. With carefully rehearsed nonchalance, I handed my leave pass to the corporal on duty.

Next day, I was charged with being absent without leave for three days and was marched into the adjutant's office. The adjutant was away on leave, and the officer given the chore of handling the matter was very new and very young. I guessed that he had only just arrived from England. He knew absolutely nothing about Rhodesia or South Africa. Never at a loss for words, I soon had him thoroughly confused about distances and dates. He couldn't understand why I had hitchhiked from Johannesburg when his wall map showed a perfectly good railway line.

"You mean you can't get there from here?" he asked.

"No, sir," I replied. "I actually…I got back faster by hitchhiking. It's only about 500 miles."

He stared again at the map and then said, "Well. Yes. That's good. But you were late getting back. Three days' loss of pay. Dismissed."

Post Script

Two months later, along with three dozen other servicemen who were being shipped back to England, I was on the train to Cape Town. It was a hot and boring trip through the eastern edge of the Kalahari Desert with only quick glimpses of Mafeking and Kimberley. Eventually we reached Cape Town and were allowed one day to see the sights before boarding one of the boats of the Union-Castle line. On our way back to England, there was one short stop at the delightful island of Madeira, then we sailed into the cold and rain of England.

At a depressingly ugly camp in the north of England, we handed in our uniforms and were given our official discharge papers and a one-way railway ticket. There was no ceremony or final parade. Nobody even said, "Thank you." We got on the bus to the railway station and each of us went our separate ways.

I lost touch over the years with my relatives in Rhodesia and South Africa after I emigrated to North America and concentrated my travels on Latin America. I wandered everywhere between Mexico City and Cape Horn, but except for a visit to Egypt in 1990 to gaze in awe at the ancient monuments, I have never been back to Africa.

But great changes have occurred on that vast continent. Between 1955 and 1959, the Rhodesians built one of the world's largest dams across the Zambezi River at Kariba, creating a lake 175 miles long. The power is shared by Zambia and Zimbabwe. About ten years later, the Portuguese built a similarly enormous dam across the Zambezi at Kahora Basa, upriver from Tete. This dam produces more power than Mozambique can use, so most of it is sold to South Africa over power lines that extend for 870 miles.

The sleepy little town of Tete is sleepy no more. Enormous coal deposits have been uncovered in the area and a modern bridge now spans the mighty Zambezi. The north shore, where I was stranded in the bush for a couple of days in 1952, has become a sprawling shanty town larger than Tete and populated by emigrants from Malawi and Zimbabwe. The coal is exported by rail to Beira, and the infamous road from Mtoko has become a busy but still unpaved highway.

The missing link in the rail line from Bulawayo to Beitbridge was finally built by a private company in 1999 and has proved very profitable. A flood control dam has been built across the Limpopo River east of Beitbridge and a new road bridge has been completed. The old bridge is now used as a railway bridge. The little village has grown into a busy border town famous for its traffic jams.

Diamonds have been discovered at Marange near Umtali in the eastern hills, and the resulting diamond rush has led to official corruption, a high crime rate, and serious ecological damage.

Everywhere, restrictions on movement and residence have been lifted and people have moved from the countryside to the urban areas, which have all grown very large and often dangerous. The Kibera slum in Nairobi is one of the largest slums in Africa.

In South Africa, an excellent system of roads has been built, but it bypasses some of the smaller town I visited. Also, quite a few of the old town names have been Africanized. Elizabethville, for example, has been renamed Lubumbashi. The Congo has likewise seen great changes. Constant war and insurrection have made the old routes to the Atlantic unreliable. Road and rail routes through Zambia are more attractive. The rail line from Lubumbashi into Zambia is now busy, and the lonely road I traveled on has become a busy highway through crowded border towns. Mokambo, the tiny place where I spent a whole fruitless day, is now a small town with its very own railway station.

Appendix One
Colonies and Protectorates

Not every piece of African land taken by the British immediately became a colony. Some lands, like British Somaliland, were protectorates. Declaring a land a protectorate was simply a useful way a great European power could make sure no other great European power could claim that territory. British control over its protectorates was minimal. Trade was encouraged, but immigration was not encouraged. If, however, the territory proved to be of value, then the protectorate would become a colony, and the British government would take control of the economy and allow immigration.

Governmental power was often given to a chartered company, such as the British South Africa Company (established by Cecil Rhodes and chartered in 1889) or the British East Africa Company (created after the Berlin Treaty of 1885 and led by William Mackinnon). These chartered companies often had their own military forces. In time, however, the chartered companies disappeared and their territories became colonies.

All the colonies were different. Some were completely controlled by London, some had minimal local control, and some (those usually called crown colonies) had almost complete local control. In 1902, after the end of the second Boer War, the Union of South Africa quickly became a completely self-governing dominion in the British Empire.

In the first half of the 20th century, the two most important colonies were Kenya and Rhodesia. Kenya was created in reaction to the German take-over of Tanganyika, but when it was discovered that much of the land was highly fertile, entire tribes were removed from their homes and lands, often by force. The best land soon became know as the "white highlands." Huge coffee and tea plantations were created, and thousands of indentured laborers were imported from India to build railways. The Indian "coolies" were treated little better than slaves, and the Africans were heavily taxed and also subject to forced labor. Very quickly, Kenya became known as the place where only upper-class Englishmen were welcome, and many a titled gentleman had a country estate in Kenya, where it was fashionable to spend the cold English winter "roughing it" in the warmer African climate. Many of the estates were owned by absentee landlords, and although most of the estates were well run and profitable, some were retained just for shooting (i.e., hunting large African animals). After the First World War, any discharged officer who could raise 1,000 pounds could apply for free land in Kenya. Men of lower rank were not welcome. Not surprisingly, the white population was quite small (barely 100,000) and was outnumbered by Indians. Kenya was considered the most racist of all the African colonies.

Rhodesia was the product of Cecil Rhodes and his British South African Company. It was Rhodes' ambition to occupy and develop all the land later called Northern and Southern Rhodesia and Nyasaland. In fact, Rhodes sought to control all the land between the two Portuguese colonies and German Tanganyika. He called this huge region Zambezia, but the name never caught on.

Rhodes and his British South African police were successful in Southern Rhodesia, but the company had only a minimal presence north of the Zambezi River. Both Northern Rhodesia and Nyasaland eventually became British protectorates and immigration was discouraged.

Rhodes was a dyed-in-the-wool imperialist, but he almost always acquired his land by treaties, many of them of very doubtful legality and often accompanied by bribes. Somebody's signature or mark on a bit of paper was all he required before the settlers—both British and Dutch (Boers)—arrived in their wagons. Working-class men with strong backs were particularly welcome. In time, a number of mines were opened, and much of the land was being farmed by owner-farmers. Rhodesia prospered, and in 1923 it was declared a self-governing colony with the right to have its own coins and postage stamps.

After the Second World War, immigration from England increased, and the white population grew to nearly 300,000, three times that of Kenya. Rhodesia had become the breadbasket of central Africa and exported food to all of its neighbors. Other exports were gold, platinum, and tobacco.

The crash came in the 1960s, when the European nations that had raced to grab chunks of Africa began to race to give independence to their colonies, whether those colonies were ready or not. In 1964, Northern Rhodesia became Zambia, and Nyasaland became Malawi. But in Southern Rhodesia, the white population was not prepared to simply hand over everything to a black majority. In 1965, Rhodesia declared itself an independent state. Civil war followed. After almost fifteen years of often bitter guerilla fighting, the whites gave in and the Republic of Zimbabwe was declared. The black leaders promised reconciliation and that the takeover would be legal and peaceful, but under the dictator Robert Mugabe everything of value was confiscated and any resistance was put down by force. In a very short time, what had once been the most promising land in Africa was ruined as white families fled, farms were abandoned, and the mines and factories closed. The people living in the former breadbasket of Africa were now facing starvation and massive unemployment. Inflation in Zimbabwe reached the highest mark in history—ten trillion percent.

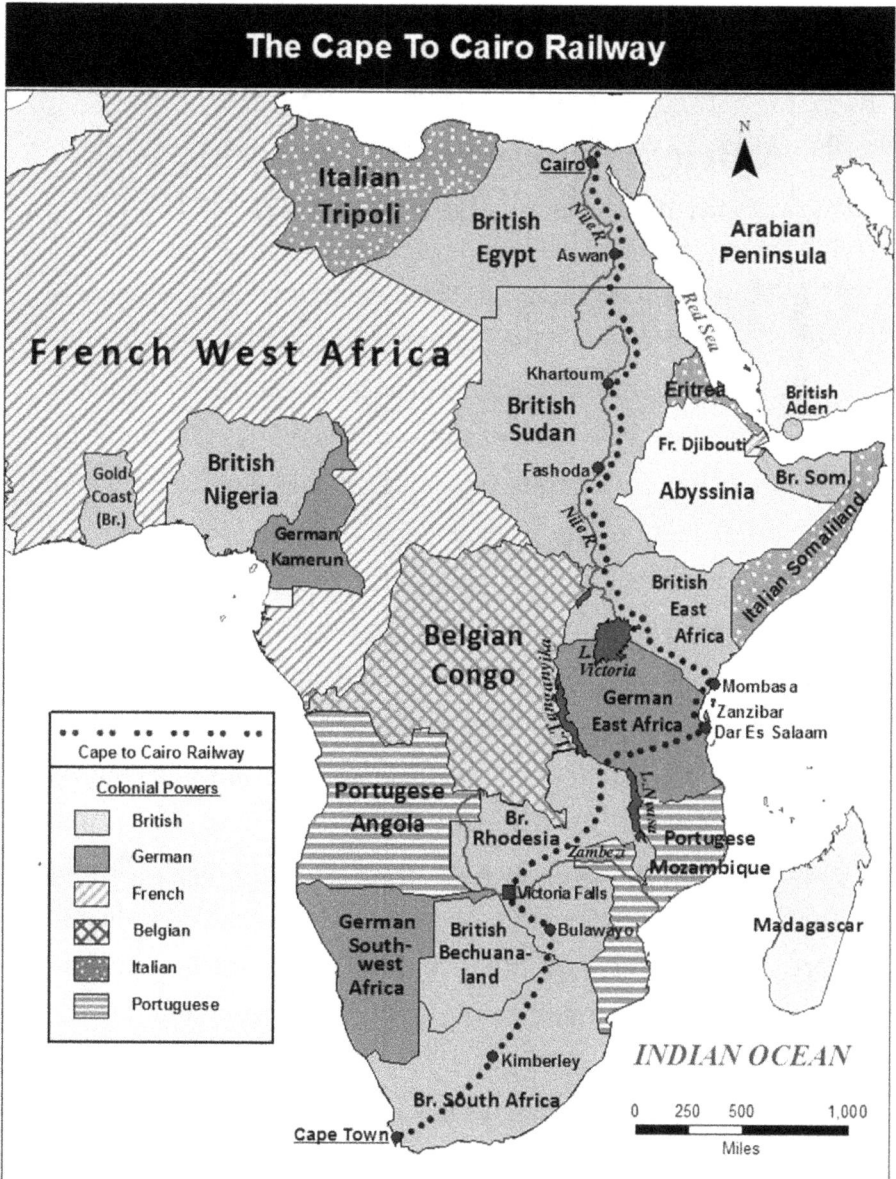

The Cape To Cairo Railway

Italian Tripoli

British Egypt

Cairo

Aswan

Arabian Peninsula

French West Africa

Red Sea

Khartoum

British Sudan

Fashoda

Eritrea

British Aden

Fr. Djibouti

Abyssinia

Br. Som.

Gold Coast (Br.)

British Nigeria

German Kamerun

Nile R.

Italian Somaliland

British East Africa

Belgian Congo

L. Tanganyika

L. Victoria

German East Africa

Mombasa

Zanzibar

Dar Es Salaam

L. Nyasa

Cape to Cairo Railway

Colonial Powers

	British
	German
	French
	Belgian
	Italian
	Portuguese

Portugese Angola

Br. Rhodesia

Zambezi

Victoria Falls

Portugese Mozambique

Madagascar

German South-west Africa

British Bechuana-land

Bulawayo

Kimberley

Br. South Africa

Cape Town

INDIAN OCEAN

0   250   500   1,000

Miles

N

Data provided by:
ESRI, Google Earth

Map Illustrator:
Robert A. Cisneros

Map 4: The Proposed Cape to Cairo Railway

Appendix Two:
A Brief History of the Scramble for Africa and the Cape to Cairo Railway

Towards the end of the 19th century when there was a mad scramble among the European powers to divide Africa up into colonies as England, France, Germany, Portugal and even Italy all struggled to lay claims to large portions of the "dark continent." But the scramble was not as wild as it seemed. Each of the powers had definite plans and each needed specific parts of Africa to carry out their long-term objectives.

The best known plan was the Cape to Cairo plan. This was a serious attempt to create a 5,000-mile-long belt of British-controlled territory extending from Cape Town, at the southern tip of the continent, north to Cairo, Egypt. It would be linked by railway and telegraph and would include almost all of East Africa, thus protecting the Suez Canal and the Indian Ocean for Great Britain. The Cape to Cairo scheme was very popular and received wide support, especially from Cecil Rhodes, the prime minister of the Cape Colony. It was an extraordinarily ambitious scheme, and it nearly succeeded.

Since the 16th century, Portuguese had controlled the coasts of Angola and Mozambique. Portuguese traders in Mozambique had been slowly working their way up the Zambezi River, and by 1760 they had settled in the trading city of Tete, which is 260 miles up the river. In 1877 the Portuguese explorer Alexandre de Serpa Pinto crossed the continent from Angola by following a tributary of the Zambezi. Communication between the two colonies was easiest by sea, however, and there was little Portuguese presence in the interior of Africa. With the advent of the railway and steam-powered river boats, the Portuguese hoped to link the two sections of the Portuguese empire in Africa into one large colony.

In 1890 the Portuguese produced the Pink Map to substantiate their claims to what later became Southern and Northern Rhodesia and Nyasaland. The Portuguese claim was instantly rejected, however, by the British and great pressure was put on the Portuguese, including an order to remove all their military and government officials from the area. In their determination to have a Cape to Cairo rail line and empire, the British were prepared to lose their oldest ally. In 1891, the king of Portugal reluctantly signed an agreement that severely limited the borders of Mozambique and Angola, but this angered the people so much that a few years later the king and his son were murdered and Portugal became a republic.

Far to the north, the French had amassed a huge area of colonies and protectorates in western and central Africa. They hoped to unite their West African possessions with their tiny territory on the Red Sea at Djibouti. This would create a belt of French-controlled territory extending from the Atlantic to the Red Sea, cutting right through the proposed British rail line from Cape to Cairo.

In 1898, a small French military expedition of 130 soldiers under *Major* Jean-Baptiste *Marchand* crossed the continent from Brazzaville, on the Atlantic, to Fashoda, on the upper Nile, where they hoped to link up with an expedition coming west from Djibouti, in French Somaliland. While they were waiting, a flotilla of

British gunboats arrived carrying Field Marshal Horatio Herbert Kitchener and the army that had just conquered the Sudan. The French were politely requested to leave. The diplomatic war of words that followed almost led to war between England and France but the Fashoda Incident ended with Britain in complete control of both the Sudan and Egypt.

In 1888–9, the Italians occupied Eritrea on the Red Sea and Somaliland on the horn of Africa. Since Abyssinia (now Ethiopia) was the only independent state left on the eastern flank of Africa, there was serious concern among the other European kingdoms that the Italians would take that country and have complete control of the Horn of Africa, which would create a serious threat to both the Cape to Cairo rail line and the Suez Canal. The British countered by taking a large section of Somaliland between the two Italian colonies and improving their naval base at Aden on the southern tip of the Arabian Peninsula and directly across the Red Sea from the Horn of Africa. The Italians conquered Abyssinia with great difficulty in 1935, but their African empire did not last long. At the start of the Second World War, British, French, and Belgian troops removed the Italians, and Abyssinia became independent again.

A more serious threat to the British plan was German East Africa, also known as Tanganyika. The Germans had declared the area a protectorate in 1885, and German claims extended from the Indian Ocean to Lake Tanganyika, which formed the border with the Belgian Congo (also known as the Congo Free State), so there was no way around this last barrier to the Cape to Cairo rail line. The British answer was to create, in 1888, the British East Africa

Company and lay claim to what later became Kenya and Uganda. They also declared a protectorate over the island of Zanzibar, which lies just 26 miles off the coast of Tanganyika.

The Germans had a colony in South West Africa and another in Kamerun (Cameroon), but the East African colony was the most important. At that time, the enormous and highly profitable Belgian Congo was the personal property of Leopold II, King of the Belgians. Since it was not a colony or even a protectorate, its very existence was dubious, and the borders of the Belgian Congo were poorly defined and almost unmarked. With a little luck, the Germans decided, the Congo, or a portion of it, could fall into their hands and a connection would be made with Kamerun, with the result that Germany would have a coast to coast empire running through the heart of the continent.

In 1914, when the First World War began and German troops overran Belgium, the Tanganyika-Congo problem was taken quite seriously by London. If Germany won the war, Kaiser Wilhelm II might claim the Congo as the spoils of war. Even if things went badly for the Germans, troops from Kamerun and Tanganyika could easily take the undefended Congo.

Steamers on Lakes Nyasa, Tanganyika, and Victoria were equipped with guns and their crews were trained. British troops were sent to cooperate with the Belgians, and a couple of airplanes were shipped north on the long rail line from Cape Town to Elizabethville in the Congo. The Germans also armed their lake steamers.

The inevitable confrontation between the German gunboats and those of the British-Belgian forces is one of the most extraordinary chapters in naval history. It began when war was declared in 1914 and *HMS Gwendolen,* a lake steamer on Lake Nyasa, carrying a three-pound cannon, attacked and sank the *Herman Von Wissmann,* a similar lake steamer with a one-pound cannon. The British telegraph system was faster than the German system, so the German captain did not know that war had been declared. Nevertheless, the victory was trumpeted as the first great naval battle of the war.

Meanwhile, a few hundred miles north on Lake Tanganyika, something similar was happening. The German passenger ship, *Graf Von Gotzen,* which was over 800 tons and with two screws was capable of nine knots, was armed with a modern 105-millimeter cannon and two 77-millimeter revolving guns taken from the German light cruiser *Konigsberg* which had been damaged and had retreated up a west African river. The *Konigsberg* was trapped and had to be scuttled; twenty-five years later, the *Graf Spee* faced the same fate. The Germans also had the *Kingani,* which was much smaller but had a six-pound cannon, which, unfortunately, could only fire straight ahead. The German fleet also had the *Hedwig,* which was only about 100 tons but had a six-pound cannon in the bow and a one-pounder at the stern. When war was declared, the *Hedwig* sailed across Lake Tanganyika and sank a Belgian steamer as well as a British steamer, the *Cecil Rhodes.* This left the great lake in German hands.

The British answer was to build two high-speed motor boats with the unbelievable French names, *HMS Mimi* and *HMS Toutou.* They were only about thirty feet long, but they had gasoline engines and were highly maneuverable and fast. Each had a three-pound Hotchkiss and a couple of Maxim machine guns. The little boats were built and tested in England, then shipped to Cape Town and sent by rail to Elizabethville in the Belgian Congo, where they, plus their gasoline and spare parts, were dragged 150 miles by steam tractor, oxen, and manpower through the jungle and over the mountains to Lake Tanganyika. The naval officer in charge, Geoffrey Basil Spicer-Simson, was an extraordinary character who had once been court-martialed for incompetence and who insisted on wearing a khaki kilt, much to the amusement of the natives.

The *Mimi* and the *Totou* were prepared for action. The next time the *Kingani* came by, they chased it, fought it, and captured it. The British then patched it up and renamed it the *HMS Fifi*. The six-pound cannon was moved to the stern and a 12-pounder was put in the bow. Unfortunately, this cannon was so powerful, the little lake steamer stopped dead in her tracks whenever it was fired.

In January of 1916, the *Hedwig* came by looking for the *Kingani* and was greeted by the *Fifi*, the *Mimi*, and a Belgian motorized barge carrying two cannons. They gave chase, with the *Fifi* in the lead, but she slowed down every time she fired her 12-pounder, so the *Mimi* took the lead. The *Hedwig* kept turning around to bring her bow gun into action, but the *Mimi* was more agile, and so the two boats danced around each other and wasted ammunition. With her last two shells, the *Mimi* actually managed to hit the *Hedwig*, and the German ship burst into flames and sank.

Now all that was left of the German fleet on the lake was the *Graf Von Gotzen*, but the kilted commander, Spicer-Simson, did not want to tackle her, so the Belgians and the British tried to bomb her from their tiny airplanes, but with no success. Not knowing what other surprises the British had for her, and learning that the

German gunboats on Lake Nyasa and Lake Victoria had already been eliminated, the *Gotzen* went north up the lake to hide while her guns and ammunition were unloaded and given to the German general, Paul Von Lettow-Vorbeck, who had stripped the light cruiser *Konigsberg* of many of her guns, made field carriages, and used his German sailors and African soldiers to create an army.

The *Gotzen* was scuttled, and Von Lettow-Vorbeck led his little army into the bush, where he immediately became a major problem for the British. Living off the land and moving with uncanny speed, the army of sailors created so much trouble in Tanganyika and surrounding territories that at one time nearly 50,000 British, South African, and Indian troops were diverted from the war in Europe to hunt for him. Von Lettow-Vorbeck was never defeated. The end of the war found him deep inside Northern Rhodesia, far from the sea and far from Lake Tanganyika.

A number of books have been written about this period and its strange goings-on. One of them, by C. S. Forester, was made into a movie based very roughly on the events. It starred Humphrey Bogart and Katharine Hepburn and was called *The African Queen.*

When Tanganyika was taken over as a British protectorate, the Cape to Cairo plan almost came to fruition. But times had changed, and the great rail line was never built. Investors prefer to put their money into railways that will make profits, and the Cape to Cairo rail line could never have made a profit. The rail lines that cross the Zambezi River at Victoria Falls do not go northeast to Kenya; instead, they go northwest to the copper mines near the Congo border. The rail lines that were built in East Africa were designed to link the coast with the interior, and so little consideration was ever given to a north-south line that might connected the east-west lines to each other. Even less consideration was given to a line running north to the Sudan. Along the Nile, the rail line from Cairo goes south to Khartoum, but building a major line across the enormous wilderness of the south Sudan had never been seriously considered.

The Cape to Cairo plan was completely abandoned during the 1960s, when almost all of the African colonies and protectorates gained their independence. Less than 80 years after the Berlin Conference of 1885, where the great powers had divided up a continent, almost all of Africa was free once more.

Following independence, however, there was a period of anarchy and the railways suffered from a combination of corruption and mismanagement, plus a lack of money and the skills required to maintain the rolling stock. Many lines were abandoned, but gradually the various post-colonial governments became aware of the value of a good railway system.

In 1976, the Chinese financed, surveyed, and built a railway of nearly 2,000 kilometers from Kapiri Mposhi (near Lusaka) in Zambia to Dar es Salaam in Tanzania. It is a freight line designed to carry copper from the Zambian mines for export to China. It was an extraordinary engineering effort that included 300 bridges and 23 tunnels and was completed within five years (two years ahead of schedule). The line was primarily intended for the export of copper to China, but it also has a passenger service that ranges from quite good to execrable.

When the line from Zambia to Tanzania was completed, another section of the Cape to Cairo line was put in place. Since the entire route is the same 3′6″ gauge, it is theoretically possible for a train to go directly from Cape Town to Dar es Salaam. Unfortunately, however, the Kenya and Uganda railways are a different gauge (1,000 mm) and so there is no direct train connection between Dar es Salaam and Mombasa.

Apart from the Mombasa to Nairobi line, most of the east African rail system is in poor condition with large section nearly abandoned, although there are lines that extend to Gulu, a city in Uganda that is close to the border of South Sudan. Plans were recently put forward to modernize the east African railways and convert them to the 3′6″ gauge used throughout south and central Africa.

The empty wilderness of Sudan has suddenly become important. Oil was discovered there in the 1970s, and after a prolonged and bloody war, South Sudan became independent in 2011. In the 1960s, rail lines from Khartoum had been extended as far south as Wau, and now the new government of South Sudan intends to extend the lines to Juba and then on to link up with the railways of eastern Africa. If these plans are carried out, and if there is peace between Sudan and South Sudan, and if the various railway gauges are standardized, then yet another section of the Cape to Cairo railway will have been put into place. The only remaining missing link will be the section on the Nile between the Sudan border and the Aswan Dam.

The Egyptian line from Alexandria and Cairo to Aswan and Abu Simbel is busy and very popular with tourists, but it uses the standard European-North American gauge (4′ 8 ½″). A limited ferry boat system takes cargo and passengers to the Sudanese rail head at Wadi Halfa (in northern Sudan on the southern edge of

Lake Nubia, which is the Sudanese name for its part of Lake Nasser). Not only is there no intention to build a rail line around Lake Nasser (Nubia), but transshipment would also still be necessary because of the difference in gauge. The great Cape to Cairo railway will therefore never be a completely unbroken rail line.

It is interesting to note that the rail line from the Nile at Aswan to Khartoum was built by General Herbert Kitchener's army in the war against the Mahdi in the 1890s. Cecil Rhodes, who was a friend and admirer of Kitchener and a great supporter of the Cape to Cairo railway, lent the general some locomotives that were intended for the railroad that he was building from Kimberly to Bulawayo, so Kitchener ordered the line built to the 3'6" gauge.

After the defeat of the Mahdi at the Battle of Omdurman, in which a young Winston Churchill fought as a cavalryman and Frank Rhodes, brother to Cecil Rhodes, served as a war correspondent, it was the victorious Kitchener who confronted the French at Fashoda a short while later. This little incident in a long-forgotten war was the first major step in the grand imperial dream of complete British control over the east coast of Africa as well as the Cape to Cairo railway.

www.ingramcontent.com/pod-product-compliance
Lightning Source LLC
Chambersburg PA
CBHW060154070426

42447CB00033B/1281